SWEET KWAI RUN SOFTLY

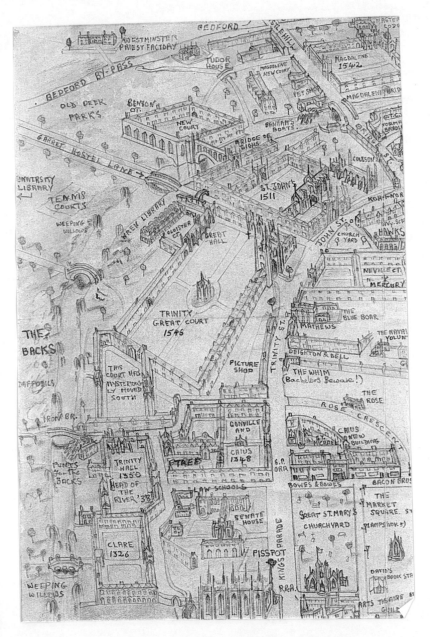

Detail from map of Cambridge drawn in 1944

SWEET KWAI RUN SOFTLY

Stephen Alexander

Merriotts Press

For Ruth

First published in 1995 by
MERRIOTTS PRESS
174 Long Ashton Road, Bristol BS18 9LT

Text and illustrations copyright 1995 Stephen Alexander

Designed and produced by Open Books Publishing Ltd,
Beaumont House, Wells, Somerset BA5 2LD

Typeset in Sabon by Michael Mepham, Frome, Somerset
Printed and bound in Great Britain
by Antony Rowe Ltd, Chippenham.

A CIP catalogue record for this book is available
from the British Library.

ISBN 0 9526763 0 3

Contents

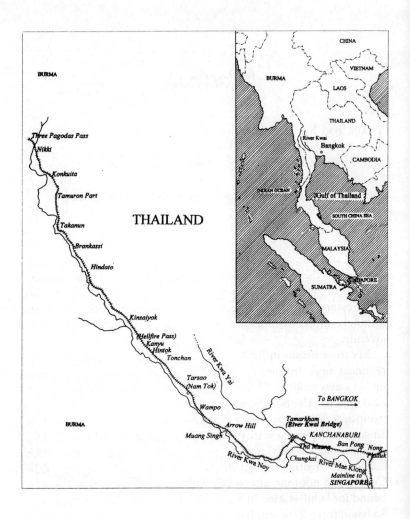

Preface

'PAUL had his Arabia, Moses his desert.' This was my father's consoling message when I was caught in the surrender of Singapore. Four years of tribulation on the Burma-Siam railway followed. Faced with adversity in such an unfamiliar form, the instincts are conflicting: to go by the book or go native, to follow the herd or exercise a degree of bloody-mindedness? As certainties crumble, faith starts to fade – in country, God, family and self. It makes no difference how willing the spirit is when the flesh, starved, over-worked and diseased, inexorably weakens. It seems to be sheer luck that decides the issue. I recall the personal tugs-of-war in the darkest days of the railway between altruism and self-preservation and, as the pressure eased off, between thoughts grown on the one hand infinitely more mature and on the other disconcertingly more juvenile.

My story begins in Bristol and Bath. I am posted to a yeomanry regiment more distinguished socially than militarily, which is shaken up by a new colonel, Philip Toosey, and prepared for action in the Middle East. The bombing of Pearl Harbor finds us in an American troopship near Cape Town bound for Basra; we are diverted to Singapore. As we go warily down one gangway the RAF hurries up another, and a month later I am imprisoned in Changi Barracks with thousands of others. I am despatched to dig up Singapore Golf Course and not long afterwards am squeezed into a goods wagon bound for 'a hill station in Siam with light work and plenty of rice'. So begin three long years on the River Kwai.

1943 is the worst, with privations on a biblical scale. Once the tracks from Bangkok and Moulmein have met, physical conditions improve but frustrations of a different kind follow – the crushing by the Japanese of all intellectual activity, incompatability between

1

our regular and by now very irregular soldiers, and in the wake of better rations an inconvenient revival of the libido. The new boredom is alleviated by surreptitious lectures, secret versifying and far from secret infatuations.

But a common enemy brings uncommon friends. Fellow prisoners from the Netherlands East Indies Army, local Thai farmers, Chinese traders, and even the odd disaffected Korean guard, present new views of Asia. From these, which are much more intimate than those held by the British Raj, I perceive that the approaching victory does not necessarily mean that the first will be first again or the last last. In July 1945, with a Thai rising planned for August, I am marched to an extermination camp – but rescued by the atom bomb. With our new uniforms we don something of our old personalities; but would the inner man ever be the same again? Would the same experiences affect in the same way such diverse characters as George Bartley-Dennis, Harold Cassel, the Lord De Ramsey, Norris Lindsay Emmerson, Philip Hay, Edward Douglas Home, Guthrie Moir, Jim Swanton, Bishop Leonard Wilson and – shorn of their regimental trappings – unemployed colonels of every size, shape and disposition?

There were many, however, for whom no uniforms were needed; among those who never left the Kwai were my batman and my Cambridge gyp. Death came sometimes like a bolt from the blue, sometimes like a thief in the night, and sometimes – as for me – it passed inexplicably by at the last moment. Survival – perhaps all victories – demanded a judicious balance between contempt for death and respect for it, between courage and circumspection, and no one understood the strange providence that determined the moment for one or the other.

After fifty years I returned to a River Kwai in the full flow of an economic miracle. But tourists were its only traffic, and Thailand was disintegrating in the whirl of a Greater East Asian Co-prosperity Sphere not so very different from that promised by the Japanese in 1942.

*   *   *

In 1942 the docks party shambled along in the Singapore sun. We passed Lavender Street. *"Autres temps, autres moeurs!"* murmured Stuart beside me. Chinese stall-keepers threw bread rolls to us and men broke ranks to scrabble in the dust for them. Indignantly I stopped my men from following suit, and soon the Nips took over – with the screams and blows that were still a novelty to us.

That night, sleepless from hunger, I ran over the highlights of an inglorious military career, now eclipsed in this twilight of Empire: Secrets of the Bath Steam Laundry; The Big Sister of Oswestry; Second Lieutenant Noël Coward RA; The Demon Barber of Lockerbie; The Hospitality of Mrs Jones; Mount Vernon Nights; The Man with the Sam Browne Belt; and Duff Cooper's Duff Poem.

Not far away Chris Hughes, a gentle soul from Chagford who sometimes took our minds off food with talks on heraldry, also lay awake. He relieved his feelings by composing a triolet:

> I ate the bitter bread of shame,
>   I bore disgrace's heavy yoke.
> Subjected race, degraded name,
> I ate the bitter bread of shame.
>   A clod, a slave, a tool, a joke –
> Forgetting not, revenge my aim –
> I ate the bitter bread of shame,
>   I bore disgrace's heavy yoke.

1

The Bath Steam Laundry

IN 1939 I volunteered as a matter of course. I didn't feel a clod, a slave, a tool, a joke then; in fact I was quite pleased with myself. What I did feel as I heard Neville Chamberlain's susurrating voice deliver the words, "We are at war with Germany", was my heart plummeting to my boots. This was partly because his drooping moustache, butterfly collar and prim manner seemed no match for rasping dictators and row upon row of goose-stepping automata but also because I knew I'd had an easy life and hadn't done much with it. It was almost as though I deserved to lose it – unless I was prepared to fight for it.

My fire-breathing father had no doubts about our role. Britain's authority in the world was ordained and thus invincible. The Ribbentrop Pact drew a snort of approval: "It's God's will! We shall crush the two Antichrists together!" A friend in the Gloucesters reacted differently. A devotee of Auden and Co, he took his dilemma to his commanding officer. He could not in conscience take up arms against the Russians; what was he to do? (He was to send his officer's greatcoat to the dyers and spend the rest of the war in the fire service.) I suppose my views lay somewhere between these two.

My father had earned the right to strong views for he had done well. Struggling out of his father's Scottish evangelical circle in Birkenhead, he had married a well-bred but penurious English wife and moved further south. As a GP in Bristol he had brought up a large family, sending three girls to the High School and five boys to Clifton College and Oxford or Cambridge. I was the youngest of the family and comparatively spoiled. The war had caught me at an awkward moment in my second long vac at Peterhouse. After my First MB I had switched from medicine – my father's choice rather than mine – but had not yet got far enough towards another career to set family – and my own – doubts at rest. My gloom at the outbreak of war was therefore offset by having my mind made up for me. My career could wait. It had been the subject of family letters, for example from my godfather, the rector of Glanmire:

> I have been thinking about you while I was ill, and the thought occurred to me – might it not be possible that God was calling you to something else – the Ministry for instance? . . . I wonder have you ever thought of it? From what I have heard and seen of you I believe that you would be a distinct asset to the Church. Will you think the matter over sincerely and ask God to direct you?

A short cut to God through my parson brother, Hugh, only confused the issue:

> . . . Ma and Pa are a bit disappointed with the Last Hope forsaking the medical profession, but they will soon get over it having had so many shocks of one sort or another from us all. Talk amiably to as many people as you can, especially nice ones, in all walks of life and you will gradually feel your way into some useful niche. . . .

Joan, the first of my sisters to get married, spared a thought for me in the middle of her domesticities:

> You should have seen Mother and Rachel watching me bath Daniel my first morning here. It was agony to both of them as they both felt they could do it so much better, and when it came to Rachel imploring me to do the napkin as tightly as possible and Mother telling me to do it loosely so that he'd have room for duty, and Mother trying to put his dress on at the same time so that I couldn't even see how I was doing the napkin, I felt a little distraught. . . .
>
> I think poster-design or household decorating would suit you if you had a spot of training, but people always think that

is so unmanly. But there, there isn't one of the family who hasn't been miserable over what they did except me, who wasn't because I didn't do anything. . . .

Later on she had more time to consider my case:

Mother has all my sympathy, not for her attitude to you, but as I am a budding mother myself I just don't know how she's survived it with so many. When I contemplate Daniel and possibly another on the way, and think that I first have to battle with laws of hygiene and physical behaviour, and then begin on the soul, teaching them honesty with themselves, if not with other people as such a thing is hardly possible in this sad world, and faith in God in the Universe and God in Man, and independence of thought and action, and good manners, and a sense of responsibility to their own life, and good taste, then I feel I could lie down in a field of buttercups and willingly sink into nothingness. She's had to try and do all that with eight utterly different characters, so can you wonder she just lays down rules for herself and sticks to them without bothering about the psychology of the case?

In these days of threatening war and the irruption of building pustules I think there are just three things that matter, the Church, agriculture and architecture. I always thought you ought to be an architect because even if there doesn't seem to be much in it, there will be, and there's *got* to be. Sometime it simply must be compulsory for all building estates to be designed by a trained and cultured architect and the plans submitted to a committee. As for agriculture, I think it's so vitally important to save it in England that if I was a man I would be a farm labourer, if I couldn't do anything else to help it. Of course all that stuff of Mother's about jobs that are socially proper, and money, is not worth bothering about. It's an attitude of their generation, quite understandable when so many of them were self-made and literally slaved themselves into their position, but nowadays it is not so important. The point is, to use every power and gift that you have and increase it as you go along so that in the end you have given more back than you started with, and not only expect security and freedom from worry. So you have the vital occupations of the Church, medicine, architecture, art, farming and industry – if it's a necessity and not a luxury trade – to choose from; and I think architecture or the Church would suit you best, perhaps not farming because you are too lazy in that particular way, and have too active a brain.

But as I say, it's agony being a mother; you are tied, body and soul – and God, the responsibility! So pity poor Mum, maddening and stupid as she is, but actually a good deal more wonderful than maddening and stupid, to have started us out with any ideals at all. Well, farewell. All the chaps felt just the same at your age about whatever they were going to do.

My brother Noel (Robin to the family), in the Malayan Civil Service, advised me to 'be rational and stick to medicine; it will keep you in touch with all sections of whatever community you're in – whether Chinese, African, Arabic, Military, Naval or merely urban. No one can believe that things will continue as they have done for much longer. If you want to know more about Europe's prospects do a course of political reading; don't waste time with newspapers; if you read *The Republic*, *The Communist Manifesto* and *Mein Kampf*, and a history of Europe, you might have some sense of direction.'

The previous year he had written, from the P & O *Ranpura* off Cochin China, to admonish me about a situation that was to bring us unexpectedly together:

Concentrate on Cambridge but at times spare a thought for the world outside and give what energy you can if not to supporting the right (nothing is a hundred per cent right) at least to opposing what is evil whether it is Mussolini, Nazism or Japanese pan-Asianism. . . . Your University has produced two great men who have appreciated China's superior civilization and have attempted to persuade English people to be just to China: read Lowes Dickinson's *Letters from John Chinaman* and Bertrand Russell's *The Problem of China*, both extremely readable and which will advance you beyond your table or the JCR in broadness of outlook. And join any organisation for the boycott of Japan: attend meetings: hiss John Simon, stamp and cat-call: join the leftists and LIVE. You have probably read John Gunter's *Inside Europe*, if not do so. Knowledge of the world is becoming paramount even in shrouded-in-cotton-wool England. My career, whatever its humdrum limitations and trying climate, has at least brought me in touch with more trends of world history and paths to Heaven or Hell than if I'd become a master at Clifton or a don at Oxford or gone (straight) into the Holy Anglican Catholic Church. (I am not mocking: I may yet become Father or even Brother Noel.)

When I saw the Japanese aeroplanes daily flying past Macau and heard the bombs reverberating, and when I saw uniformed boys and girls taking up their first-aid drill stations near the sandbagged street-corner shelters in Canton, and the general cheerfulness after the air-raid alarm had been sounded, I felt right in the middle of things. Tho' when I heard of Japanese troops looting in Nanking, raping Chinese girls, shooting batches of 'varsity students in Tientsin and compelling weeping Chinese girls in Peiping to carry Japanese flags in victory processions I felt more on the fringe. As also when Chiang Kai Shek's cousin (a lady) told me of the troubles of the rich in Shanghai: of the stench of the corpses they are not allowed to remove from their lawns, etc., etc. – peasant youths, packed like sardines, drafted on empty stomachs as cannon fodder, and the trek of millions of refugees. I returned to Macau on a boat packed with women and children, owing to rumours of an imminent attack on Canton: I spent all the time talking to adorable Cantonese schoolgirls who knock High School girls into a cocked hat. Get to know the Chinese in Cambridge; they are more mature than English undergraduates and make very good friends. . . . Well, have a good time, and disagree with everything I write if you like.

To this I replied in February 1938:

There is a widespread boycott of Japanese goods going on,

and here in Cambridge all self-respecting shops have an anti-Japan notice in the window.

I see your friend Michael Redgrave is to become a film star. . . . Birdwood is unfortunately leaving at the end of this term and a dim History professor is to become Master. This Sunday morning everything is quiet after yesterday's weekend excesses. Parker's Piece is bathed in sunlight, and is quite deserted – except for a couple of dogs buggering each other in the middle of it. The Salvation Army band has just come within hearing.

I've just bought my first picture, called 'Awakening Spring' by Rowland Hilder; framed complete it cost a guinea. All my other pictures are posters. Last term I saw a weedy-looking artist wearing foul clothes and a greasy black hat, with long flea-ridden hair and looking very seedy and starved, painting Clare Bridge – quite well too. I pitied his evident poverty and thought of offering him a pound or two for it. This term I saw the picture in Heffers for £12. He was Stephen Bone. . . .

As it happened, I could have stayed on at Peterhouse because the army was in no hurry to call me up. I had not enjoyed being in the Corps and never thought of joining the Territorials at Cambridge. My memories of the OTC are entirely trivial: taking a swig from a stone Brooke & Prudenco ginger-pop bottle at a field day on the Mendips and feeling my teeth crunching on a cockroach; getting blisters on route marches at Tidworth and in the evening laughing at an Oundle master called Arthur Marshall doing impersonations from Angela Brazil; tittering in the ranks as a wretched boy who couldn't even tie his puttees properly failed his Cert. A by giving us the order, "Er – a few paces backward – MARCH!"

A lot of work would have to be done on me before I could face those steely stormtroopers, and, as the months passed, I began to regret surrendering Cambridge so lightly. I got a job at thirty-five shillings a week in 'Priority Branch' at the Admiralty in Bath, going over by train every day. This sounded important but consisted in granting or refusing priority to industrial workers for exemption from military service. It was appropriate that what now kept the lid on my patriotic fervour took place in the former premises of the Bath Steam Laundry. Also there awaiting call-up, and an obvious favourite of the office girls, was a good-looking, deep-voiced Cambridge undergraduate called John Durnford, whose father owned a quarry near Bristol and lived off Bathwick Hill near my Indian Railways aunt and uncle. I joined John in excursions to the Assembly Rooms, where we danced with light-footed girls as ladylike as their city. Like little bits of fluff they soon floated out of my memory; I thought that with such a gay Lothario as John they would do the same, but I was to be proved wrong. I ought to have realised that his hearty manner belied an introspective temperament when he confided that the priority forms on which he wrote so busily in office hours as often as not contained drafts of verse.

The months of the 'phoney war' continued without incident until almost the end of that academic year, and I was getting so used to them that it came as quite a shock when some Whitehall warrior pressed my own priority button and I left the Bath Steam Laundry for ever. In May 1940 Number 931035, Gunner Alexander, S. C., was directed to join C Troop, A Battery, 7th Heavy AA Training Regiment RA at Park Hall Camp, Oswestry.

2

Ubique Quo Fas Et Gloria Ducunt

"ALEXANDER!" exclaimed the bombardier issuing my battledress.
"Alexander the Great, is it, or Alexander's Ragtime Band?"
At least mine is a name difficult, with its four syllables, to bandy
about. Drill-sergeants soon pick out those that are easy to project
across the parade ground.

"Hal-den-by! Where d'you think you're goin'? Try the other left!
Stand still, Ham-il-ton! You're wavin' in the breeze like a bull's
pizzle! Still now! Stand still! By the left, quick march! Phillips! Keep
that rifle up; you're marchin' like a pregnant duck! I don't mind.
You can stay here all night. I've got nothin' spoilin'! Squad, halt!
Stand still! Still, now! Brown! Look to your front! Not up there! It's
only a plane, lad! Nothin' to do with you. If Jesus Christ in clouds
descendin' came down from heaven, it's nothin' to do with you!
Look to your front!"

With other potential officer cadets I was put in a hut insulated
from the 'real' other ranks in that we shared it with contingents from
Newfoundland and the Isle of Man. "Are ye coming down the village
for a bit o' skin?" the Newfoundlanders used to ask, and one of them
had the courage to complain at the lack of meat in the canteen stew.
The rural air round the camp turned out to be deceptive on my first
visit to Whittington. "Hallo, mister!" said an apple-cheeked Shrop-
shire lad. "Gimme a penny and I'll fetch me big sister!" Without her
help we soon found our new discomforts strangely enjoyable,
becoming 'healthily tired' with square-bashing and gun-drill and

11

feeling curiously detached as though we were privileged but dutiful angels looking down into English life from a new angle.

We helped build a hutted POW enclosure, into which five hundred Czechs who were said to have rebelled against their own officers marched one day – very much at ease. A few weeks later they marched out again and it filled up with survivors from Dunkirk, and this was the nearest we came to the real war going on over the Channel.

Alan Haldenby, a Derby solicitor, was the only one of us who was to stay with me throughout the war. My immediate neighbours in the hut seemed the most unmilitary of us but were the kind of people whose intelligence or charm would surmount any difficulty. Michael Hamilton was the gentle soft-spoken son of the Bishop of Shrewsbury but he had the steely nerve to arrive with a hot water bottle, and after lights out, among the grunts and snores from the other beds, I used to hear the whisper of his miniature radio. Raymond Phillips was smaller and looked out of his element scampering about with enormous dummy shells; but he had a deep authoritative voice to make up for his lack of brawn. Of all this gently-nurtured troop I think our sergeant found these two the most bafflingly well-bred. He would sometimes gaze quietly at them with a speculative eye, as though wondering whether they would finish up as generals or in ENSA.

Our military training proceeded briskly. The bombardier who lectured on the history of the Royal Regiment confined himself largely to innuendo – '*Ubique quo fas et gloria duCUNT!*' – and health education was limited to hearty advice on contraception. Gun-drill on 4.5 howitzers soon assumed, through repetition, a beautiful symmetry. The mysteries of setting up the director, deploying the guns, range-finding and using the observation post were breezily outlined for elucidation later. The only occasions when time seemed to drag unbearably were the nights on guard duty. It was horribly difficult to keep awake after days of being made 'healthily tired', and I often felt a prey to fancies and quite incapable of dealing with a crisis.

After a couple of months most of us got a stripe and could begin to throw our weight about with newer recruits. But even with what seemed enormous new privileges it was like coming up for air when my brother Noel arrived home on leave from Ipoh and carried off Michael, Raymond and me for dinner at the Wynnstay Arms. In the lovely July evening everything from the sporting prints on the wall to the grass of the bowling green seemed to glow cosily. There were soft lights; there was sweet music; there were women in long dresses; and as we swung our boots under the delicate table and scanned the wine list we felt that life for off-duty angels was still pretty good. Unlike Mike with his hot water bottle, I had not had the nerve to bring my accordion to Oswestry, but Noel brought it up for me. The next reunion for Noel, the accordion and me was to be much less convivial.

During the three months passed at Catterick OCTU I sometimes wondered whether the misfits who had stayed in the ranks had not had the better of it. Compared with the hutted squalor of Park Hall Camp, the first sight of the sumptuous 'Sandhurst' blocks made us feel that we had indeed come up in the world. But unease soon spread. We were visited by gleeful cadets ahead of us who warned of the horrors to come – the lecturettes and examinations, the monthly interviews and weeding out, the shameless arse-crawling to instructors, the rising panic as the end of the course drew near and we might still be 'returned to unit' – weighed in the balance, found wanting and cast into the outer darkness of the non-commissioned. As the weeks passed, gaps began to appear around me as the Colonel's antipathy to regular rankers made itself felt. One quiet little man who had toyed with the idea of going into the Church was briskly 'RTUed' with the assurance that the Church needed him more than the army and that Holy Orders were the only orders he was ever likely to perform satisfactorily; a tougher character was returned to his unit as an avowed atheist and thus unfit to lead men in battle.

At Oswestry I had learned easily but at Catterick I found myself thinking more of how I appeared to be doing a job than of how it ought to be done. At a lecturette session on vehicle maintenance, when we would be thrown lecture subjects without any warning, I found my mind a total blank when faced with 'The Working of the Magneto'. Had I been quicker-witted I might have said: "Gentlemen, to understand the working of the magneto you need to know something about the petrol supply in general, so I shall give you a quick run-down on that first." Instead, I said: "Gentlemen, I am very sorry to say that I am not the best person to instruct you about the magneto, so I must ask you to learn about it from someone else." And I sat down. "Well!" said the Colonel in his summing up, "the speaker on the magneto was very cool, I must say." I was surprised, for I was not yet aware that coolness cannot always be distinguished from panic.

The senior cadet was held up to us as the perfect example of officer material; he was certainly tall and handsome, thoroughly in command of himself and of us, and at a camp concert – 'Shot 2' – turned out to be even more of a paragon, both as compère and as a baritone soloist. But it was his senior cadetship that appeared to be even more remarkable: in civvy street he had been Noël Coward's understudy. However, we soon discovered after leaving the freezing Yorkshire Moors that life as an officer is ninety per cent acting. When the moment of truth arrives the adrenalin is just as likely to flow in the effete as in the extrovert. Who can say with hindsight whether Noël Coward and Dickie Mountbatten might not have swapped roles to everyone's advantage?

There was another resplendent character at Catterick in the person of its adjutant, Captain R. K. Jones, a copy-book Regular whose boots outshone even the Colonel's. As a small boy at Clifton I had admired him from the touch-line, playing rugger with shining ones like Trevor Howard. Would it, I wondered in my disillusion with the magneto, be judicious to encourage him to reminisce over his exploits on the rugger field? Fortunately, such a desperate measure proved unnnecessary, and it was rugger that made it so.

"You have the right background," said my Battery Commander at a final interview, "but you lack self-confidence and drive. And so – ," he frowned, "I could hardly feel myself justified in recommending that you finish the course."

My heart sank to my still black boots. The vision faded of the precious pip, the Herbert Johnson hat, the brown boots, the first-class railway warrants, and the cocktail lounges and girls in long

14

dresses; I saw myself bundled into a truck – button-stick, blanco, black boots and all – and expelled from Cambrai Lines.

"However," the Major went on, "the Colonel has given you quite a good chit."

He flashed it across the desk and I just had time to read the opening: 'I like this man, but . . . '

"And I've seen you on the rugger field. You seem to have more gumption than you show in your lecturettes. So I've decided to give you another chance. That was Obolensky in the Signals, wasn't it, you were marking on the right wing?"

Catterick seemed to cultivate an unnecessarily demoralising atmosphere, and I have few pleasant memories of it. The beauties of Richmond and the Swale valley did not compensate for the ugliness of all those camps, and the charm of the dales did not survive the icy moorland exercises.

The memory of one eerie moment remains. We had a drill-sergeant named 'Chalky' White with a voice like a rusty saw. You could hardly hear it close to, but when deployed on the square it developed an extraordinary timbre and volume, its power of penetration seeming to vary in direct proportion to its distance from the squad.

One afternoon we were resting on an exercise three or four miles up on the moors when we heard, borne to us on the wind, a long-drawn-out vibrant cry, ending on a short, sharp, rising note.

"What's that?" said someone. "A bittern?"

"Listen! There!"

"That? It's another two-legged bird altogether; it's Chalky White on the square!"

In October I celebrated my twenty-first birthday at the Catterick Bridge Hotel, and the barrack-room gave me a copy of Osbert Lancaster's *Homes Sweet Homes*. But the party was blighted by thoughts of an exam on the following morning.

In due course I left Catterick with a commission. Without too much difficulty I put behind me any doubts about whether I deserved it, as I was measured by the Simpson's tailor for my uniform: the ennobling greatcoat, the still dull Sam Browne, the hugging breeches, the fawn puttees which we wound from knee to ankle in homage to the horse artillery, and the brown boots henceforth to be shone by a batman. "Bless Mr Simpson!" I thought, "They can't RTU me now!" I saluted myself in the mirror and decided that Number 164313 2nd Lieutenant Alexander, S. C., would do. At any rate he ought to do for the 135th Field Regiment, whatever that was, to which he was now posted. Alan Haldenby and I were to report to it on 31st December 1940 at Holt – wherever that was.

3

A Fine Mess

FIRST we were to come down to earth with a bump. When Alan and I went to see my parents in Bristol we found there was a real war going on. Our blacked-out train crawled into Temple Meads station in the early hours, and we emerged into silent streets. There had been an air raid. Wardens and firemen had gone home and hoses lay about vomiting water. As we walked up to Clifton, humping our holdalls, fires were still burning: the leaning tower of Temple Church was lit up from below, and a roofless St Mary-le-Port shone across the water at Bristol Bridge.

The warmth of my welcome shook me. My normally undemonstrative mother flung her arms round my neck, and I felt a complete fraud. My father, working harder than ever at the surgery, was less bellicose than on previous visits. They knew as little about Holt as I did, but it sounded pleasingly bucolic, set perhaps among wooded hills, and nearer to the warm south than the bleak, stony wastes of Blubberhouses Moor.

> 'Twould blow like this through holt and hanger
> When Uricon the city stood:
> 'Tis the old wind in the old anger,
> But then it threshed another wood . . .

Holt, however, turned out to be on the northern edge of East Anglia. Prognostications for cosy living or cheerful leaves were not good. Nor did they improve when Alan and I reported for duty at midnight, after a long train journey over ever more flat and featureless country. We were greeted by a disconsolate red-haired Scot.

"Just my luck to be orderly officer on Hogmanay! 'Tis the first Hogmanay I ever remember missing. And look around ye! Not a soul in sight! The place is dead. All the officers are away to London. And no doubt the swede-bashers are in Norwich, reeling down the Prince of Wales Road!"

Jock Monro, as I found out later, was inclined to look on the gloomy side of things. Nor was the term 'swede-bashers' strictly accurate, for though the 'feet' in our 53rd Brigade were indeed from East Anglia, the 135th Field Regiment was formed from the North Hertfordshire Yeomanry, with one battery from Hitchin and one from Peterborough. They were Territorials and somewhat jealous of their territory, especially the Hitchin crowd. However, the outsiders like Jock, the subalterns from OCTUs, and the Troop Commander (our only Regular) were eventually invited (rather as if they had earned their Colours) to 'put their Harts up', that is to say to wear the becoming bronze shoulder badges of a leaping hart.

This badge had already been the cause of embarrassment. Shortly after my arrival I had walked into the mess, deserted except by an officer not much older than myself, who had greeted me somewhat pompously. Taking a quick look at his shoulder badges I noted two pips and underneath them what I took to be a slightly squashed crown. "Oh, dear," I thought, "the Colonel!" and I sprinkled our sticky conversation with 'Yes, sir's' and 'No, sir's' which he appeared to accept as his due. It wasn't until the room started filling up with a posse of full colonels that I realised that what I had taken for a crown was in fact the bronze county hart, and that my condescending messmate was one Lieutenant P. K. ('Peaky') Laing; our relations remained sticky thereafter.

There were other, more homely subalterns who were Reservists from World War I, and an unexpected family link was supplied by the Information Officer, Stanley Hall, who had been at the other Hertford – at Oxford – with my ICS brother. But on the whole the atmosphere was still pretty seigneurial. My first charming if unmilitary troop commander was Tom, Earl Fitzwilliam, whose land agent, Sam Egar, was also with us, and the battery captain was the Lord De Ramsey. Whatever we outsiders thought of their social clannishness, we had to respect the sense of duty that had prompted them to face the discomforts of pre-war Territorial service. After all, they could have pulled strings to join the BBC or the Ministry of Information, or simply continued to farm their ancestral acres in a 'scheduled occupation'. But here these gentlemen of England had been, dossing down in empty village houses, parading in draughty drill halls, and offering themselves as hostages to fortune long before we had thought of doing anything so decisive.

The 135th Field Regiment included the avuncular Colonel Hudson; Captain James McMullen of McMullen's Beer; Lieutenant Michael Cory-Wright (a name familiar on South Wales coal trucks); gentlemen farmers like Major Hugh Peacock and Captain David Cherry; and the City brigade: Malcolm Northcote (Adjutant), Granville Keane and Seymour Dearden. There were also several barristers and solicitors, and as gentlemanly a padre as anyone could wish in Struan Robertson, formerly rector of Doulting in Somerset. Carl Robson, the former *Daily Telegraph* correspondent in Berlin, was a sardonic and soft-spoken man of great charm, as was my battery commander, Terence Sanders, an engineering don from Cambridge. To break the Etonian mould there was the Harrovian Philip Hay, one of what we termed the Newmarket brigade because they wore canvas-topped Newmarket boots rather than the full leather riding boots of the older generation, or the mere knee-length puttees of us lesser mortals.

Philip was very tall and slim, with a mop of fair hair and a falling lock incessantly combed back with long, slender fingers. He had a cleft chin in a face of 'good bones'. One could see him as a Regency beau, but in fact his tastes were very different. When not playing piquet with Michael Cory-Wright he could be discovered reading *Swann's Way*, or writing letters in a duplicate book. "H'm!" said Stanley Hall, "what is so deathless about Philip's prose that it has to be duplicated for posterity?" His writing was very small and neat and modelled on the script of Baron Corvo. ("What's that you're reading, Philip?" "*The Desire and Pursuit of the Whole*." "How d'you spell that?" "Spell what?") The duplicates, he averred, were for rehashing to other correspondents but I rather favoured Stanley's suspicion. Philip liked to relieve the sombreness of his uniform with touches of colour: a canary silk shirt, a mulberry handkerchief worn at the wrist, or sea-green socks. He appeared one day in service dress but with corduroy trousers the colour of *vin rosé*.

19

"Really, my dear," said Terence, with his gentle smile, "those trousers!"

"You don't like them?"

"Well, I think just a little too – er –"

"Unmilitary?"

"Well, I think the men might be a little – er – nonplussed, don't you?"

I'm not sure that they would have been more nonplussed than they were already by all these beautiful people, visited from time to time by elegant, quiet wives in big black cars. Philip himself had never learned to drive and was only now beginning to tackle this distasteful task. An even more distasteful task was the one so often pressed upon us by our elders: to take part in organised games and lead the men in PT. Philip steadfastly refused to follow these promptings.

"But don't you take any exercise at all?" asked his exasperated Troop Commander, faced with the alternative of finding someone else or having to play soccer himself.

"Oh, yes; I play tennis when I can."

"But, my dear fellow, why didn't you tell me? We can organise a battery championship at once."

"There is the slight problem of a court."

"But there are plenty of courts round here."

"No, I mean real tennis. As far as I know, the nearest court is the Stanleys', twenty miles away."

The men must also have found the vocabulary of their officers a little quaint. Seymour Dearden was the one who started the rot, developing a kind of Bertie Wooster slang and an affectation of immense weariness so that almost any kind of circumlocution was used to avoid short, sharp, unfriendly consonants. Thus to Stanley he would say, "Stanners-anners, my dear fellow, could you make a long arm and sling over the butter-dish-if-you-don't-mind-awfully?" This sort of thing was very catching and it wasn't long before Sergeant Major Murkin found himself addressed as 'Murkers' and Sergeant Ramsbotham as 'Ram'. When Philip called his Troop Sergeant 'Tippers' the redoubtable Tiplady gave me a sideways look.

Of course, while sneering at these exquisites, we were happy enough to accept the pleasures of their company: the hand-made

20

cigarettes, the pinches of snuff from silver boxes, the voice of Edith Piaf on their gramophones, and the odd hamper of eggs and game from Abbots Ripton. Ailwyn De Ramsey, responsible for the hampers, was a useful man to have as Battery Captain when exercising the guns on cold, drenched and darkling moors. Looking at the map, he would say, "By Jove! We're quite close to Sniffy's place", and a despatch rider would be sent off to sound out 'Sniffy' on the possibility of a night under cover. Instead of bivouacking under hedges or sleeping in our vehicles we might find ourselves in a cosy outhouse at Skipton Castle. Once, after manoeuvres on Cartmel Fell, Stanley Hall was despatched to Holker Hall, where the butler asked him to wait as "his Lordship was still at breakfast". Stanley watched a succession of steaming dishes being borne into the breakfast room and began to wonder if his night manoeuvres and the very existence of the 135th Field Regiment RA were not all a dream. However, in time his Lordship emerged and not only were the men duly installed in the stables but officers were accommodated in the Hall itself. Later that night, as I lay between soft linen sheets, I stretched out my hand for something to send me to sleep. Inside *The Short Stories of Saki*, in a confident sloping hand, was the owner's name: 'Diana Cavendish'. I had already abstracted a sheet of embossed paper from the desk, on which to write to my mother.

Telegraph & Station	Holker Hall
Cork-in-Cartmel	Cork-in-Cartmel
½ mile	Lancashire

Dearest Mother,

You may wonder what we do on these exercises. On this one I got into my wireless truck and went up to Carnforth in convoy with the guns. From there we went to the coast and harboured for the night. I slept in the Isolation Hut of a Home for Poor Leeds Children. Next day we moved east and took up a battle position. That night I slept with the guns in a field, and the next day we moved down to Hornby. We harboured that night at Hornby. The officers slept at the Vicarage. Very nice, too, in a charming village – a typical country rectory.

Next day we moved up to south of Windermere, along a frightful track, and did a night occupation with the guns. We spent three days in a field. On Sunday there was a Service in the field; the sun shone, and the day was beautiful. We were called upon at all hours of the night to fire on SOS tasks – with blank ammunition. At half past five this morning we fired a barrage – with blank. It has rained steadily since three this morning. We all got very wet, and had very little sleep. Today we moved into our last harbouring area for the night. So here we are at the Duke of Devonshire's place – each with a bedroom in the Bachelors' Wing; comfort, kindness – heaven after dirt and tiredness and thousands of cow pats. There is a house-party here tonight and strange figures flit about the passages. The house is vast – with thousands of rooms. Only the centre part is old. The rest is Victorian and ugly. . . .

PS We go home tomorrow, so don't inflict letters on the D. of D.

The regiment's gentlemanly aspect changed to a more professional one as its Territorial base began to slip away from it. Soon we were to move the men from their seaside hotels and abandoned factories up to Scotland. We left behind our mixed collection of coastal defence guns – the 4.5 and 6 inch howitzers, 18–pounders and French 75s – and were equipped with 25–pounders and Morris quads, the beetle-shaped lightly armoured four-wheel-drive tractors that pulled them and carried their six-man crews. All this new machinery made us feel much more glamorous, but it tended to separate us even further from the veterans of World War I. We headed north, conscious of our new fighting power but subconsciously expecting too much of our new acquisitions. Perhaps we thought technological advance called for less rather than more physical toughness and enterprise. As for our destination, I doubt if any of us had heard of it, though it was only just over the Scottish border. It was a market town in Dumfriesshire called Lockerbie.

4

Lockerbie

THE regiment's move north was only my third experience of Scotland – land of my grandfather but of no known existing relations. At fifteen I had been invited to join a friend and his parents at Killin for a motor tour of the Western Highlands. I went up by night train to Stirling, dozing fitfully on the bench seat, noting at each awakening that the severe sandy-haired schoolteacher opposite had moved further under the rug of the solicitous Irishman who had joined us at Crewe. As we crossed the border in the dawn light I felt – or thought I felt – the tug of paternal ancestors. It had already pulled me through *Guy Mannering* and *Rob Roy*, half way through *The Antiquary*, and at a gallop through Stevenson's novels. When my hosts took me to the Highland Games at Crieff I began to think that the novels' romantic passages were by no means overdrawn. But after that there was no striding through the heather or riding up the burn. My Plymouth Brethren host and hostess rarely emerged from their Hudson Terraplane, except to eat – and that in temperance hotels – and stopped the car only when we came to a good view. In spite of their kindness and the beauty observed from afar I was quite glad to leave the stodginess of their Scotland for the livelier and more sinful south.

I had happier memories of a second visit with three Cambridge friends, camping in Galloway and amusing ourselves by telephoning the pretty Post Office girl at Ballantrae from her own call-box. Passing through the *Nine Tailors* country we found ourselves wholly unable to understand the reply when asking a road-mender the way near Gatehouse of Fleet. It seemed incongruous that the Western

Highlanders spoke not only Gaelic as their first language but much clearer English than these Lowlanders.

Lockerbie had an air of sober prosperity. The food was better than it had been in the south; there was plenty of butter, haggis was off the ration and we lived well. But for amusement we had to be content with the Saturday night shilling hops where the girls, with their lilting voices, were pleased to see us but remained tiresomely abstemious as far as drink was concerned. There were only two occasions when they would enter a public house: on Hogmanay and Burns night; then they more than made up for their restraint, and I was shocked to see such gentle creatures in so sodden a state. Alan Haldenby and I concentrated at the dances on Nettie and Bessie, and I felt a little nervous when having my hair cut in town because the barber was the eighteen-year-old Bessie's father. But in any case my ardour cooled after seeing her home one night. Kissing her at the gate with rather more passion than usual, there was a click and a caving in and a strangled scream. She pushed me away and thrust a finger and thumb into her mouth. "It's ma' teeth!" she said, clicking them back into place. All her top teeth were false.

Once a week I exchanged the prim tones of Lockerbie for accents that reminded me of my incomprehension near Gatehouse of Fleet. With a sergeant knowledgeable about small arms I went up to the Eskdale moors to give instruction to the Home Guard – although as they were mostly farmers and shepherds they knew far more about shooting over the local country than I did. On these occasions neither side understood a word the other said, but when we moved to the pub after a couple of hours of mutual toleration, communication improved wonderfully.

From Lockerbie our military exercises introduced us to Hawick and – on the specious excuse of running-in some new motor bikes – to Edinburgh. They took us in fact on a kind of grand tour. Travel was still a luxury before World War II, even in our own island, and the natives were not always friendly. While Yorkshire housewives would send out jugs of tea when our convoys were stalled by their houses, and shout with laughter if we offered to pay for them, one farm in South Wales did a roaring trade at a penny for a cup of water, threepence for a bread and butter sandwich and fourpence for half a glass of milk.

At the end of an exercise, with the guns hitched up and the field officers safely ahead on the homeward run, we others would sometimes liven up our journey. We could take a turn at driving a Morris quad, an exhilarating experience (in small doses) with all that power underneath, gears needing double de-clutching, and the gun and trailer swinging and bumping behind. Or we could swap a wireless truck for the Sergeant's Norton, and zoom up and down the convoy. One moment the convoy would be crawling sedately along, the next the devil would be let loose and trucks officially governed down to forty mph would zip past each other, bullet-proof tyres whining and wireless masts waving, at sixty-five; even the quads would quicken their insect crawl to a lumber, and the lumber to a gallop, until they thundered along like charging rhinoceri, guns swaying wickedly behind them. Then someone's conscience would prick, hands would wave, and in a few minutes the convoy would revert to its 'butter wouldn't melt' procession.

From this wildness born of the border country our next move sounded a little tame. We were to re-group before service overseas, and were to go south to Cheshire – to Macclesfield, Congleton and Alderley Edge. Our destination may have sounded tame, but we soon found that there were to be no more high jinks on the convoys or musical chairs with the quads.

5

Toosey Takes Over

THE regiment was expanded from two to three batteries, and I was billeted at Alderley Edge. Its suburban opulence made Lockerbie seem quite bucolic in retrospect. The mansions wrapped in shrubberies along the Wilmslow Road or peering through the trees running up the Edge looked at first sight resentful of our intrusion, but they soon opened their doors to dispense Manchester hospitality. Often there was a daughter of the house who was less inhibited about visiting pubs than the lasses of Lockerbie. The memorably named Fluffy Shelmerdine, for example, of the Old Hall was often to be seen with one of my fellow officers (and not always the same one) at the seigneurial Roebuck Inn of Mobberley, and an urbane coal baron, Sir Robert Burroughs, and his wife kept open house at Bonis Hall in Prestbury with their daughter, Sheila. Through a mutual friend I met Peggy, a medical student who lived with her parents on the Edge, and in her white tennis shorts she bowled me over at once.

But there was something very prim about Alderley Edge; neither village nor suburb, it seemed to be designed not so much for living and working in as for the scene of an Agatha Christie plot. A body might well surface in the oppressive Queen's Hotel bordering the railway line or more likely lie there undetected for years.

On a firing exercise at Sennybridge, I saw a familiar face from the past among a group of Cambridgeshires – round, bespectacled, cheeky. It saluted me with elaborate courtesy and broke into a grin. I realised with a feeling of having changed into reverse by mistake that it was my Cambridge gyp, Harry Asplin. This sudden reversion to civvy street insouciance was symptomatic of our amateurish firing on the ranges that week. On a night shoot one troop fired 180 degrees off target, rattling a few dustbins in the village. At the post mortem afterwards the Divisional Commander of the Royal Artillery, Hubert Servaes, was very grim.

"Who was responsible?"

"I was, sir," said 'Butch' Gamble, a bright and breezy London solicitor.

"They were your guns, were they?"

"Yessir!"

"Can you explain what happened?"

"Oh, yes, sir!"

"Well?"

"Well, sir, it was like this. *Prima facie* . . . "

"Oh, sit down and shut up!"

The CRA may have been irked by the prospect of Butch's legal smokescreen but he was no Regular Army blimp. He had been a thrusting Liverpool businessman before the war and he now decided that a kindred spirit was needed to take over the regiment and shake it up. There were only six weeks before we went overseas but the man he posted to us was just the one for the job. Lieutenant Colonel Philip Toosey, at thirty-seven, was energetic, personable and ambitious. A pillar of Baring's Bank in Liverpool, it was his fate to be an up-and-coming man in a down-and-going situation twice over – first at Dunkirk and now with us. Perhaps the quality he conveyed was charisma rather than leadership, for I felt there was something of the showman in him; but we never worked closely together long enough for me to see if this was really so, or if I was merely nonplussed by characteristics absent in myself. Anyhow, his bearing went down well with the troops, and the officers soon found that they could take it or leave it. The older ones departed, and everyone else now felt Toosey's keen dark eye upon their successes and failures. My new battery commander, Major Osmond Daltry, proved both efficient and likeable.

With Toosey's arrival the feeling of fiddling while Rome burned left us. While I had been immersed in the domestic details of military life, Dunkirk had come and gone and so had the Battle of Britain.

In April 1941 came the first family casualty – a sister's brother-in-law killed in the fall of Tobruk; Crete fell – inexplicably – in May, and in June Germany even more inexplicably invaded Russia; in July, far, far away from Alderley Edge, but close to Noel in Malaya, the Japanese quietly co-habited with the Vichy French in Indo-China. All this time the nearest we came to active service was in the aftermath of the Liverpool air raids. Accustomed to the anodyne bulletins of the Ministry of Information, we were shaken to see their effect on the ground as we trundled into the dark and messy city one night to stand by for 'Duties in Aid of the Civil Power' and to hear first-hand accounts of looting and riots.

Our fighting arms began to improve, and by autumn 1941 we were up to establishment; the pace of life accelerated, the guns and vehicles were repainted for desert warfare, and the word went round that we would soon be embarking for Basra. Some of the younger married officers were a bit glum but most of us, at least outwardly, were philosophical. One recently married young bombardier failed to return from his embarkation leave but others, including 'Tippers', complained bitterly at being left behind on medical grounds.

I gathered that we were likely to call at Cape Town, where my eldest brother George (Bim to the family) might still be on long leave after serving with the 1st/6th King's African Rifles in the Abyssinian campaign. So I alerted my mother, whose letters to us all were largely family cross-references. (We kept our family bitching for each other, which helped to explain her inordinate pride in her children.)

Saturday 25th October 1941

We are off at last so don't send anything else here. I am sending home a cabin trunk with my unwanted stuff. If by any chance it doesn't arrive, you might enquire of Mrs Jones, 176 Chester Road, Macclesfield, if it has gone.

Thank you for a fine leave. Bristol was looking very lovely, so were the Assembly Rooms and I now feel very homesick. However, I'm glad to be going at last, but it is the parents who suffer.

There was a newly-commissioned ATS officer in the carriage. Ah, she was so lovely! She will probably marry a Lord.

If I had a fortune I would have asked her to marry me. But, alas! we said Goodbye at Shrewsbury, for she was going to Wrexham. And she gave me a conspiratorial smile as I handed down her brand-new valise to her; on the outside of it was tied a hot-water-bottle.

To my father I had mentioned going through Leek on one of our exercises. It had been his first medical post after his marriage and it sparked off memories:

Did ever I picture when I was at Leek such a world as that in which you are launched!

The Boer War was raging, to be sure, and I was perturbed about it. I was not sure of our honour in the matter. I thought our little brother in South Africa should manage his quarrel and that the event would be better for him if he did so than if he called his parent country in! But though that quarrel might smirch our honour it could never threaten our safety or menace our existence. England was above the heads of other powers. Her dignity was not to be affronted. May you live and enjoy an England as superior and as safe as we, when I was young, thought England to be. . . .

I am still pursuing the futilities and the successes of that practice of medicine you have left behind. It is largely perhaps a woman's trade; there are more of them about, now that men are called up. People come to us doctors as if we could give all they asked. So came a wife, and asked butter and milk and eggs for her husband, a fat old man who needed little of anything. Only to certain diseases, I said, could milk be given. She said her husband had been a lead worker and such workers had to take milk. We could live, I said, on bread and water. What did she reply? "I know it says, 'thy bread shall be given thee; thy water shall be sure.'" I could not so collect myself as to say our land was not flowing with milk and honey at present.

By this time Peggy and I had become close. But now I had been well and truly called up and must leave her to pursue her studies

29

unhindered. It had been fun, being a couple, and was beginning to be more than fun, but the partnership for which I had been trained so long was claiming me. Great events, I found, depend on momentum more than choice, and soldiers are conditioned to go along with it. If there was a dilemma, 'Tell me not, sweet, I am unkind' was one way of resolving it. I embraced my sword, my horse, my shield with admirable fortitude.

The bustle of departure swept me along, and as I packed my books I ran through other apt quotations: 'He threw his empty revolver down the slope'; '"Good morning! Good morning!" the General said, as we met him one day on our way to the line'; 'Ben Battle was a soldier bold, and used to war's alarms; but a cannon ball took off his legs, so he laid down his arms'. Inevitably, however, more sombre lines intruded: 'I have a rendezvous with Death'; 'It seemed that out of battle I escaped'; 'The thundering line of battle stands, and in the air death moans and sings; But Day shall clasp him with strong hands . . . '. I suspected that, even discounting Yeats's assertion that war was no fit subject for poetry, no poet had yet managed to convey the real horror of it.

> On Waterloo's ensanguined plain
> Lay twice ten thousand of the slain,
> But none by sabre or by shot
> Fell half as flat as Walter Scott.

For our last few days before the regiment took the train to Gourock I was in Macclesfield among the officers farmed out to local families to sleep. In the reshuffle before embarkation I had been posted to First Line Reserves at RHQ, and I was sorry to leave the familiar battery mess, even if I had never felt entirely at home there. It is a moot point whether 'Reserves' are chosen more for their tactical dispensability or idiosyncratic social habits, but I should think I qualified on both counts. The others at RHQ were my Hogmanay host, Jock Monro; Roger Smith, an Audlem solicitor; and a former sergeant-major from Darlington named Wilkinson; Wilkie was prickly but proved to be a tower of strength in a tight corner.

I rang up Peggy to say goodbye with the minimum of fuss. She was paralysed by a cold but determined on a last meeting, and her father lent her the chauffeur-driven family car for it. I had not bargained for the funereal circumstances of that last farewell. The black Daimler looked in the darkness like a hearse. A glass partition divided us from the silent chauffeur, and Peggy coughed and sneezed as I held her shaking body, trying to think of something to say. ('Man's love is of man's life a thing apart, 'tis woman's whole existence'.) When at last the Daimler pulled away I looked after it with stinging eyes. Then I turned to the problem of Mrs Jones, my hostess for the night.

Mrs Jones lived in a bow-windowed thirties house, polished up to the nines. It was full of frills and furbelows – as was Mrs Jones. She was stout and old – at least thirty – and she too was polished up to the nines. Mr Jones was 'away on business'.

I had already fended off her offers of food, coffee and hot-water bottles and stayed out as long as I could. When I re-entered on tiptoe, the door to the lounge was ajar and lights shone within.

"Is that you, Mr Alexander?"

"Yes."

"You're back then?"

"Yes."

"What you need is a nightcap."

"It's very kind of you, but – "

"It's no trouble. I often have one about this time."

I suppose this was the first time I noticed that a man involved with one woman seems to attract others. Thus married men often live like pashas, while many a bachelor is born to blush unseen. As I stood at the foot of the stairs between a Peter Scott and a Russell Flint, I felt myself breaking into a sweat. Mrs Jones opened the door of the lounge wider. I caught a glimpse of shaded lights and of glasses set out on a trolley; soft music came from the radio, and a red glow from the electric fire; Mrs Jones's bosom in its jewelled frame loomed nearer, and a steam seemed to rise and engulf me – like smoke from a 25–pounder gas shell. What could I do? Was the sweet sorrow of my recent parting to be followed so grotesquely? Yet how could I escape? It was Mrs Jones herself who solved my dilemma.

"Come in, do!" she said, placing her hand firmly on my upper arm.

"Ow!" I cried. "I've just been innoculated. If you'll excuse me, I think I'd better go straight to bed. I'm feeling a bit feverish."

As I turned the light out a little later, I heard the radio go silent, some bangs and clatters downstairs, dragging footsteps coming upstairs, and at last a door slamming along the passage.

> But Day shall clasp him with strong hands
> And Night shall fold him in soft wings.

6

Yanks

WE embarked at Gourock for Basra. The biggest ship in our convoy was the *Andes*; we were on the smallest. Apart from the Irish ferry it was the first ocean-going ship I had sailed in. The saloon of the Polish *Sobieski* (officers only) displayed murals of the Castellan of Cracow and his son John, the Saviour of Vienna, while the bar sported the upper half of a Doumergue girl. In the early days there was a terrific swell and the submarine watches at night were very uncomfortable; but after a few days I felt I'd been at sea all my life. On November 3rd I wrote home:

I am still in the Atlantic, and didn't know there *was* so much sea. The officers are all pretty comfortable, tho' the men sleep in hammocks in stuffy holds. The food is staggering. The lunch is one, two, three, four, five, *six* very large and beautiful courses, and dinner is four courses and coffee, etc. There is no rationing, and we all feel very guilty. I have to refuse at least two courses. The sea has not been calm, and there has been much sea-sickness. I haven't had it very badly. Harry, my erstwhile gyp, is on the same boat. A friend of mine, Roger Smith, fell off a ladder while we were on submarine watch, largely because I shouted something at him and he was looking at me instead of at the ladder. He was in an awful bloody mess when we picked him up, and will have to rest at the nearest hospital instead of coming with us. I felt a frightful shit. We have been lucky in the weather, and the scene is always beautiful. My accordion is so far undamaged, except for the case.

We had grown so used to the tough and cheerful Poles that we heard with some dismay that we were to be trans-shipped in Halifax to American transports. When our British convoy melted away in mid-Atlantic and dozens of American warships took over in a great flurry we felt abandoned. It was dark and wet in Halifax docks when we arrived, and at noon the next day, November 8th, we began our second embarkation. With the 53rd Brigade (Brigadier Duke) of 18th Division (Major-General Beckwith-Smith), we filed into the huge maw of the *Mount Vernon* and down into her bowels; space became ever more constricting for the wretched men. How we missed our little *Sobieski*, with its gin for us and beer for the men! Roger Smith, suffering from concussion, had gone ashore to hospital but insisted on rejoining us before we sailed. I often wondered how much he regretted that decision.

The troop carrier *Mount Vernon* had been the SS *Washington* and was one of three great passenger ships of the US Lines in the convoy; the others were the *Wakefield* (SS *Manhattan*) and the *West Point* (SS *America*). The *Manhattan* had taken Duff and Diana Cooper to their American lecture tour (to the disapproval of Chamberlain: "In a few weeks time, when things get pretty hot here, a man of fifty might be criticised for leaving his country.") Later on, the *Washington* had carried their children and those of the Mountbattens to safe houses in America. We had three smaller troopships and a massive escort consisting of an aircraft carrier, two heavy cruisers, eight destroyers and a fleet oiler.

All this was the fruit of a meeting off Newfoundland in August between Churchill in the *Prince of Wales* and Roosevelt in the *Augusta*. Thomas Allison of the *Mount Vernon*, who kept a diary of events while convoying what the Americans called 'Winston's Specials', described the meeting:

> Because of the spacious compartments aboard the *Prince of Wales* and the President's infirmity it was decided to transport all the American contingent via destroyer to the British battleship. McDougal approached the man-of-war for a

'Chinese Landing'. That is, to have the bow of the destroyer secured to the stern of the battleship. While McDougal was near her landing, a CPO on the destroyer noticed a sailor dressed in pea jacket and blue rain hat standing by idly. The Chief yelled, "Ahoy on the deck of the *Prince of Wales*, bear a hand and secure this line!" The Chief then ordered one of his men to throw a line to the deck of the battleship. Seeing this, the idler hurried to the line and made it fast. This idler was Winston Churchill!

On September 1st Churchill had asked for US Navy troopships and escort to carry twenty thousand British troops to the Middle East. 'Agreements were worked out for the troops to be carried as supernumeraries. . . . The troops would conform to US Navy and ships' regulations. Intoxicating liquors were prohibited.'

Our route to Basra was to be via Port of Spain and Cape Town. Not all went smoothly. The *Mount Vernon* had only manually-aimed World War I guns and it was fortunate that they were never used in earnest. One of the carrier's aircraft ditched in landing, and there were several collisions among the smaller vessels. On the *Mount Vernon* 'Edward Hemly, AB USN, was waiting to go before the Executive Officer for a minor breach in naval regulations when he bolted and cleared the boat deck railing portside.'

Avoiding-action was taken one morning when an unidentified man-of-war was reported forty-five miles dead ahead, and aerial photographs identified her as the Argentine cruiser *Belgrano* (the former Italian cruiser *Varese*). Several submarine scares led to nothing, and Thomas Allison tells us why. In May 1941 the British had captured a U-boat 'with the Ultra secret German deciphering machines used to vector U-boats to Allied convoys and instruct Nazi supply ships. This secret was not known to the US Navy until January 1942 and the British advised the convoy on safe courses to all ports.'

We landlubbers were less concerned with naval tactics than with the sweet and sour element of American cuisine: the all-purpose food tray with pineapple slithering over cuts of ham, sweetcorn spreading like vomit, iced tea, and all too often the dreaded hash.

But memories of plum duff and stew faded, and the men began to appreciate the freshness and variety of the food emerging from the ship's vast kitchens. The officers remained more choosy, perhaps because they dined in separate canteens, served by black stewards in a style particularly foreign to them. There was a commotion one day in the service queue, which ended in one steward seizing a knife and lungeing at another. "Good heavens!" I thought, "what will happen now? Flogging? Irons? Keel-hauling?"

"Hey, hey!" cried a petty officer, waddling up and putting himself between them. "Cool down there! Why d'you do that?"

"Ah ain't going to be called that by no man!"

"Aw, c'mon, Sam. Cool down!"

"No, ah ain't!"

"Sam, c'mon! Gimme that knife. Now, get hold of those plates."

"Well, I . . . "

"That's it then, Sam. Keep moving now. OK boys, break it up."

But the real trouble lay below. While officers shared staterooms the men were squeezed into the saloons and empty swimming pools. To add insult to injury, the five-tier steel-netting bunks were framed in delicate garlands and pink cherubs. There was a shortage of water, and the 'heads' stank abominably; ventilation, which suffered further from the black-out, had not been designed for tropical climates. Most of the day men found themselves queueing for something – meals, the laundry, the heads, the doctor, salt-water showers – or standing by for boat drill; and most of them in a huge ship like this were a very long way from the nearest mustering point. Deck space was so restricted that open-air exercise had to be staggered, and it was many days before the men's distress was tempered by improvements, by ingenuity and by the give-and-take that makes one get used to almost anything – provided everyone is in the same boat.

Dearest Mother,

We are beginning to get into the heat, and strange little white bodies are dressing themselves in unfamiliar tropical kit. One has only to compare the magnificent bodies of the crew with the scrawny and pallid physique of the Tommies to feel surprise that our army is reputedly the second best in the world. However, I suppose training counts more than physical perfection, and I hope our training will prove so.

We are cramped aboard this ship and the men's quarters stink to high heaven. But the food is good, though rather greasy. It seems very odd sailing down into summer from an English October. No doubt in a week or two I shall yearn for a fine cold day again. Already the ship reeks of stale sweat. I have run out of anything to read – except *Peter Simple*, which I'm enjoying again – not that a subaltern has much time of his own on board ship. He is continually harrassed with silly little jobs. Having spent half the day cutting out bits of other people's letters, I feel it would be unfair to slip in some of the interesting titbits which security forbids me to repeat.

Did you get my trunk from Mrs Jones?

After seven days we entered the Dragon's Mouth between Venezuela and Trinidad and sailed west along the Gulf of Paria in the early morning. Compared with the foetid atmosphere below decks, life ashore looked Elysian. The sun gilded lush hilltops where white houses with red roofs peered at us from behind green protective palms. Borne on the warm breeze there seemed to come a distant hail from Robinson Crusoe and a nearer one from Jim Hawkins, then, nearest of all, the heavy scent of mangroves and fever and barrack graveyards. At Port of Spain we lay offshore to refuel and there was no shore leave, but Ailwyn De Ramsey's social contacts were once again deployed. A case, allegedly of faulty ammunition, went ashore to Government House, to be replaced by a more effective fighting spirit. After a couple of days we were off again for Cape Town.

We crossed the line [I wrote on December 5th to Bim] a couple of weeks ago with the usual celebrations and the ship still reeks of sweat and old socks. However, the chaps are cheerful and write long letters home 'hoping this finds their girls well as it leaves them at present in the pink'. I am in a cabin with a pushing reporter, a dour ranker named Wilkinson, a land agent who dislikes the unavoidable sweetcorn as much as I do, and a QM who is 'fucking browned-off, boy!'.

I left them all pretty well at home and had (oddly enough) quite a riotous embarkation leave. I felt very guilty when Mother said goodbye to her youngest hope and disappointment, and as for after the war – with no qualifications and no jobs, no beauty, no class, no free enterprise agriculture but only co-operative chaos – God knows what we are all going to do, whoever wins . . . What will Japan do? I have no faith in America – none at all. David Pitcher, the land agent, says that half her naval petty-officers two years ago were Japs, and what I have seen of her military power is all 'bum-and-bang-me-arse' as old Fred Proud, whom we left behind, used to say. . . .

The weather got worse as we went south, and by December 5th a Force 7 gale was blowing. We lost our steering for twenty minutes – a very nasty feeling; but on 7th our American hosts got quite a different sort of blow – the news of Pearl Harbor. For us, of course, this new ill wind blew rather differently. My father sent his views to Noel in Malaya:

Today Japan has attacked; we have replied. Better now than later, we say to each other. America finds the futility of aloofness; too long has she borne the fraud and ambition of the Japs; our next thought is for you. I assume you are at rest in the matter. You have long foreseen trouble and been impatient of dalliance. You will hardly carry through your duties with war around, without incurring danger; so we shall be wishing you a double daily portion of courage and good health. At home we want for nothing needful. I have indeed a very small stock of wine but I discovered the other day that whisky and cider is an admirable mixture, heightening the quality of each. . . .

A book in my hand is Oman on 'History Writing'. To him there is no providential purpose to be found, only a succession of happenings. 'He that gathereth not with Me scattereth abroad.' Oman looks on: he does not come to the help of the Lord against the mighty. . . .

I could enjoy a trudge from Triscombe Stone to Bicknoller Post.

My own letter was less reflective:

Shepton Mallet 66   Doulting Vicarage
Cranmore GWR   Shepton Mallet

Dear Father,

I write on the Padre's notepaper. He is a nice man, who knows his Lady Horners and drives a Rolls round his parish.

We hope to go ashore at last for a few days in a week or so. We are now heartily sick of flying fish and nothing else to look at (though we saw an albatross this morning). I sleep in a cabin of five not very stimulating companions. However, life is pleasant enough. Training continues and the ship's library has some Scott, Stevenson and Thackeray.

We crossed the line a week or so ago, and there was much shaving, throwing about of dye and hosing down. One of the crew jumped overboard and was drowned. We follow the ship's news eagerly and are wondering what is to happen to Libya and Japan (so, I expect, is Robin).

If our landfall in the Gulf of Paria had enchanted me, the first sight of the sun and clouds on Table Mountain was infinitely grander. Here stood the sentinel to an even braver and airier new world, and I could hardly wait to hitch up the wagon and trek into the great open spaces. But we were given no chance to do so. As Thomas Allison put it, 'the negro members of the crew were taken by bus to a selected area for recreation', while we stepped ashore to find a queue of cars awaiting us. I was disappointed when I saw Adderly Street; I had subconsciously been expecting cape carts, saloons and hitching posts rather than Chevvy taxis, the Junior Conservative Club, and department stores equipped with escalators. My world of Smollett and Hickey, of Henty and Rider Haggard, was not, after all, to be regained. But there was little time for introspection. The whole town seemed to have turned out to take us wherever we wanted to go: to the shops, to lunch in leafy suburban houses, to our first Van der Humms at Del Monico's – and my first colour bar. That night there was a ball at the Kelvin Grove and Marshal Smuts himself addressed us:

"Ladies and gentlemen, there is one thing for which we can be profoundly grateful to the Japanese. They have done something that nobody else in the world has been able to do; they have – BROUGHT AMERICA INTO THE WAR!"

The applause by British and South Africans was not echoed by the American crewmen, and I remember the whole occasion as being rather muted. The next day we were all depressed. News arrived of the sinking of the *Prince of Wales* and the *Repulse*. Suddenly the beach at Muizenberg (the white end) lost its attractions. Was Singapore to be our Port Arthur?

After four days we were off again, and our American escort dispersed to its own theatre of war, leaving us in the company of the *Dorsetshire*. On December 14th she brought us new orders. It came as no surprise to hear that I was to join Noel in Malaya; indeed, the thing seemed in a curious way ordained and I felt a warm glow of family solidarity. We were fated, then, to see off the Japs together – or not, as the case might be. Basra was abandoned, and the *Mount Vernon*, leaving the rest of the convoy to go on to Bombay – taking our guns with them – made for Mombasa at twenty-one knots. We docked on Christmas Day.

Monday, 29th December 1941

Dearest Mother,

How amazing it is that Malaya was so poorly prepared when everybody out there – e.g. Robin – knew its weakness and Japan's strength five years ago. So many people were scornful of Japan – including America – and even now think she will be mopped up soon. I shouldn't be surprised to hear that Singapore has fallen within a month.

Soon after leaving Cape Town we put into another port. I bathed in the hottest sea I've ever known, from dazzling white sands with palm trees at the edge (and at the edge of the water other things not quite so pretty – this being a Moslem society – which one had to step over rather carefully). There was a pleasant white cathedral built in 1905, most of whose bishops seem to have been drowned or murdered. At the local club I

40

saw a card left many months ago by Major Atthill, Diana's papa, who taught us at Catterick for a short time and then went out to Abyssinia. It's shocking to eat well and do nothing while you people live so uncomfortably at home.

Passed by Censor
No.1476
S. C. Alexander
164313

Tuesday, 30th December 1941

Dear Bim,

I just missed you at Cape Town. What a pity. We unexpectedly spent Christmas ashore in a second African port, tho' very different from Cape Town. This was a really one horse hole, but as it gave us our first view of a genuine native quarter we were all rather thrilled. The English women were pale and sweating things, and the whole place was pretty desolate as the shops were mostly shut.

An interesting parson there – who lived in Japan and combined Intelligence with Religion apparently – was very fearful of Japan. He said they took all they wanted from China in six months and only continue fighting because China makes them, their average man is far better educated than his English opposite and illiteracy is practically non-existent, and their fatalistic attitude makes them worse enemies than Germany.

We were first of all to be nearest you, then nearest David, and now it is to be nearest Robin. I think – at the moment – this is good news, because the thought of fossilizing still longer with a lot of nattering and ambitious officers and bored men in an outpost of empire seems worse than an at least *active* experience, however unpleasant. I won't think this in a month's time, I dare say. I've just read *Testament of Youth* which I enjoyed, but I felt a few kicks in the pants would have done Miss V. B. no harm.

Happy New Year (ha ha!)

It was not a very merry Christmas in Mombasa. Guam had fallen on December 10th and Wake Island on 23rd. Japan had attacked Burma on 11th and took Hong Kong on Christmas Day. The only bright spot in the news was the British capture of Benghazi on Christmas Eve, which seemed to mark a revival of our fortunes in the Middle East.

We set off again next day. Joining us for Singapore were four merchant ships, one carrying fifty-one boxed Hurricanes, and one, a Dutchman, a reminder that the resources of the Netherlands East Indies were at our disposal. We watered at the Maldive Islands and were soon afterwards joined by the *Exeter*.

Now the days were positively balmy. In the evenings the men would congregate on deck for a sing-song and perhaps for a session of the long-running cabaret act by an odd couple in the Norfolks; one was tubby and apple-cheeked and the other saturnine, with the guileless menace of the old pugilist. They would walk round each other for a bit, feinting and sparring as spurts of inspiration came and went, while the crowd, filled with a sense of well-being and eagerness to be amused, barracked and applauded, gradually working them into a corner until suddenly they would connect and they were off: a trip to the Derby, a demonstration of the Indian Rope Trick, or a walk down the Prince of Wales Road on a Saturday night ("You can tell by our hats we're a right pair of twats" or "Sing cock-a-doodle-do, it's nothing to do with you, I tell you what, it's a jolly fine cock and a cock-a-doodle-do!"). But the most encored of their acts was a Cuban rumba, with Apple-cheek as Carmen Miranda and Don Saturnino as her partner. Men were perched at every deck level looking down onto the 'stage', and higher still, off-duty crew watched too, bathed in gold against a darkening backcloth of rolling sea. As the light faded from reds to blues a last radiance ran out, over the grey cruisers loping along in the distance, to the horizon.

A less suitable preparation for jungle fighting could scarcely be imagined, and every day the radio brought news of more 'strategic withdrawals' down the Malayan peninsula. The Dutch presence was increased by the battle-cruiser *De Ruyter* and more destroyers – the *Tromp* and the Australian *Vampire* – and finally by three Dutch minesweepers. All this attention made us feel we were nearing the moment of truth; after weeks of fattening we were being politely but firmly shepherded – "After you, gentlemen!" – to the slaughter-house. Manila fell on January 2nd. On January 12th we entered the Sunda Straits and, as one wit put it, heard the gates clang shut behind us. We certainly heard the drone of engines as ninety-five Jap bombers and fighters, already signalled to us from Singapore, approached – and passed over. They passed over because at the crucial moment we were blotted out by a tropical rainstorm. And why not? Such providential protection would not have surprised my parents. I wrote them my last letter from the ship.

. . . What a waste it is, coming all this way and seeing practically nothing of the lands we passed. Had I left behind me an interesting job, or a wife and family, or even a girl I was crackers about, I should doubtless have been very homesick. As it is, 112 Pembroke Road has taken on very rosy hues, but they are subdued by the fact that I was unemployed there and passed my time sowing a not very wild oat or two. When I think about the end of the war any longing is nullified by apprehension for our condition and, more selfishly, for my position in it. There are three thugs in my cabin and two and a half months in their company has made me very tired of them. It is for such as these that England will be turned upside down to give them their rights. . . . However, enough of that! We have lived in sunshine and health for two months, with no bombs, no rationing, no pain, all good chaps at heart, and now we shall justify two years' boring training and two years' salary at 11/– a day. And I'm very pleased at that but can't help moping sometimes, because uncertainty is rather a bloody thing. Cambridge seems very long ago; I wonder what I'd have done there. Yesterday a Welsh corporal in the MPs said 'Excuse me, Sir, were you ever at Catterick?' He was technical storeman there. How he remembered my face from so many I can't think. We still see nothing but ocean and wonderful sunsets. Sometimes we pass desert islands in the middle of nowhere, just flat spits of sand about three miles long, with palm trees and perhaps one or two canoes. A big wave could sweep right over them, but I suppose they never do. . . .

The next morning a mine floated by a few feet away; it was detonated behind us by a destroyer. Soon we passed the dense jungle of the outer islands of Singapore; they looked enigmatic and impenetrable. As we neared the city in the early light, its office blocks and godowns glittered like Venetian palaces. We had arrived at the City of the Lion – or Shonan to the Japanese.

The rest of 18th Division arrived from Bombay a fortnight later, and were not all so lucky with the weather. As for us, our last sight of the *Mount Vernon*, as she prepared to cast off, showed RAF ground staff going up the gangplanks we had just come down. At the last moment she had to dispose of a stowaway, a rating from the *Prince of Wales*. Then, rattling in the last gangplank, and carrying away the cosy beds, ample kitchens and simple routine of our six weeks' easy living, she made – lickety-split – for the Sunda Straits.

7

Raffles Country

COMPARED with the improvisations of Mombasa, Singapore looked immensely competent and strong – but nightly formations of twenty-seven Japanese bombers were already coming over with impunity. The enormous docks and godowns, the splendid roads flanked by generous 'malarial' drains, the white-domed municipal buildings and dark Gothic cathedral, the pink-sugar railway station, the banks in broad avenues and the beflagged clatter of narrow Chinese streets all gave the impression of self-confidence and bottomless resources. But underneath, the infrastructure was fragile; there were grave public works problems and fatal gaps between civil and military administration. Vital preparations had not been made for fear of alarming the civilian population and, in government and army offices alike, people still busy with red tape were disinclined to go out in the midday sun.

Of all this I was happily unaware, as we went under canvas at Nee Soon, six miles north of Singapore town, but it was a shock to realise that after barely a month the Japanese were already halfway down Malaya's five hundred and fifty miles of 'impenetrable' jungle. Penang, it appeared, had been evacuated in an unseemly British-first panic and the conduct of General Heath and his Indian Corps was variously described as masterly, in effecting without tanks or air support a retreat to defend Singapore rather than suffering annihilation upcountry, or disastrous in letting Jap tanks through at Slim River only fifty miles north of Kuala Lumpur and losing all central Malaya. There had been no pockets of resistance or retaliatory landings in the enemy's rear, and the general air of demoralisation

showed there was something very wrong at the top. The appointment of Duff Cooper as Resident Minister for Far Eastern Affairs,
or 'Commissioner', was Whitehall's attempt to improve matters.
Nobody seemed to know where the Commissioner or the Governor
stood in relation either to Whitehall or to each other. I knew little
of Duff Cooper, except that he had resigned office over Chamberlain's policy of appeasement to Italy in Abyssinia, that he had been
very fierce about poor 'Plum' Wodehouse's Riviera broadcasts, that
he had a flashy society wife, and that he was a small man with a little
moustache. And I had no chance to learn more because, as more
bombs fell on Singapore and refugees poured south and discipline
crumbled, the futility of his mission became obvious. He and his
wife did not wait to catch the *Manhattan/Wakefield* a second time
as – by a curious coincidence – they could have done, but departed
by plane on January 11th. I wondered if Duff Cooper remembered
some lines he had written in 1939:

> More gladly though would we give all
> That yet we have to give.
> Oh, let the old men man the wall,
> And let the young men live!

As one of the young men concerned, it did just cross my mind
that it might not have been a bad precedent for a politician, instead
of beetling back to resume the role of Whitehall warrior, to share
for once the fate of his constituents.

It was not so much the heat of Singapore that took us aback as
the unsuitability of our equipment for it. The heat had been worse
at Mombasa, and anyway we had become acclimatised to the tropics
by our long voyage. But at sea there are no mosquitoes and there is
always a breeze, either from the wind or the motion of the ship.
Ashore, we had to get used to periods of blinding sunlight when
everything seemed on the point of shrivelling to a cinder and the
guns felt red-hot, and to evenings clouding over in a suffocating
stillness, when the world closed in, birds fell silent and there was no
sun to dry sweat-soaked uniforms. The air, charged with menace,
resisted any kind of action. Then, with barely the warning of a few
fat drops thumping onto leaves, asphalt or canvas, the skies would

open. The temperature would drop exhilaratingly as rain thudded down like bullets onto roofs and roads, and beat trees – bananas, papayas, palms, rubber – into water spouts. Just when it seemed the flood would go on for ever, it would stop, leaving every flowing gutter, every gleaming blade of *lalang* grass pulsating with life; lizards, giant ants and enormous russet centipedes emerged sleek and unscathed from the puddles, while cicadas and tree frogs opened up their frenzied counterpoint like machine gunners making up for lost time. As the roar of the rain receded into the distance, the damp heat rushed in again, stickier than ever and mocking the elaboration of our tropical clothing. Our 'Kitchener' pith helmets looked and felt ludicrous compared with the bush hats of the Aussies. Our thick khaki drill was both too tight and too loose, closing on sweating armpits and crotches but opening to welcome insects up the thigh or burn the skin on sunbaked seats.

It was as though we were fighting a battle against the climate, instead of making the most of it, and it was the same with the rations. We cooked and ate as though we were in England. None of the army's experience of living off the land in overseas campaigns figured in our training – not even the adoption of a Middle Eastern diet for our planned operation in Basra. As we heaved our huge valises aboard the trucks, indispensable for even the shortest move, I observed how comfortable the Chinese stallholders looked in their singlets and sarongs, and wondered how far, kitted out as I was, I could propel a rickshaw or sprint down a jungle path.

The contrast between the desert-coloured neatness of our equipment and the green fecundity around us was echoed by that between the colonial formalities of Singapore and the chaos upcountry, heavily camouflaged in the jargon of official bulletins but vividly revealed by the stragglers from it who began to come our way. And the numbers game was so confusing; we seemed such an insignificant few to be added to so many: thousands of civilians still going about their business in spite of the bombing, and over a hundred thousand Commonwealth troops involved – some said many more, counting the odds and sods who wouldn't know one end of a rifle from the other. There were no tanks and hardly any planes, and the forward troops were already streaming back towards Singapore. Where did our eight hundred men and the rest of 53rd Brigade fit in? Or even the rest of 18th Division when it arrived? The heartland of Malaya which we had been diverted to defend had already fallen and, far from moving up in strength, it looked as though even a piecemeal operation, without waiting for the rest of 18th Division to arrive, would be tricky on roads and railways already clogged and under constant air attack. As each optimistic report was succeeded by a strategic withdrawal, we turned our attention from a dispiriting future and busied ourselves with adapting familiar routines to unfamiliar surroundings. We spent a few days at Nee Soon assembling equipment – and learning to drink *stengahs* at the nearby mess of the Hong Kong and Singapore Royal Artillery.

Toosey, with his guns still in Basra or perhaps Bombay, now had to battle not with the Japs but with the local ordnance store to get hold of some 25–pounders. They proved elusive, and a less zealous CO might have been content to wait in the fleshpots of Singapore until they materialised. Stuart Simmonds who, for all his Wildean eye for paradox, could play the martinet as well as the next man, accompanied him on his almost daily journeys to Ordnance, whose staff learned to dread their approach. After many abortive visits they arrived one day to find the office empty and an uncanny silence reigning.

"That's funny, sir! Doesn't seem to be anybody here."

"I smell a rat, Simmy. Let's comb the place!"

They looked in cupboards and behind partitions and at last found the warrant officer in charge cowering under a spare desk. The guns were collected a couple of days later.

On my first evening in the Nee Soon mess I was buttonholed by a chap who was upset at having lost, or having been accused of losing, his Bofors gun upcountry. He was the first of many men I was to meet who sought relief from shock in endless postmortems of their adventures – from the last official order received to the flight through the jungle and the night marches, in barefoot silence, down the roads through the rubber. One moment this chap was in full spate, glass in hand, the next he had keeled over. He was carried out by the Indian staff with no more ceremony than if he'd been a planter's chair. A stout, pop-eyed man took his place.

"Dear, dear! That's happened every night this week. Never mind! Have another drink, old man, before the bloody Nips get it!"

Several officers were in mess kit, and smartly dressed 'boys' hurried about the lofty fan-cooled room, handing out drinks.

"It's a good thing, don't you think, old man, to keep up appearances? I do my bit in my humble way, got the best Sam Browne in the regiment, polish it myself, have done for years. Pity one has to take it off in the mess, otherwise you could have seen it for yourself. Have another *stengah*, old man!"

His pop-eyes were beginning to swim in front of me; or was it *my* eyes that were swimming? After long abstinence on the *Mount Vernon* I was in poor training for Singapore mess life. I drifted away.

"Oh, there you are!" said Pop-eyes some time later. "I was saying just now it's a pity I had to leave my Sam Browne in my room. Cheers! Like to come up and I'll show it to you? Won't take a minute."

See his Sam Browne? Why not his etchings? I drifted away again.

The next morning one of our few remaining bombers, returning to the neighbouring airfield from the north, exploded and scattered gruesome relics round us. The fighter planes, mostly Buffaloes with a Wildebeeste or two, used to take off as the Jap bombers appeared, and circle pathetically until they had vanished again. At such times we were grateful for the concrete anti-malarial drains.

In Nee Soon we were joined by a colleague of Noel's in the Chinese Protectorate – Colin Dakers, now in the Straits Settlement Volunteer Force. He was the first of several liaison officers attached to us to help remedy our ignorance of the local scene; another was Bill Drower, a senior of mine at school, who had worked in Japan and learned Japanese. With their help, our local muddle sorted itself out, and the batteries moved north over the Causeway to Rengit and Pontian Kechil, with RHQ at Johore Bahru. I remained with reserves in Singapore. Colin guided me to strategic spots like the hospital and the Raffles Hotel. One of our men had been wounded – in the art of love, not war – and it was a weird experience to walk into the splendid hospital building, with its verandahs, pools and patios, green lawns and banks of red cannas, spotless linen and virginal mosquito nets, and to see under the whirring *punkahs* strapping soldiers, their muscled torsoes covered in tattoos, lying in comfort while their less randy fellows were being bombed and bayonetted upcountry.

After a few days we were lent to Third Indian Reserves Centre's tented camp at Changi, commanded by the gentlemanly if ominously named Colonel Pine-Coffin. It was an Indian Army camp – there were Sikhs, Jats, Garhwalis, Ghurkas, Punjabis, Frontier Force Regiment and many more – and it gave me my first experience of the uniform discipline that holds together such disparate troops. It also provided my first experience of being treated like a god – by a magnificently moustachioed and venerable *havildar*. It seemed inconceivable that these noble beings, so neat and restrained on parade, could also be responsible for the 'Indian National Anthem' – that dawn chorus of universal hoicking and spitting – which I was now to hear each day.

The rubber trees round our camp had the odd air of a municipal jungle; I soon got used to geckoes jerking up and down the tent pole, to mosquito-net management, and to the unrelenting chorus of cicadas and tree frogs. The officers' mess introduced me to Indian food, a delight after the stodge of British Army rations and the sloppiness of the *Mount Vernon* cuisine. But the war intruded as Indian Army officers began to fill the mess after shambling back in rags from upcountry. Few were Regulars and many were suffering from experiences that had liberated inhibitions normally held in check. As their strength returned, and between louder and louder shouts of "*kiahai!*" to the mess waiters, the horrors of the campaign were refought.

"That slinky Chinky in the Ocean Ballroom in KL, d'you remember her? Tricky little bint. Kept saying, 'You seek. Why you seek?' 'I'm not sick,' I said. 'Then why you jiggy-jig so red? Eh? You seek!' 'I'm not bloody well sick, and it's a bloody fine jiggy-jig, you silly little cow. I'll show you what it can do!' 'No, you seek!' 'I tell you I'm not!' I said, 'I caught it in the door of the major's truck.' 'Major fuck? What major? You fuck major?' 'Truck!' I said. 'I shut it in the door, see? It's bruised, not sick!' 'Not seek?' 'No.' 'OK, I love you!' 'That's more like it.' 'But you pay another twenty dollar!' 'Another twenty dollars!' I said. ' Why?' 'Cos you seek!'"

It was in this camp that my family reunion at last took place. Noel, working in Muar just north of Johore State, had joined Ferret Force, one of the specialist volunteer groups that found themselves overwhelmed by the speed of the Japanese advance and were disbanded. Returning to Singapore, he had reverted to civilian status, and he now arrived in an enormous Chevrolet driven by one of his colleagues, Russell Forsyth. (He had never learned to drive himself.) It would have been nice to have had an optimistic appreciation of the situation from these 'old hands', but they were a good deal more pessimistic than I was. They said plans of organised behind-the-lines activities had been abandoned in favour of official escape parties to India, which would re-equip and train there for clandestine landings upcountry later. Some local experts were already leaving for Sumatra, but most were resigned to waiting for the end, either remaining in SSVF uniform or reverting to civilian status. Noel had lost most of his belongings at Muar but had hung onto his latest letter in verse from his friend Martyn Skinner, who farmed at Ipsden in the Chilterns. He gave me a copy, together with the published volume of the first two cantos, *Letters to Malaya*, and we parted with a flip family fatalism. "Here we are," ran our unspoken thoughts, "together in the shit! But the family has been all right so far and the Good Lord will see us through. We've observed the proprieties from the lowest (St Mary-le-Port) to the highest (All Saints, Clifton) and He can do the same for us. And if He doesn't, well, we owe it to the family to come through anyway." That evening, in the stuffy blacked-out mess tent, I retired to a corner to read Martyn Skinner for the first time, as he envies Noel his life in the fabled East:

> The world of China, and a world that gleams
> With blossoms and pagodas, silks and streams,
> Mist-headed mountains, torrent-clad defiles,
> Isle-dotted lakes and temple-dotted isles . . .
> Lakes where a poet undisturbed would glide
> Through scenery tranquil as a vase's side; . . .
> With some grave mandarin I'd sip my tea,
> Lake-fringed in his alfresco library . . .

Learning what Lao said, Confucius taught,
I'd touch the world of China too, in thought . . .
Fold up the screen, the hanging scroll upwind it,
Your world has gone and where else will you find it?
Where else forget that ever day had hours?
In Shanghai's water-front of office-towers?
In clearings bright with missionary bricks?
In vales where pylons with pagodas mix . . .?
Where the calm mandarin on business keen
Lolls Homburg-hatted in a limousine,
And the robed angler, wearing rims of glasses,
Rocks in his sampan as the steamer passes . . .?

Not long afterwards I visited the tent of Colin Dakers. "Your brother," he said, "is not the world's greatest administrator but he has an amazing knack of making friends in all walks of life. The Chinese like him enormously. If they've got to be persuaded to do something awkward, Noel's the chap to talk them into it. They'll do things for him that they wouldn't for many of his superiors. Have you seen the latest instalment of *Letters to Malaya*? There are some lines describing Noel at school, where he is made to say – yes, here it is:

‘ . . . in a minute
You'll have my Oxford days and schooldays in it,
And show me, just exempt from canes and classes,
Collecting friends as some do books or brasses;
Or High Church ritual discussing keen,
An Anglo-Catholic of just fifteen.’

He's very like that; a very stimulating person." His face clouded over. "And a wonderful chap at a sticky party."

Was Colin, I wondered, thinking of the parties Noel had told me about during my artist sister Margie's visit before the war? Her touch with a pencil was surer than her touch with men. She had gone out to Ipoh on the 'fishing fleet' and lost her heart, not to the sensitive Colin but to an amiable philanderer, who soon afterwards left Malaya and was murdered by bandits in Persia. Large families take mutual support for granted, but also mutual ridicule; and Margie had her share of both. Finding herself alone at a late stage in one of Noel's parties, she had looked into the dark garden from the verandah. "I say!" she cried. "Where is everybody? What are you all doing out there?" There was a moment of stillness as the cicadas throbbed; then the garden rustled into life and couples converged on the house to make studiedly casual farewells.

Whether Colin was one of the people in that garden I don't know, but he had soon married and settled down to the life of a local administrator. It was clear that he knew how to make himself comfortable in a tropical environment. His tent had none of the unpractical furniture and baggage that mine had (a heavy canvas valise with mould-attracting leather straps, thick bedding, pyjamas and a niggardly square mosquito net); he had a lot of cosy matting lying about, hardly any bedding and a sarong instead of pyjamas, but a splendid round mosquito net big enough to accommodate his 'Dutch wife' – the bolster which old hands use lengthways to insulate their limbs from each other and absorb the sweat. Among the toiletries neatly laid out on his folding table was a wooden spatula, which he told me was a tongue-scraper and quite common in the tropics. I did not follow his example in this, but soon adapted to other local customs: the use of cigarettes, for instance, to discourage mosquitoes, Moslem lavatories – but with toilet paper, Malayan showers with a bailer and jar of water, the inefficacy of Tiger Balm and the efficacy of Tiger Beer. But I never got used to our absurd tropical uniforms and great big clumping boots.

Domestic discomforts, however, were soon dwarfed by increasingly bad news. Troopships were bombed coming in, evacuee ships going out; the last Brewster Buffalo was shot down and the still-boxed Hurricanes were shot up; power lines were broken and water mains blown up, with dark rumours of the reservoirs in Johore being cut off or poisoned; Chinese villagers, seeking to allay the evil spirits behind their Japanese attackers with firecrackers, were mistaken for enemy snipers and fired at by their 'protectors'. And still the leapfrogging back to Johore went on, and the funnelling of troops withdrawing from the peninsula, across the Causeway and into the false security of Singapore Island.

One of my jobs with the Indian troops was to erect a tented camp on the Tampinis Road. Who should move into it but the 148th Field Regiment who had been with us in our convoy on the *Wakefield*, but had been directed to Bombay. They had not left Bombay until January 9th. The convoy, led by the cruiser *Exeter*, was at the Sunda Straits in late January and the three fastest troopships went ahead to Singapore, where on 30th they had to put in at Keppel Harbour since the Naval Dockyard was by then under constant attack. The *Empress of Asia* (formerly *Empress of Japan*) was hit and went down off the Semilan Islands, and the *Wakefield* lost five men, with nine injured, before she could clear again for Batavia in Java to pick up more refugees. A pang of nostalgia struck me as I thought of those floating hotels heading back to civilisation without us. Who would be sitting in their quiet cubicles while we had the shit bombed out of us on alien shores?

About the time the *Wakefield* was docking, the Causeway was blown, with the 22nd Indian Brigade on the wrong side of it. They were forced to return by boat. At this stage I was recalled to the regiment, now back in the north of the island after suffering three officer casualties, Stebbing, Bolt and Raynor, at Rengit. On my way I met one of our subalterns, Macdonald, looking noticeably thin after returning from Rengit by sampan. It had been taken in tow outside Singapore by a naval launch which had gone too fast, overturning it and drowning three of his men. With him was the Padre, now very changed from his urbane peacetime self, and "tired of being the CO's batman".

I found the regiment dug in by the reservoir at Nee Soon, and next day went up to Advanced RHQ near the Naval Dockyard to join the Colonel, Freddy Fitch – another of our SSVF advisers – and Stuart Simmonds. Stuart was controlling the firing with aplomb – and also, as he disarmingly admitted, with the indispensable help of a grizzled sergeant. (Without the sergeant next day, he was intrigued to find his more fanciful fire-plans were received with equal respect by all concerned.)

There had been a lull before the Japanese managed to reach the blown Causeway – bicycles, after all, are slower than trucks – and our guns were now registered on it and fired when anything moved by day, and intermittently at night. But we soon had evidence of the ant-like activity that was to become so familiar in the years ahead: no sooner was one Japanese column destroyed than another swarmed onto the Causeway to replace it.

Only a few days earlier, and even as the rout upcountry accelerated, Stuart had had occasion to observe how, down among the 'scarlet majors at the base' normality was still a fetish. Sent back with despatches to Percival's HQ in Fort Canning ('The Castle of Confusion'), he decided to treat himself to dinner at Raffles Hotel. His appearance in sweaty field kit caused consternation to the major-domo, but he was ushered to a corner behind some palms, well away from the band; and just to make quite sure he would not disconcert the diners in white tuxedos and mess kit, two more waiters appeared and delicately adjusted some screens round his table.

8

The White Flag

'THE skilful evolutions of war,' observes Gibbon, 'may inform the mind, and improve a necessary though pernicious science. But in the uniform and odious pictures of a general assault, all is blood, and horror, and confusion.' Gunners, of course, tend to avoid much of the blood and horror, unless overrun or bombed, and it is all too easy for them to criticise the 'poor bloody infantry' slogging through the jungle into bullets and bayonets, and to blame them for infiltrations and withdrawals. When I examine 2nd Lieutenant Alexander on his role in all this confusion his revelations are scarcely the stuff of history. I see, for instance, from my surviving scrappy notes, that the failure to retrieve photos from a Chinese shop which was always closed during air raids seems to have irked me more than the raids themselves. But I quote these scraps verbatim because their immaturity and disorder are a reflection of the situation around me:

At 7 MRC we met our first beaten officers – the Leicesters, East Surreys and 137 Field – all bloody-minded and endlessly retelling their lousy experiences. . . . Frank Mitcham (4/9 Jahts) walked off with my Dunlopillo mattress which I had leant (*sic*) him. This was infuriating. . . . Air raids were now very persistent; the bombs were many but small. The papers still burbled about victory and reinforcements were pouring in – but what reinforcements! The Indians were useless. . . . All work stopped for air-raids, coolies did nothing but loot the vast stores at the Docks, ships were not properly unloaded. Shenton-Thomas, the Governor, deserves to be shot, the bloody old fool . . . ! I was MCO between HQRA and Regiment and made a gigantic balls-up which the CO has never allowed me to forget. The CRA, 11th Division, a hopeless muddler, gave me orders, saying '135 Field Regiment, less one battery. . . .' This battery I assumed to be 499 who were staying behind anyway, but he meant 336 to stay and support 53rd Infantry Brigade. I repeated these orders to the CO, who was livid and tailed him for the rest of the day to find out the actual situation. . . . While I was waiting for Seymour and Philip to bring up the guns the GPO of the 88th told me that his Troop Commander had shot a Sherwood Forester for running away. . . . Bullets started flying about . . . we searched all the huts in vain – obviously fifth columnists who quickly retired to the *kampongs* – bloody Tamils and Malays!

At our position near the smoking Naval Dockyard our forward HQ were rather pleased with themselves and critical of everyone else – a natural state, I suppose, of many belligerents. Having fired some twenty thousand rounds we were congratulated for our zeal by Wavell, and were preening ourselves on our performance in action. But except at Rengit, where we suffered over a hundred casualties, we had had few of the horrors of being cut off and hoofing it back through the jungle that gunners further upcountry had had. We felt confident of settling down to a Gibraltar-type siege; there remained stacks of ammunition and loads of food, and if the reservoirs were cut off, there was rain every evening. Perhaps if we had had closer contact with enemies only seen through binoculars we would not have been so critical of the Australians on our left for withdrawing with scarcely a shot fired when the Japanese landed at night through the 'impenetrable' mangrove swamps, laughing and shouting in English so that no action was taken against them until it was too late. We heard that some of the infantry had deserted and got drunk in Singapore, while the Garhwalis endeavoured to hold their line. Their gunners, too, after minor shelling and only one casualty, had limbered up and withdrawn, leaving us to cover their front. We soon had to shift from our snug positions shelling the

Causeway and boats and counter batteries, which we could out-range. A general panic had set in, all started by one Jap battalion and perhaps some fifth columnists alleged to be Tamils. So we in our turn were withdrawn a few miles back to the Mandai Road. I felt this was a grave step because we lost the moral advantage of feeling a sea barrier all round us, of being on a tight little Jap-proof island – like, say, Malta – with no room for strategic withdrawals any more. My own resolve in facing the enemy for a last-man-last-round stand in a strong position was badly shaken. The protection of the blown Causeway was of course illusory, but now there was no longer any doubt that henceforth there would be equivocation, civil distur-bance and second thoughts about death or glory.

> Life, to be sure, is nothing much to lose
> But young men think it is, and we were young . . .

I thought it was the middle-aged who really had most to lose and who probably kept their weather eyes open; and perhaps our seniors – both civil and military – had aged prematurely in that climate.

Of course, the total absence of planes would have done for us sooner or later, but the Japanese – it emerged afterwards – were even more surprised than we were when the island caved in like an eggshell at the first tentative crack. Back we went again from the Mandai Road to Sembawang aerodrome, which the RAF had left a week before; it looked from the beer on the table and the food in the stores as if they might be back at any moment. The roads were chaotic and one night, on the motor-bike, I lost my way to Nee Soon in the sea of Great-Trunk-Road-style Indian drivers and found myself halfway back to the MacRitchie reservoir and bogged down in the wagon lines. The bombing had become devil-may-care and for the first and only time I saw Sikh Bofors gunners actually bring down planes.

Stuart and I installed RHQ in a comfortable abandoned house (the toys still on the verandah) on the outskirts of Singapore, while Toosey stayed at HQRA in the town itself. I found him there, closeted with the CRA, 'consoling himself with whisky and talking wildly about the hopeless infantry, the criminal AIF [Australian Imperial Forces], the brilliant 135th Field Regiment, and his own vow never to surrender, never to be captured alive and never to leave by boat'.

I was glad to get away soon afterwards from recriminations at RHQ and return as troop leader to my original battery, now at the old Japanese Sports Ground near the Serangoon Road. But bad news awaited me. In the latest retreat our B Echelon party of twenty-five, including Colin Dakers, had been left in ignorance of the withdrawal and had sat, perhaps over-trustingly, near the Naval Base until overrun by the enemy. 'The Japanese sent back BQMS Cluff with an ultimatum to Percival: unless Singapore surrendered by midnight they would paste it.' Singapore was not surrendered and it was not pasted more than usual, but Colin Dakers was shot; the other ranks, except for one who escaped, were bayonetted. One recovered from his wounds and eventually rejoined us in Changi camp.

Meanwhile conditions near the Serangoon Road were becoming desperate too:

> The guns came in at dusk. Suddenly we were sniped by a machine gun and rifles. This was the first time shots had whistled about our years (*sic*). We were all caught on the hop and terrified. Chamberlain opened up with the Bren but nearly shot up the Command Post and so stopped. I ran back to E Troop and explored in the Bren carrier. Nothing else happened so we carried on getting the guns into army huts for cover. The shots came from one of the huts behind us and continued intermittently for the rest of our stay there. . . . After a bit we got used to bullets phutting through the *attap* of the huts. We got the last gun in at 0100 hours and then the infantry started their favourite game. This is played by a fifth columnist firing a shot in the woods and then all the feet firing their Brens at each other all night. There were, of course, no Japs nearer than a couple of miles. Next morning we only had two shoots, but everyone else was banging away, except when the planes were over, which was often. Pillings [Second in Command] came over to see us, very cool. He told us that Osmond and party had been told to get away and had gone to

the docks. The CO had refused to go – one up to him! This left us feeling beheaded. . . .

The day continued quiet, with occasional sniping, lovely weather, and shelling on the town. Bill Hunt [my Cockney batman] dug us a latrine and trenches were improved. Food was good. About teatime they started shelling us . . . very accurately . . . some Gurkhas came back across our front in the middle of it . . . several were hurt. Two of them came into the CP trench and stayed with us, turning up on all the parades . . . SAA dumps were going up all round us. 88th B Echelon thought it was tanks and fled to the town. Philip Hay [GPO] and I sat in the trench and were convinced our end had come. We talked calmly of a fight to the death and I felt quite happy. Philip went off to his trench in a lull. Then shells came though the CP and guns and shrapnel thumped all round us. Ellis and Wiltshire were hit slightly. E Troop appeared to be in trouble and their telephonist was histerical (sic) I went round with a rum ration; some of the men were bloody-minded but Ellis and Dando were perfect. After a couple of hours Philip came running in breathlessly and said I had to go to E Troop at once. Off I went, knowing nothing and missing my rum and food. . . . I found Alan [Haldenby] safe, to my relief, but the Troop was in a flap. The telephones were giving trouble and at one point Seymour came bumping back from his observation post on Sgt. Ramsbotham's ('Rammers') Norton. He let it fall in the middle of the track and moved really fast for once. "The Japs are massing before attack! There are thousands and thousands of them out there! Midnight's zero hour, m'dear chap! Must put the birdseed down!" But after our firing nothing happened. I waited for two hours (very angry over missing food and rum unnecessarily) before taking Pammenter's gun forward to act in an anti-tank roll (sic).

I felt very envious of the people in the CP trench as we set off for Serangoon Road Roundabout at 11.45 pm. . . . We passed a road block of old lorries and chose the position. After sighting the gun I was determined to get a good trench dug. We struck water at 12 inches so started again in a tumulus. We finished at 0200 hours. All was still quiet. . . . Stood to at dawn and improved trench. . . . Breakfast was sent down to us. Began to feel more hopeful – if the Japs had not attacked they must be bluffing. . . . Natives from a *kampong* looted a big hospital behind us in about ten minutes (the patients had been evacuated). . . . We stopped them too late. A Chinese doctor and padre came back to salvage stuff and I got a key to the hospital and we had excellent showers. It was a good building with a large garden in the middle of it – used to be a school.

The pillage of the hospital shocked me greatly. Like many institutional buildings in Malaya, it presented an air of quiet and verdant opulence – until I realised that from the far side of it an ant-like column of Tamils was making off with its more portable contents. This betrayal, as I saw it, of mutual colonial obligations drove me shouting into the building, waving my revolver and firing it in the air – the only shot I ever fired in anger. The white *longhi*-clad figures vanished in a flash, leaving mattresses half off the beds and towels lying in the doorways. An eerie silence fell, and as I emerged I felt hidden eyes watching me from the rubber trees. It was in fact these trees that had sent me to the hospital in the first place, because the Tamils near our position would insist on taking shelter under mortar fire by standing erect behind trees; hence the gashes from shrapnel that sent them to me for treatment. (This was also the bad habit of my distinguished namesake in Burma. Field Marshal Slim writes that General Alexander 'refused to take shelter in a trench, preferring to stand upright behind a tree. I was very annoyed with him for this, not only because it was a foolhardy thing to do, but because we had been trying to stop the men doing it.')

Another incident that had happened on our way to the gun position has stuck in my mind like a silent film sequence. Rumbling along the bombed road in the quad we saw an officer and two men standing under a lofty street light and telegraph post whose wires hung trailing to the ground. The heavy lamp was hanging by a thread and, even as I watched, it fell plumb onto the officer's tin hat. He dropped like a stone, and as we drew away I saw the two men unfreeze and run forward to lift him up.

Recce planes were continually flying over very low; the Bofors always missed. A few bombs were dropped. I went off to try and spot a mortar over the hill but saw nothing. Everything was very peaceful – a large pool with native huts all round it – flowers and sunshine; a Malay was cutting a *zeiss*'s (*sic*) hair in the garden. In the afternoon the shells reached us again – very light but all around us. A lot of the Tamils got shrapnel wounds. I patched one old boy's nasty gashes in his arse and got him off on a civilian bus. His son showered blessings upon me. They had probably been shining lights all night. Got some sizzling hot sausages from a Chinese house. I heard rumours of surrender but pooh-poohed it because (a) I wanted to; (b) the Japs had let up on bombing for the last week thus lending aid to (c) news that the Americans had landed at Penang and were cracking down the mainland; (d) no attack had been made the night before. The Feet near us thought we should surrender. Someone had heard a queer order to the effect that a lookout should be kept for a car full of fifth columnists dressed as British staff officers and bearing a white flag. If spotted, this car was to be fired on. Were they really fifth columnists or were they indeed from the 'Castle of Confusion'? I stopped Sam Egar in his truck. He had been recalled from the OP, he didn't know why; this looked gloomy. Shelling continued and ambulances came back continually. No signs of any tanks. Pammenter was a bit jumpy and very talkative. We loaded with A/P before dark. A silly message came from Ailwyn saying 'don't destroy the gun until told to'. I should destroy it when I thought proper, i.e. with my dying strength. We had a good trench, four rifles and a dozen grenades, so we could give some trouble from the trench if not from the gun. Went to sleep early. Was awoken at eleven by arrival of Sugar on 'bike: 'Destroy gun, but don't fire it, and return to CP.'

I was staggered – this must mean a second Dunkirk. We took out the firing mechanism and sights and telescope and clinometer and broke the cross-level bubble and piled into the quad. 'Happy' Hart drove us back. I was uneasy because the

Feet had not come streaming back, firing had almost stopped and we heard cheering in the distance. Then we reached the roadblock and found several trucks with their lights on. My heart sank to my boots. Found Stanley, Alan, Philip, Ailwyn, Granny, Seymour, (Graham had gone off that afternoon to try and escape) and some food at the CP. They confirmed the surrender. 'Thank God it's over,' said Philip.

The next day some Japs, the first we'd seen, came to look at the guns. An officer, beaming affably, shook hands with Sgt. Ramsbotham. I don't think they realised that we had destroyed both guns and quads ourselves. A Chinaman put on a gramophone playing Old Favourites, which the men all sang loudly. I found that RHQ had looted my two kit bags, which made me just as angry as the surrender. The peace was amazingly sudden; one couldn't get used to walking about upright and careless. The next day we moved to Changi.

Before going, HQRA 11 Div. directed us to unpack all printed matter, letters and photos and send them for censoring to the Chinese High School. Simple soul that I was, I gave in everything, including *Letters to Malaya*. But, not for the first time, the information was wrong; the Japs didn't want this precious stuff and it was all left behind.

I went to Changi with the baggage in one of our two trucks up the Serangoon Road and down Tampinis Road. There was a blackened, oily, naked body lying in Serangoon Road and a Sikh lay with a bayonet through him; otherwise nothing, except a few crushed cars and shelled buildings and trailing wires, to denote a war. We saw a couple of dozen Japs altogether and thousands of hale and hearty Gallant Englishmen marching along (the Aussies hopped lorries, the bastards). Passed three IRC again, and finished in the very camp where I'd bought beer from the NAAFI for 148 Regiment.

"Who are you?" said Becky [Major General Beckwith-Smith].

"135 Field Regiment, sir."

"Ah, Toosey's boys!"

The camp had been blasted to hell by bombs and the

explosion of an ammunition dump. Graham came back after being caught by the Japs in his escape bid. Next morning, February 18th, we moved to a spacious Married Quarters bungalow; and that evening I went down with dysentery. My sixteen days of fighting and five weeks of the Malayan Campaign had ended and captivity began.

9

Still Life in Changi

CHANGI lay above the unspoilt beaches at the eastern point of the island, fifteen miles from Singapore town. In peacetime it must have been a salubrious spot, once past the forbidding civilian gaol. The commodious barracks, with their ample lawns, playing fields and parade grounds, had been designed on a generous scale for a population of about eight thousand. Fifty-one thousand British and Australian prisoners of war were marched there, while the Indian troops remained near the town. Bombings and demolitions had already destroyed the plumbing, and piped water was not restored for six weeks. We were left to sort ourselves out there, and eventually to wire ourselves in, and the whole military hierarchy soon managed to establish itself in a Heath Robinson version of Fort Canning. No amount of ingenious improvisation, however, could increase the miserable rations, and real hunger stalked the camp. This exercise in remote control became understandable as the enormity of our defeat began to sink in. Over our huge if disparate collection of Commonwealth troops, the Japanese had triumphed with only thirty thousand men. After roughly nine thousand casualties on both sides, there remained a hundred and thirty thousand prisoners of war for the Japanese to guard. No wonder they were grateful for our assistance!

As for me, it was lucky that I had been detailed to go in that three-tonner to Changi. Had I marched, the dysentery would have weakened me even more than it did. On the other hand, if I had caught it a week or two later I would have been despatched to the overcrowded RAMC 'hospital' and had a rough time there. As it was, as soon as I felt the symptoms that were to become horribly familiar over the next three years our MO, Sidney Pitt, prescribed liquids only and left me among familiar faces in Quadrant Road. By the time I recovered three weeks later and was ravenous again, the mess was down to twelve ounces of rice a day and precious little else.

I had missed the first bout of starvation that hit us between combat rations and prison fare. Stuart and other 'outsiders' unfamiliar with exotica like *escargots* had watched with wonder as the 'yeomen' experimented with tropical snails.

"Would you say, Deardy, that this thing is a snail?"

"What's that, m'dear feller?"

"This creature like a legless caterpillar."

"Nasty look in its eye, old boy."

"And a pretty turn of speed."

"This one's got legs but doesn't seem to know if it's coming or going."

"Probably a hermaphrodite."

Though the gourmets knew how snails should taste, they did not know how to cook them. In any case ingredients were lacking, so their creations of squish and cinders were soon abandoned. The change in diet slowed our natural functions; once every two or three weeks became the norm – and what a 'once' that was! Our outside privy assumed the air of a maternity ward. One by one we would stride determinedly into it, only to return baffled and exhausted past the next expectant patient. Our daily menu was something like this: breakfast – rice pap, sometimes 'limed', often mouldy and pepped up with garden fertilizer which Ailwyn assured us was harmless and full of vitamins, a teaspoon of tinned milk and sugar, an army biscuit, a flat teaspoonful of marmalade, and plain tea; lunch – rice, a tin of bully between sixteen, a sweet of rice and grated coconut; supper – rice flour pasty (the 'flour' milled with the transmission of a truck), beef tea from our minute cold-storage Jap beef ration, citronella water and a rice-and-fertilizer biscuit.

In the afternoons, before working parties became frequent, there was a difficult choice between having a siesta and dreaming about food or going for a walk and working up even more of an appetite.

Graham Searles and I sometimes compromised by escaping from the mess but walking only as far as what I called the Bluff or, in my more nostalgic moments, the Sea Walls. Up there the illusion of freedom was still strong because Changi camp covered a large area and had not yet been fully fenced in, while the Japanese kept themselves to themselves – provided we did the same. We were up there one afternoon, staring out to sea, with nothing except our stomachs to suggest that we were prisoners. Behind us in the distance elegant sprays of bamboo and palm-girt porticos suggested an urbane Georgian landscape rather than pock-marked facades of barracks with smashed sewers and maggoty drains. The nearest island was thick with jungle and we might have been two Crusoes as we gazed at it and beyond to other islands – stepping stones to Java – perhaps already overrun but still nearer the dusty sanctuary of Darwin in Australia. Java!

With the Nips there, the quotation would carry a new significance.

> What though the spicy breezes
> Blow soft o'er Java's isle,
> Though every prospect pleases –
> And only man is vile.

"I thought," said Graham, "it was Ceylon where every prospect pleases."

"I believe it was at first; then Heber went there, found the breezes weren't spicy, and changed the name. Scanned better too."

"I wonder how the Dutch are getting on."

"Missing their grub even more than we are, I should think. Noel used to rhapsodise about a Dutch palaeontologist called Professor van Steyn Callenfels, whose Saturday tiffins were famous. They began with *stengahs* at noon, with the *rijstafel* arriving at three and going on until five . . . the next morning."

"Oh, don't!"

Noel, I presumed, was interned over the hill in the gaol with the civilians. Was this really the beginning of the end of the British Empire where my four brothers and umpteen cousins were making a living? Or was it only a nibbling at the edges and would we return as sadder but wiser rulers? And where exactly did the Americans stand?

"Of course," said Graham, who had worked in Peruvian Railways before the war, "we weren't resented in South America. It was the North Americans who were the sahibs – the *gringos*. We were the descendants of the Legión Británica who had fought for their freedom. It was a marvellous job!" He described the joys of trundling down the track on inspection trolleys, the slug of *aguardiente* to combat the dawn chill; the sun streaming through the mist as the villages came to life; the men emerging to visit privies and the children to pee in the yard; the women lighting fires and, as the light grew and the temperature rose, throwing off their ponchos to look incredibly old and ugly or incredibly young and beautiful.

"Bloody marvellous!" cried Graham, not normally an imaginative man. And we relapsed into daydreams – his (perhaps) of Cochrane, O'Higgins and Colonel Jaime Rooke waving his severed arm in the air at Ayacucho, mine of Stamford Raffles, Frank Swettenham and . . . Shenton Thomas. But not for long. Man – and moderately vile man by the look of him – intruded on the scene. Below us on a track to Changi village came an old Tamil humping a sack, followed by three of our fellow-prisoners. Even as we watched they jumped him, bowled him over and seized the sack. Bursting with righteous indignation I leaped up and ran down the slope.

"Come on, Graham! We must put a stop to this!"

The Tamil lay whimpering on the ground. There were only rags in the sack. One of the men said shamefacedly, "We thought he'd got food."

As we walked back I held forth about our responsibilities to poor Tamils. We had seen them sheltering ineffectively behind rubber trees in the battle, and they had the right to expect protection from officers like us who were representatives of their King Emperor. Now our men had let the side down badly.

"Ought to be ashamed of themselves! I'll have them put on a charge! Good job you're here to back me up!"

"Oh, d'you think so?"

With the hour of siesta over, our regimental headquarters in an old kitchen was humming with activity. A signaller made out orders; a clerk typed inventories; and in the washhouse next door we found the Colonel and Adjutant waiting for something to turn up and engage their talent for organisation. They looked up hopefully as we entered, Toosey with his restless dark eyes and Malcolm North-cote with his calculating ones. As I poured out my story I could feel their interest fading. It was logistics they liked to sharpen their teeth on, not morals.

"And where was this?"

"Over there, sir. Below that bluff over the track leading to Changi village."

"And how many men d'you say there were?"

Silly young prig, he must have thought, as if I haven't got enough to worry about without Alexander's absurd notions of Empire and the white man's burden!

"Three of them, sir. I've got their names and numbers. All in the Sherwood Foresters."

"Oh, all right. I'll have a word with Major Dillon. Malcolm, make a note of the names, will you? And you saw this too, did you, Graham?"

"Yes, sir."

"Got anything to add?"

"No, sir."

As we went back to the mess I began to realise the depth of the chasm between colonial and military attitudes that had made such a shambles of the Malayan campaign. Imbued with the one and indoctrinated with the other, what kind of competition was I for the single-minded soldier-ants of General Yamashita?

In the mess the military atmosphere had begun to soften, but other things – Japanese working parties, agriculture, lectures – had not yet emerged to claim our attention or take our minds off the subject of food. We found our brother officers engaged in their usual distractions. Granville Keane and Michael Cory-Wright played endless games of piquet; Ailwyn De Ramsey and Sam Egar whetted their appetites on plans for a pig farm; David Cherry and Seymour Dearden outbid each other in lip-smacking descriptions of sumptuous meals at Prunier and the Café Royal.

"What I really yearn for," sighed our rapidly thinning padre, "is a NICE WILD DUCK, with orange sauce!"

"Ah!" cried Philip Hay. "Now there I agree with you. I will not tolerate puddle-duck!"

We related our little adventure to Stuart, and he was no more sympathetic than the Colonel. He was already favouring the intellectual side of a character precariously balanced between military efficiency and ironic detachment. The poor Colonel and Adjutant, he said, could not be expected to share my moral preoccupations. The more efficient they had been on active service the more they needed to continue their military routine to retain a sense of purpose in their lives. We who had been inefficient junior officers were free to experiment and develop new interests.

"Senior officers and sergeant majors build up this amazing momentum," he explained, "which carries them through absolutely any circumstances without any kind of deviation. They talk about contingency plans but there were precious few of those in Malaya. And the government in its hierarchical way was even worse – that disgraceful Penang evacuation for instance! But when a catastrophe does occur they're like chickens with their heads cut off. They carry on running round in circles. Psychiatrists say chickens are so devoid of enterprise that if you draw a line on the ground and put a chicken down with its beak on it it can't move away from it. Some of us are like that. We become hypnotised by routine."

As we moved away he took pencil and paper and started to play about with this idea. 'Eye upon chalkline,' he wrote. One, two – three, four, five; perhaps a sonnet? 'Eye upon chalkline, hypnotised is hen – '.

I lay on my bed-roll and found myself thinking of chickens, not as poetic symbols but as Peterhouse chicken omelettes, roast chicken, fried chicken, boiled chicken, curried chicken, cold chicken, even raw chicken, for God's sake!

As a matter of fact I was not all that far from the Peterhouse kitchen because our cook came from Corpus. Later on, when rations had improved, he managed to produce a cocktail with delicacies picked up on outside working parties and thus set Stuart off on his long affair with his muse:

Craftsman sublime, you have our humble praise!
This latest triumph hath o'erfilled the cup;
Now, not content to roast and bake and braise
Successfully, withal, you gathered up
The meagre offerings of a prison cell
Adding perhaps a dram of potions looted,
Muttered into the pot some secret spell
And into a liqueur your dross transmuted.
Pour out the precious golden liquid slow,
Raise to the lips this proof of man's endeavour;
Reply, parched throats with heart's ecstatic glow –
For while he lives then perish shall we never;
And never shall our troubled spirits fail
While cooks for us the gallant WILLIAM MAILE!

Alas! We little knew what the future had in store for us, nor how many troubled spirits were to fail; among them Gunner Maile, who was never to see again his own little fenland river.

In Changi the shadow of the latrine loomed over us at an early stage. I was shocked by the death from dysentery in the RAMC hospital of the stalwart BSM Murkin, a man held in much respect, even awe, by the men. His age told against him and it was unnerving to see his stern composure falter and collapse. At a grave not far from his an equally elderly major, 'Daddy' Brieghel, was arranging flowers over a son who had died of gangrene. Nor did the consolation of religion seem to be as effective as we had hoped. I heard of a padre who was 'one day administering the last sacrament with shit pouring down his legs, and a few days later dying himself and cursing the war, the army and God'.

Yet farce and horror were never far away from each other, and padres were exposed to one as well as the other. The Senior Chaplain was strolling towards Changi gaol one afternoon when a truck drew up beside him. A voice cried *"Kora!"* He had not heard the Japanese for "Hey, you!" before and kept on walking. With a louder *"KORA!"* a bristly face protruded, and a hand was extended horizontally with the fingers flicking up and down. This too was new to him. (It is in fact the Asiatic gesture for 'Come here!' The first time I saw it I thought it meant 'Sit down'; I sat down – and got a clip on the ear.) The Japanese jumped out angrily, pointing to the red cross which all padres wore at their waists. Bundling the Chaplain into the truck, the Japanese drove down the road to a wood and led him deep among the trees. There he dropped his breeches and produced his ill-conditioned weapon. The Chaplain needed all his expertise in religious drama to explain that his red cross signified not 'doctor' ('*ayesha*') but 'Christ-man'. It was a crime in the Japanese Army to go sick, especially (with comfort girls on army issue) from the wounds of venereal disease, and our real MOs were to be constantly pestered by the Japanese in this way. Sometimes they were able to put this ill wind to good use by making the *kampong* warrior obtain, besides the drugs needed for his own treatment, those more valuable to us.

No doubt in those early days the paraphernalia of military organisation was beneficial. Role-playing is safer than idleness, and make-believe morale better than demoralisation. But it looked peculiar to some outsiders. H. Robert Charles had been a machine-gunner on USS *Houston*, which went down with the *Exeter*, *De Ruyter* and *Tromp* in the Battle of the Java Seas. He reached Changi in August and was horrified: 'British officers could wear their rank and parade and preen in full uniform as though they still owned Singapore. We Americans could barely believe our eyes as we watched British soldiers stand at attention and salute their own officers, the officers actually prancing around expecting it.'

In our own mess we lived in separate sections for HQ and the three batteries, and once a week we spruced ourselves up and invited the Colonel along the path for a phantom dinner. Typewriters rattled away, orders of the day were despatched and inspections were carried out just as though we were in a normal camp. All this kept a lot of people harmlessly employed and gave the rest of us something to criticise, instead of criticising each other. There were also plenty of labour-intensive fatigues – firewood, for instance, being collected in a lorry chassis pushed by gangs who could probably have carried more by hand. For a short time we even enjoyed the luxury of swimming on Changi beach; but this came to an end after the ominous sound one day of machine-gunning from near Changi village. Massacres of Chinese – a hundred and four at first and sixty-four the next day – had reached our self-absorbed little world. Two Chinese survived and were hidden in the camp.

Bringing in the firewood at Changi

One reason why we saw so few Japanese inside the camp area was that troops of the 'Indian National Army' of Chandra Bhose, who had flown in from Japan, were used to guard it. Soon after the capitulation the Indians who had gone over to him – by no means all the Indian Army, and certainly not the Ghurkas – had paraded through the streets of Singapore with their pipe bands and their buglers to celebrate a great Indian Independence Meeting. 'Indians!' they were adjured, 'What awaits you? Mahatma Gandhi has been arrested. . . . The craftiness of the British, manifested as it has been in all its ugliness, has fanned the flames of your love for your fatherland. . . . We know that the Nippon flag which flutters behind you is spurring your love for your fatherland. Nippon is always the ally of justice. Indian friends! Let your Indian brethren fighting in your fatherland know of the strength that fills you in marching side by side with the banner of Nippon.' We were ordered to salute our INA guards, who wore a Rising Sun badge sewn onto their old uniforms, whenever we passed them, and a Sikh officer was said to have beaten up British officers who had failed to do so. But when I saluted a sepoy he had the grace to look as embarrassed as I was. During the battle the Japanese – or, as we had inevitably taken to calling them, the 'Nips' – had dropped leaflets on the Indian Army, saying that the British and Australians were evacuating the island

and leaving them to their fate, and on the Australians, saying that the British and Indians were doing the same. On the British they dropped pictures of women looking like Theda Bara, and asked why we should leave them for the Far East, which All Mighty and Respected Imperial Nippon Forces were liberating to fulfill their destiny in the Greater East Asian Co-Prosperity Sphere. We were also enjoined to 'pack up our troubles in our old kit-bag and join the Nippon Army'.

There were remarkably few recriminations over the campaign. I think we all felt to blame for our ignorance of jungle warfare and lack of fighting spirit. We did blame Gordon Bennett, the Commander-in-Chief of the Australian Imperial Forces, for deciding it was his destiny to fly back to Australia to 'let the folks at home know and profit from our adventures'. And some were disillusioned when a message was received through the Red Cross within a few days of the capitulation. Was it about evacuation of the wounded? Was it about food? Was it about books for external degrees? No, it was to enquire after the wellbeing of Captain the Lord De Ramsey. The string-pulling in high places, however, was the more understandable since Lilah De Ramsey's baby was due at any moment.

Many RHQ staffs busied themselves compiling war diaries. In our own case the debacle over Colin Dakers and B Echelon was reported simply as 'for some reason unknown, B Echelon were not informed of the withdrawal'. Action in another battery was described by its commander as 'a hand-to-hand dawn engagement with the enemy in the best traditional style', but the troop leader told me it had been a ghastly mistake, with gunfire over open sights directed at Ghurkas instead of Japanese. I wondered if the two Ghurkas who had taken refuge with us had been the targets of our own gunners. How much could war diaries in general be relied upon? And how much had reliance on them distorted military history? Meanwhile, great pains were taken over arrangements for ceremonial parades for drill, for church, for fatigues and, above all, for a grand march-past before visiting Japanese officers, riding high in our former staff cars. Orders were a curious mixture of the practical and the lunatic; possibly the latter were designed mainly for Japanese eyes, but they were issued ostensibly in all seriousness. One, signed by a brigadier, instructed beach patrols to 'warn off any Allied craft approaching the shore and report their presence to the Japanese'.

The scope for pushing bumph around was called into question soon enough, and one of the ironies of later experience was that paper itself became worth its weight in gold. An India paper Bible, cannibalised for cigarette paper, fetched £150, though – as the faithful pointed out – its injudicious use brought proof that the wages of sin are death. Printers' ink contains arsenic.

10

Shakespeare – 37 Plays

ON a hill not far from Quadrant Road, fenced off and officially out of bounds, a concrete dugout housed a gigantic Barr and Stroud rangefinder, a memorial to the end of the 'Impregnable Bastion of the Pacific'. One day I climbed through the wire and walked up to it. A little breathless from the climb on an empty stomach and from the heartburn that was dogging us all, I prescribed the soldier's remedy of curing one irritation with a worse one, and lit a cigarette which exploded satisfyingly inside me. (A local 'AN-DATH CORK-TIPPED' cigarette and genuinely cork-tipped because it had 'J. CORK' printed at one end, it was my interim indulgence between running out of English cigarettes and going completely native by rolling my own with black tobacco, known as 'Sikh's Beard' or, less delicately, 'Hag's Bush'.) When my head had stopped swimming I walked down some steps into a little office full of signal pads and sheets of paper. They were to prove invaluable for both physical and mental purposes. They should not, of course, have been wasted on physical use at all, but it was months before we were introduced to Moslem rites of sanitation by the Netherlands East Indies Army.

We were very badly off for books, having handed ours in to HQRA. We had picked up a few in a bungalow at Telok Paku, and I remember enjoying the bitter-sweet nostalgia of Sassoon's *The Old Century*. Also going the rounds were vivid journalists' reports like William Shirer's *Farewell to Berlin* and John Gunter's *Inside Asia*. I was so carried away by these that I expected to be led in the sweep of history right through to the final settlement; it came as a fearful jolt to find at the end of the book that the war was still on and I was still in Changi. Some books were read eagerly for quite the wrong reason; they would be skipped through in search of culinary descriptions.

"What's that you've got there, old boy? *Eothen*? Try this Ethel M. Dell; there's a much better tribal feast in it. You'll find it about half way through."

A particular favourite was Kenneth Roberts' *North-West Passage*, with a well-thumbed description of orgiastic stuffing after a period of starvation. Our conversation fared little better than our reading habits. Whatever we started talking about, we soon veered into sickening reminiscences of meals in England; while others yearned for underdone roast beef, baroness pudding or *canard à l'orange*, my own tormentors were bacon and bread and cheese.

The English language *Singapore Times*, renamed the *Shonan Times*, printed propaganda for the Japanese way of life and the 'Greater East Asian Co-Prosperity Sphere', and bulletins of Nip victories. This was demoralising but not always convincing. One article extolled Japanese virtues – 'The Nippon Zin Are Kind To Animals'; but on a working party I saw one Jap guard throw a cat over a rooftop and another bayonet a dog. Another article exhorted us to 'LEARN NIPPONGO NOW! If you don't learn it now you never will!' One after the other, the fall was announced of Java, Sumatra, the Philippines, Borneo, New Guinea, Timor, Port Darwin, the Aleutians and Rangoon. Several days running we read, 'By the time you read this paper Alexandria will have fallen'. Then the subject of Alexandria was dropped in favour of a serial called 'Singapore Assignment' by a Japanese journalist on the *Malayan Tribune*. This exposed the arrogance and muddle before the war which led not only to military disorder but civilian atrocities, and claimed that a goods truck of Japanese internees was left in a siding at Port Swettenham for twenty-four hours with the doors shut. When they were opened several of the passengers had died of suffocation. Of British officers an American woman journalist was quoted as saying: "They won't look so beautiful when the mud of the jungle bespatters their nicely cut uniforms!"

The progress of the war was followed on hidden radios but not passed on to those 'without the need to know'. This gave scope for rumours: rumours from Chinese civilians, from communicative guards, from 'the boghole', from interpreters of dreams and from a 'soothsayer' in the 2nd Cambridgeshires; he was put on a charge for spreading defeatist propaganda when he foretold the end of the war as late as 1944.

As the number of outside working parties into town increased, our military bureaucracy started to crack. It became obvious that paper would not last for ever, nor would uniforms worn by people working as coolies; and Japanese demands for labour made military 'bull' a thing of the past. A natural aversion to being ordered about reasserted itself, fanned by bolshiness towards those senior officers who stood on their dignity or evaded unpleasant duties, especially those requiring contact with the Nips. The fringe elements in camp – uninhibited Aussies and those like the Argylls who had had their wits sharpened in hard jungle training – were establishing a black market by barter across the wire, and as the military machine began to falter the social machine was warming up. We started to seek kindred spirits beyond regimental bounds.

On one of the outside working parties some 5th Suffolks discovered our ill-fated books and brought them back to Changi. The officer who sorted them out to form a library was Guthrie Moir, whom I had known at Peterhouse. By a coincidence, Philip Hay managed to rescue Martyn Skinner's *Letters to Malaya* inscribed to Noel, and gave it to me at about the same time as I heard that Noel was indeed in Changi gaol. The book became a sort of Bible to me in the next three years and, like the Bible, its lines seemed both topical and timeless. Again and again when reading it I would be carried forward to images of post-war life which relegated the squalors of the Japanese Great East Asian Co-prosperity Sphere to the past; and again and again I would come to with a pang of disappointment. For this bond with Noel I was immensely grateful to Philip – without him my *Letters* might have met a very different fate.

Guthrie Moir was also one of the instigators, with Henry Fowler and Ian Watt, who had to juggle with the conflicting logic of Leavis and a French mother, of the 18th Div 'University'. In a little mosque,

I attended their lectures on English Literature, with Stuart Simmonds and Philip Hay. We learned from Ian that literary works are
not things to be enjoyed unthinkingly, but dissected and related not
only to their own social background but to ours, too. Would
Wordsworth have been so trusting of Nature if, instead of reclining
above Tintern Abbey, he had been caught in the monsoon in the
Malayan jungle? Would Dorothy have slept in William's sacramental
hammock and mosquito net when he had had to paddle down a
tropical river to report to the DC? Auden, rather, should be our
guru; had he not seen through the delusions of physical beauty no
less acutely than through those of capitalism and, of course, patri-
otism? And was there not a class feeling in the more traditional kind
of war poetry that invalidated it as art?

When Byron wrote about Waterloo he was only interested in
'Beauty and Chivalry', in the aristocrats like 'Brunswick's fated
chieftain', and in dainty debutantes with

> . . . gathering tears, and tremblings of distress,
> And cheeks all pale, which but an hour ago
> Blushed at the praise of their own loveliness.

As for that overgrown public schoolboy, Newbolt, his hero who
fell among thieves was clearly very well off, besides being a frightful
prig:

> He saw the April noon on his books aglow,
> The wistaria trailing in at the window wide;
> He heard his father's voice from the terrace below
> Calling him down to ride.
> He saw the gray little church across the park.

(That, I knew – which was more than these clever-Charlies did –
would be the snug Arthurian chapel in the lake at Orchardleigh,
where Newbolt wondered whether to propose to the squire's daughter. He wrote – at twenty-six – to his old housemaster to ask his
advice before going ahead.)

And Julian Grenfell, too, was proprietorial in his poem 'Into
Battle'; not at all a bad poem, but it was the squire striding through
his coverts who could 'take warmth from the sun and life from the

glowing earth' rather than the poor old ploughman who homeward plodded his weary way. But, we might say, what about that ringing tale of the China wars and the 'Private of the Buffs'? Wasn't he 'poor, reckless, rude, low-born, untaught', and yet didn't he die 'as firm as Sparta's King, because his soul was great'? Yes, but the poet saddled him with colour prejudice:

> Yes, honour calls! – with strength like steel
> He put the vision by.
> Let dusky Indians whine and kneel;
> An Englishman must die.
> And there, with eyes that would not shrink,
> With knee to man unbent,
> Unfaltering on its dreadful brink
> To his red grave he went.

"Don't you think," said Philip, "that that line about 'dusky Indians' is rather topical? A note in my edition quotes the China correspondent of *The Times* as saying they are Sikhs. 'Some Sikhs, and a private of the Buffs, having remained behind with the grog-carts, fell into the hands of the Chinese. On the next morning they were brought before the authorities, and commanded to perform the Kowtow. The Sikhs obeyed; but Moyse, the English soldier, declaring that he would not prostrate himself before any Chinaman alive, was immediately knocked upon the head, and his body thrown on a dunghill.' Isn't that a fine period piece?"

"I think it's pretty near the bone," said Stuart, "when here we are, officers all, slinging one up every time we pass a Sikh guard!"

It was, I thought, even nearer the bone, with its talk of 'remaining behind with the grog-carts' and being 'knocked on the head', of our misadventure with B Echelon and Colin Dakers.

"Now," said Ian, "let us get on," and he turned with relief to the Romantic Movement, and how, though we might not think it immediately obvious, Auden was the major heir to its poets. He shared their 'inner eye', their power of seeing through superficial preconceptions to the deeper truths. We should ask ourselves what those truths were to the Romantics. What did Keats mean when he wrote 'Beauty is truth, truth Beauty; that is all ye know on earth and all ye need to know'?

"It's all very fine," Stuart complained afterwards, "Watt spending hours on philosophical nuances in the meaning of 'Beauty is truth, truth beauty' and on a psychoanalysis of Keats for saying it. But poets are like racehorses, one picks the winners not so much for their pedigree as by studying form. Keats wrote that line because he felt a poetic urge to do so. It would have sounded good anywhere and his training told him to put it where he did. 'There's a quotation for them', he must have said, 'and a damn good one too!'"

Although it was the subalterns – the second lieutenants and lieutenants – who supplied the lecturers and most of the students, a few senior officers came along to see what we were up to, and to sit stoically through the lectures. Guthrie Moir gave a series on Oscar Wilde – in all his amusing, tragic and tender aspects – and at the end of the last lecture a Colonel Hingston remarked to a Colonel Harris: "D'you know, I once saw a copy of *The Importance of Being Ernest* on Delhi railway station." Henry Fowler lectured on Shakespeare, and at the end I glanced at Colonel Hingston's notebook. Only the first page was disturbed. 'SHAKESPEARE' it was headed, and underneath: 'Thirty-seven plays. Died 1613.'

I sympathised with that entry; I read all Shakespeare's plays straight through at that time and an inexorable feeling of *déja vu* crept over me. Apart from the flights of poetry, all the plots and characters began to seem alike and I could almost see the next line coming; and tragic events followed ludicrous coincidences or mis-understandings, as in Hardy's novels or even – yes, the conviction grew – the whodunits of Agatha Christie. Here were the characters; this was the plot; there were the motives; those were the means; here were the crimes; and this was the *dénouement*. I thought that if we went to the theatre as free from preconceptions as Colonel Hingston was, we'd enjoy Shakespeare all the more.

Our tutors were not above a bit of sharp practice. "Margaret, are you grieving over Goldengrove unleaving?" intoned Ian Watt, and we were invited to guess the author of this and other poems, giving them a sort of points system of merit. I was impressed alike by the eclectic choice of poems and by the critical analysis applied to them, and it wasn't until much later that their provenance in I. A. Richards's *Practical Criticism* was revealed, and the book itself, with its fold-out appendices, made available to us.

Financial arrangements in these early days were fluid. Malay dollars were still legal tender, to the chagrin of those who had burned thousands of them at the capitulation. The dollars we had brought into camp with us were supposed to be handed in to a common fund, with a minimum kept for personal use. Not everyone adhered to this order; I kept a hundred, and on my first working party bought for the kitty some cigarettes (a dollar for ten), jam ($2.50 a tin) and bread rolls (25 cents each).

On my first working party, in April, the locals were friendly, making surreptitious V signs with rude gestures towards our guards. But most of the guards, still at that time engineers who had been in the campaign, were themselves not unfriendly; they were a bit shy of us and hadn't made up their minds how we should be treated, offering us cigarettes and giving us plenty of ten-minute rests. My own overseer was horrified when, partly to set an example but mostly out of sheer boredom, I took a shovel and started digging with the men.

As we passed the walls of Changi gaol I imagined Noel behind them, reading philosophy, teaching Cantonese or, perhaps, scrubbing the floor. Back in England Martyn Skinner, as I learned later, was writing a variation on the same theme:

> Now over Ipoh have the war clouds burst
> That seemed last year to threaten Ipsden first.
> 'Tis not my farm that scorched and jagged stands,
> But your white villa that's in hostile hands . . .
> Bunches of wires drape the piano's face
> O'erclustering a prelude still in place.
> Maps overwhelm the walls; half-seen behind,
> Your silken scrolls their landscapes still unwind
> Slightly askew. A Buddha props a gun.
> Across a picture hangs the Rising Sun.
> (Concealed, two sages stare serenely on.)
> Your desk is rifled. Papers, torn from bands,

Old letters in a dozen different hands,
Piled in a heap, the orderly await –
To bear them to the cook-house stove their fate,
With here and there on service more obscene
A bundle set aside for the latrine;
All mine among them – when I wrote on tissue,
Alas, how could I have foreseen the issue –
Two hundred letters, with but few superiors,
Doomed to be squandered on a camp's posteriors!

After a couple of months in Changi deficiency diseases appeared, particularly among the high-livers. Although Seymour Dearden had made himself tolerably comfortable on his Dunlopillo bed-roll – "Couldn't leave that behind, m'dear chap. Couldn't live without m'Dunners!" – he was unhappy with our condition.

"Life in Singers is too, too squal. I'm living for the day, m'dear chap, when old Engers and America will have everything in a great big bag and let me get back to m'whiskers and sodas." One day he wrote a note for Doc, who slept in the next room. He gave it to his batman to give to the Doctor's orderly. It read: 'Come and see me, Doc, I'm ill.' Much perturbed, Doc hurried in, only to find Deardy playing cards and smoking and, as ever, delighted to see him. But his ankles were swollen and when they were pressed the dents stayed in. This was our introduction to beri-beri and we were suitably impressed, being as yet ignorant of the real killers, the malaria/dysentery combination, jungle ulcers and cholera.

Hunger rather than illness still dominated our thoughts. The story went round of a colonel on Divisional HQ staff who was observed one morning stealing into the mess where plates of steaming rice-pap had been laid out, and in their midst a meagre bowl of sugar. After a quick look round, he put two spoonfuls of sugar in his pap, gave it a stir, sucked and replaced the spoon and slipped out again. When the others had come in he re-entered from the garden, rubbing his hands. "Good morning, gentlemen! And what have we for breakfast? Porridge, eh? Splendid! You fellows should get up a bit earlier and take a constitutional; do you a world of good. Pass the sugar, will you? Same ration as usual, I suppose."

Conditions at Changi ceased to be my concern at the beginning of May when five hundred of the regiment moved to Sime Road camp to build a Shinto Shrine to Victory in the grounds of the Singapore Golf Club. So we missed the 'Selarang Incident' which arose from a command by Lieutenant General Fukuei Shimpei, 'Commander of all POW camps in Malaya', that everyone should sign a form stating, 'I promise on my honour to obey all orders of the Imperial Japanese Army and that I will not try to escape'. When this was refused, the Nips ordered every man jack in Changi, thirty-five thousand in all, onto the parade ground at Selarang Barracks. There they stayed, packed like sardines in the sun, for four days. Latrines had to be dug through the asphalt, and when men became dangerously ill and the Nips remained adamant about signing, the doctors advised the senior officer, Colonel Holmes, to give in. This he did, ordering everyone to sign 'under duress', and the other camps in Singapore were ordered to follow suit. We had to repeat this promise at nine-month intervals thereafter, and I suppose our captors thought this justified them shooting or bayonetting prisoners who did try to escape.

Just before the Selarang Incident all officers above the rank of colonel were shipped off to Japan, including our much-loved Divisional Commander, Beckwith Smith. He died six months later.

11

Sime Road

THE move to Sime Road brought our first exercise in jockeying for position. We had no idea whether the devil we knew was better or worse than the one we didn't. Ailwyn De Ramsey stayed behind to run a pig farm and lecture on agriculture in the 'University of Changi', and others, like Stanley Hall, followed us later. As for Noel, I left him in Changi gaol.

In our weakened condition we found the twenty-three-mile march hard going, although our heaviest packs went by truck. The Chinese tossed bread rolls to us, and a few senior officers managed to buy food. The guards were considerate, even lending their bicycles to the weakest of us. But, in spite of regular halts, by the time we reached Sime Road several had fallen by the wayside and our marching had become a shamble.

The effort proved to have been worth it. The camp had been HQ for the RAF Far East. Its badly shelled wooden huts were sprinkled with decaying bodies, but by the time we had cleaned up and repaired the huts its advantages became plain. Our officers' mess was a verandahed and mosquito-netted hut on the crest of a rubber plantation, and looked down a valley to a picturesque Chinese farm at the bottom. Until our last few weeks there we enjoyed a good deal of freedom and, when not on working parties, could go for walks across the golf course and up Race Course Hill where there was an even better view to tantalise us. We could also go round as far as Thompson Road, and until the Nips started to take an interest in our movements, a few venturesome spirits actually got into cinemas in Singapore.

DULCE DOMUM
THYME RD., BUKIT TIMAH

Rubber

Old Shells

Canoa Bed

In Adam Park at the Lanarkshire Yeomanry camp I found John Durnford, whom I had not seen since Bath Steam Laundry days. In charge of transport, he knew his way about pretty well. With Guillermo de Mier, a Mexican friend of Prince Bernhard of the Netherlands who had somehow finished up in the Gordon Highlanders, he had made contact with a Portuguese ship sailing to South America. Her skipper had promised to take them with him, but when they had made their way during the night to Keppel Harbour, they found the ship had shifted her moorings, and they only just managed to get back to camp by daylight. But our working parties did not take us far afield or encourage similar enterprise. Many people in last-minute escape parties had come to a sticky end or been brought back and punished. By now we felt totally isolated, and even our SSVF friends with their local knowledge no longer thought it feasible to negotiate for boats and navigate across the Jap-infested Indian Ocean. Moreover, no letters arrived to exert an emotional pull across the widening gap between us and freedom. Our own writing was restricted to pre-printed postcards.

SIME ROAD

IMPERIAL JAPANESE ARMY

I am interned in —————————————
My health is excellent.
I am ill in hospital.
I am working for pay.
I am not working.
Please see that ————————————— is taken care (*sic*)

This left little scope for subtle messages, though in the last space one joker wrote hopefully 'AUNT LOUSYGRUB'.

Before this restriction a few of our cards had been delivered home through the Red Cross. There was an early one from me:

NO.164313 LIEUT. S. C. ALEXANDER
DEAREST MOTHER, I AM UNWOUNDED.
ROBIN WAS SEEN HERE AFTER THE SURRENDER.
DAKERS WAS KILLED. I MISS MUSIC BUT THE
WEATHER IS FINE AND SO ARE WE.
WITH LOVE TO YOU ALL FROM

STEPHEN

And a card from Robin written as late as November eventually reached my father: 'Glad to hear Stephen is well and putting on weight. My main activity is reading Greek, poetry and philosophy – if you can, send *Process and Reality* or Inge's *Plotinus*. . . . Tell Mother I hope she will remember the family birthdays on my behalf.' It was just as well my parents didn't know how much weight I had lost again by the time this card arrived in 1943. I was half-starved when I received one card from my mother, saying: 'How lucky it is that you were always fond of rice pudding.'

Noel had heard that I had put on weight after my dysentery because I had managed to get a letter to him through Leonard Wilson, Bishop of Singapore, who still had freedom to visit the camps in his diocese. (The Bishop relied on Chinese charity for his subsistence. It was funds of this kind, which he and Eurasian members of his flock so fearlessly smuggled into Changi gaol, that later got them into trouble; the military police, the *Kempitai*, accused him under torture of running a network of agents.)

We had made a little chapel, St David's, from a damaged shed walled with asbestos slabs; on these, Bombardier Warren executed in grey vehicle paint mixed with charcoal the kind of murals that I personally found too institutional, not to say downright soppy, for our circumstances. Well drawn but androgynous figures in working clothes represented biblical characters. To the left of the altar sat an aproned NAAFI Virgin and Child, and 'buckets, universal, metal, one'; the Magi worshipped in tin hats, ground-sheet capes, webbing equipment and turned-up anti-mosquito shorts. To the right, two Red Cross stretcher-bearers lifted Christ, a clean-cut sergeant-like figure, from the cross in the light of 'lamps, hurricane, one'; grave-diggers stood by with pick, shovel and *chunkeols* at the ready. I went down there one day and was watching the artist at work when Sezuki, the interpreter, came in. He looked closely at the figures through his glasses and gave a snigger. "He! He! I see what it is. You are the disciples of Jesus. He! He! Very modern!"

It was here that the swarthy Bishop and his boyish Chaplain, John Hayter, came one day for a confirmation service. They were a charismatic couple, Wilson himself managing to be both amusing and spiritual. A striking preacher, he almost persuaded us that faith in Christ was so far above the conflict of mere mortals that our troubles were irrelevant – or might even be helpful – for our salvation.

He was certainly a change from a legendary predecessor, who had a Mrs Proudie of a wife. Jealous of the privileges of her bridge partners, the 'ladies' of the Governor and the Commander-in-Chief, she designed a flag to fly on the bonnet of the Bishop's car, and announced that she wished to be known as 'The Bishop's Lady'. On the afternoon of a King's Birthday Party when the Bishop was away upcountry, she was driven to Government House, and directed her *syce* to the accustomed gateway. Here a sentry blocked the way.

"But I always use this entrance when I come to play bridge!"

"Sorry, Mum, not today you can't. All cars are to go round the other side."

"But this is ridiculous. Do you know who I am?"

"No, Mum."

"I'm the Bishop of Singapore's Lady!"

"Can't help that, Miss. Even if you was his wife you couldn't come in this way today!"

Below St David's was the men's cookhouse where it was sometimes my duty to inspect the food. It had greatly improved when regular working parties started and pay – little as it was – began to come in. Even so we were always hungry, and were shocked when a neighbouring adjutant remarked, "Of course, I require more sweet potatoes for the Colonel. We always do that you know, and make up the difference to the men's rations with rice. They can eat more rice than we can."

The Rations Officer, 'Granny' Keane, did not always find catering arrangements easy to understand.

"What proportion of rice flour to maize flour do you use in the pasties, Sergeant Sands?"

"Fifty per cent rice flour, sir, and twenty-five per cent maize flour."

"Oh, yes? And what about the other twenty-five per cent?"

"We keep that in reserve, sir."

One day, on the long slopes above the cookhouse, I passed a party of Malay Volunteers scything the *lalang* to make fodder for the Japanese horses kept at the racecourse. "*Apa khaba?*" I sang out to the nearest chap, "*Engkau sudah pergi ada t'ada?*" ("What's new? Been to the privy yet?") A flood of Malay came back, and my new acquaintance turned out to be a friend of Noel in the Chinese Protectorate, a middle-aged Irishman named McEvott. He was a man of ascetic appearance and great charm, whose accent in English was so thick I thought at first he was putting it on.

"Yer brother is a very stimulating person. But begob, he's not always easy to live with!" And he quoted a Latin tag, which I pretended to understand.

I was embarrassed that this civilised man, with half a life of experience behind him, not to mention fluent Cantonese and no doubt some Tamil as well as Malay, was labouring like a coolie in the hot sun while I, a young squirt with one pip up, lived in an officers' mess and only went out on a working party one day in three. But among the Volunteers, experts on Malaya were often wasted in this way through being 'in the ranks'. A year later they were to have a dreadful time labouring among real coolies; the lack of discipline and hygiene among the coolies inevitably spread infection to the Volunteers and far too many died, including McEvott himself.

As for Noel, the *Letters to Malaya* now lacked half their inspiration, and Martyn's imagination had to work overtime.

> I see you there, each hour a weary load,
> Musing of Plato or of Pembroke Road . . .
> Yet whatsoe'er your lot, or bad or worse,
> Still now and then I'll send a screed in verse;
> Set down my views, imagine your replies,
> And launch them with blue labels through the skies . . .
> Maybe they'll never reach you, but come back
> After long months in sorting-box and sack
> Unread, delayed, as if I sent their verse
> Not for your liking, but a publisher's.
> Yet still I'll write; and when the war is done,
> And shaved your beard and silent every gun;
> When by this window once again you sit,
> No curtains drawn although the lamp is lit,
> Why, how these lines you'll chuckle to explore,
> How smile to see what Martyn thought in war;
> Wonder to find his fancies flew so wide,
> And cry 'Look here!' to read what you replied;
> Lay down this page, a sip of wine enjoy,
> Then tell the truth about Malaya's Troy.

Few of us in Sime Road camp were familiar with Trojan allusions but we felt ourselves fortunate as life became more tolerable. The food situation improved again, and we turned our attention to other creature comforts. The scenery was pleasing; the golf course with its clumps of trees resembled English parkland, while to the north-east the McRitchie reservoir stretched away to wooded hills holding the tropical jungle at bay. We were eventually made to wire ourselves inside an official perimeter, but we had plenty of space and saw little of the Japanese. Sitting on our verandah at night, talking and reminiscing under the Southern Cross, was pleasant but made the night a long one – long enough for melancholy reflections to set in.

But after three weeks someone discovered an electric substation within the perimeter, together with drums of cable and other supplies. A technical squad was formed, repairs were made, and electricity laid on to the huts – and, at their request, to the Japs' guardroom. Fired by success, the squad went on to develop water services from some old mains, and an improvised pumping station. In time, and with equipment scrounged from the golf clubhouse, a more sophisticated system for a twenty-four-hour water supply was established, and showers and water closets installed. So successful did this become that a bill was solemnly presented by the water company through the Japanese, solemnly accepted by us, and forgotten by everyone.

Unbeknown to most of us, in the flurry of electrification a new secret radio had come into being. The adjutant of the 2nd Cambridgeshires, John Beckett, and one of his signallers, Corporal Rogers, smuggled out of a dump – under the eyes of the guards and concealed in the grassbox of a lawnmower or disguised as refrigerator parts – metal valves, condensers and resistances, together with a complete radio relay cabinet. In spite of the confusion in colour-coding between Australian, American and British parts, they installed a working set in the roof of a washhouse. It was used sparingly and only for BBC headlines, to reduce risk of detection, and news was passed on imaginatively as though it had come from civilian contacts.

The news itself was a very mixed blessing. The fall of Mandalay in May seemed at least partly redeemed by the battle of the Coral Sea, which was very differently reported in the *Shonan Times* from the BBC version of events. In June the sea battle of Midway seemed distinctly to the Allies' advantage, but in Russia the Germans were besieging Sebastapol. In October came Alamein, and in November the US Marine landing at Guadalcanal. But the Nips talked as if Burma was theirs and India within their grasp, and the BBC was annoyingly reticent on the subject.

Our new electricity supply was used to light camp concerts, at which the Aussies proved particularly uninhibited. ("Do you really love me, dear, or is that your revolver I can feel?") It also inspired Bill Peacock and Malcolm Northcote to lay down a racecourse on the concrete base of a bombed hut. We painted the course and built jumps, tote, bandstand and bar. Wooden horses were carved and numbered and colours were made up for the jockeys. The course was floodlit and Bill and Malcolm sat at a table throwing dice, one for the horse and one for the moves. The whole camp flocked to the meetings, sweeps were run for the hospital, and even the Nip guards used to sidle up and ask us to place bets for them.

The supply of mains water and electricity to the mess hut had one disadvantage: it tended to preserve the protocol that would have withered sooner under shared discomforts. As it was, it survived to make preparations for the next move less effective than they might have been, had they been more communally oriented. Petty jealousies were encouraged by two persisting divisions, one of rank and one of region. Captains and above lived in one hut, and subalterns in the other; and there was still a Great Divide between original Hertfordshire Yeomanry and other officers. It charged the atmosphere, so that the slightest spark could set off an explosion, as for instance between Wilkinson, son of a poacher, and David Cherry, gentleman-farmer. Wilkie had guts and was good with the men in even the worst conditions; he was good with the Nips, too. He was not quite so good with Yeomanry colleagues like David Cherry, Philip Hay, Michael Cory-Wright and the Padre, who had no difficulty in whiling away the afternoons trawling for mutual friends and discussing anything involving large amounts of money. We used to marvel at the inexhaustability of these talking *Tatler* pages. David was annoyed one evening to find his sugar bowl missing from his table. After a time he spotted it on the other table – the sheep and the goats dined apart – placed at Wilkie's elbow.

"What's this?" he demanded in his prefect's tone.

"It looks like a bowl of sugar."

"What's it doing here?"

"I have no idea. Why ask me?"

"You must have heard me asking for it."

"Must I, then?"

"Why didn't you tell me it was here?"

"Now look here, Cherry!" cried Wilkie, jumping to his feet, "in this mess you and I are equal. I'll not be spoken to in that tone of

92

voice! If you want to throw your weight about you've picked the wrong bloke! And if you want to make something of it, I'll trouble you to step outside!"

There was a stunned silence, a stammered apology from David, and a period of studied politeness all round. But touchiness was still in the air. We spent our 'wages' mostly on the sugary molasses mixture called *gula malacca*, Malayan tapioca-flour cakes, and, when we could afford them, tinned milk and marmalade.

"Look here, you fellows," said Bill Peacock one day, "I want you to use a bit of tact and not put your marmalade on the table for a bit. The Colonel's spent all his money and can't buy any more for the moment. It upsets him to see all these pots sitting about."

There was also the Sad Case of the Disappearing Cocktail. We had 'acquired' a refrigerator and were eager to exploit its scope for gracious living. We brewed beer from old fruit, rice water and yeast, bottled it and put it in to cool. The senior mess at the same time had made an altogether more sophisticated cocktail, embracing carefully hoarded old brandy, and they too – unbeknown to the mess secretary and secretly, lest unhallowed lips should sip it – had placed their concoction in the fridge. As the hour of dinner approached Michael Cory-Wright instructed the mess waiter to decant our beer into a jug, and when the Colonel came in he was pressed to sample the brew. Everyone was delighted with it until the time came for the senior mess to have their own cocktail; it was not in the fridge. The waiter had decanted all the bottles together.

Living regimentally may have been good for morale but it made for an incestuous society, so the experts attached to us from outside were especially welcome. Those from the Straits Settlements or Malay Volunteer Force were sometimes civil servants, like the geologist Freddie Fitch, and sometimes from the private sector, like Bobby Greene, a partner in the Singapore law firm of Braddell Brothers. Rubber planting was represented by the slow-spoken, fifteen-stone Henry Royle, whose knowledge of plantation life was extremely useful. At this time he was probably our hardest-working officer, because he was in charge of the squads whose jobs included clearing up the camp, planting allotments and keeping anti-malarial work going. He knew exactly what he was doing and exactly how much work men could do. Since Henry's gangs were working for the good of the camp, he had little patience with procrastination or time-honoured army habits like tea breaks.

"Fucking slave driver!" they would complain, "treats us like his fucking coolies!"

It was men like Henry who told us about local diet, government idiosyncracies and the different habits of Malays, Chinese and Tamils. And it was from Henry I had learned the Malay for privy – '*ada t'ada*', a 'have-have-not' – and 'one for the road' – '*satu ampat jalan*', that is to say (ho! ho!) 'one FOUR the road'.

As we lay on our charpoys at night, we would encourage these outsiders to reminisce about their work – and would wonder what was happening now in their neat bungalows, immaculate mines and regimented plantations. We began to feel quite like old hands ourselves, at least in theory.

"Henry," asked a perky Londoner one night, "what are those funny-looking bean things growing behind RQMS Beech's store?"

"Those? I should think you probably mean the *kangkong*."

"*Kangkong!* What on earth are they?"

"They are those funny-looking bean things growing behind RQMS Beech's store!"

Bobby Greene revealed to us the more urbane sophistications of legal and commercial life. He had exchanged dachshund puppies with his wife before she embarked on one of the last boats to leave Singapore. Her puppy, now his, was named Ludwig, and all this time, however little Bobby had to eat, he always fed Ludwig first.

12

In The Rough

THE work we did for the Japanese gave me a certain sour
satisfaction. The Shinto shrine we were to build on a little island
in the lake involved transplanting the sacred greens. I thought golf
a waste of time, skill and money; so it did not grieve me unduly to
cut out the turf and carry it round the lake. We also built roads and
two ornamental red bridges with green knobs on, and the carpenters
among us worked with Nip engineers and Chinese carpenters on
the pretty little shrine itself. Some jobs were nastier than others,
either because they were physically taxing (like stone-breaking) or
monotonous (like carrying baskets of earth from A to B for hours
on end), so efforts were made to share them out fairly. Officers were
in charge of the gangs but were not expected to work physically
themselves. Subalterns were on duty more often than their seniors,
and grew to dread those days, not so much for their discomfort or
monotony as for their nervous tension.

On that first working party I was prevented from sharing the
work by my *gunso* (sergeant), Nakamura. On meeting, we had eyed
each other appraisingly. I saw a fresh-faced, well-made little man,
quick on his feet – which were shod in cloven-toed rubber boots
fastening at the back. He saw a tall, straight and arrogant man in
floppy shorts and impractical hat. On the whole I got on better with
nice-looking Nips than with the cartoon characters, who really did
exist and seemed, in their turn, to prefer prisoners as ill-favoured as
themselves. But, as in life elsewhere, the awkward bloke was often
the one to be singled out for undeserved punishment.

At any rate our job was explained and we got going; it was

road-making that day, with a tea break every couple of hours. The signal for this was the Japanese shout, '*Yasumé!*', and I made my first error when, on hearing a loud '*Yasumé!*', I passed it on to the men, who promptly sat down. Up rushed a furious Nakamura, and before he laid into me I just had time to realise I had mistaken the neat, cloven-footed *hanchau* (corporal) from the adjoining gang for Nakamura Gunso. He did not, as an even more furious Korean guard did later to a Major Roberts at Tamarkham, make me stand in a trench so that he could hit me in the face more conveniently, but he managed quite well without the trench. About an hour later he approached with a furtive air and invited me to squat beside him. Offering me a cigarette (Capstan full-strength), he puffed a bit at his own and then mimed that I must not tell the Japanese *shoko* (officer) that he had hit me.

That first working party was a microcosm of misunderstandings to come. We worked from eight in the morning to six in the evening, and I found myself next to a gang of bolshie Queenslanders.

"Is there an NCO here?" I asked.

"NCO? We shot all our NCOs."

Eventually an officer appeared, and while we were talking a great bruiser shouted at him:

"You're an effing shite, you are. Take your pip off, Mr Beverley, and we'll have it out right now!"

"Aw, shuddup!" Beverley bellowed back.

Later on Brigadier Duke came tramping round with his pronged stick to see how the work was getting on. (He was to leave for Japan shortly afterwards.) When he reached the Aussies he attracted a good deal of flak.

"Morning, Mr Duke!" some of them shouted.

"Morning, Duke!" cried others.

Still others, as he passed grinning fixedly, leaned on their shovels, spat ostentatiously and chanted, "Shite! Shite! Shite!"

On another occasion we were being paraded, hundreds of us, for a formal count, and as each adjutant went up to report to the Brigadier and saluted him, a howl of derision rose from the Aussies. This quickly spread to our own troops – and who could blame them? Food was lamentable, we had not learned to give and take, and the timing – the suspense – of the thing was irresistible. The smarter the adjutant, the more punctilious his halt, the more meticulous the raising of his right arm and the more abrupt the final quiver of his hand, the louder came the ironic cheer.

We were fearful that such barracking might develop into real ill-feeling, but it remained an escape valve. Of course there was a 'them and us' feeling between British and Aussies, Aussies and Indians, and Indians and – I should think – everybody; and also between subalterns and field officers, and men and officers. But privileges, whether real or imagined, did not really survive the rigours of our later trials. The 'them and us' comparison soon lay not between ranks but between those who went out to work and those who remained in hospital or in camp jobs – some legitimately as patients, medicos or experts, but some as malingerers. It is true that field officers were in a stronger position to malinger than others, but they tended to be older anyway, and the old sweats in the ranks were no less adept at insinuating themselves into Nip-free sinecures. The tragedy was that the most conscientious of the officers and the strongest of the men – the workhorses of the working parties – were often the first to die, largely through ignorance of the stealth of tropical disease. We soon learned to temper our zeal – the officers in setting an example, and the men in getting the job finished quickly – with the need to conserve our fading strength. That first day ended badly on a note that was to become all too familiar – a miscount. (So much misery was caused by standing about being counted that the strongest of all my resolutions for after the war was never, ever, to stand in a queue.) On this occasion tools were being counted: the *chunkeols* and shovels and picks and baskets and crowbars. Some were missing, or imagined to be missing, and eventually the Nip in charge lined up all the officers and gave us each a ritual bash in the face before we could lead the men off to supper.

Misunderstandings grew less frequent as we got to know each others' little ways, but this very familiarity sometimes bred contempt. When some bad hats on an Aussie working party sneaked off, the whole party was promised heavy punishment unless the missing men were found. On occasions such as this old Padre Adams, a former missionary in Japan, was very helpful. He now produced the equivalent number of men.

"We couldn't find the original culprits," he explained, "but these men have volunteered to take their punishment instead and thus save the rest of the party from communal punishment. They have done this in the spirit of *bushido* which is so respected in Japan."

"*Ah so des-kah?* Very good – *ena!* These very brave men. OK. All men go."

In general we got on pretty well with the Nip engineers. When they were in chatty mood they asked us how old we were, if we had '*wifus*', if we had babies, and if we had photos. And just as we soon learned to count in Japanese and use words like *meshi* (rice), *bioki* (sick), *yasum* (rest), *benjo* (latrine) and *arigato* (thank you) – but not *kora!* (hey!) or *baka-yaro!* (stupid fool) – they soon learned that '*empi*' (stones) in English were 'bastards', '*bangi*' (spades) were 'buggers', '*tanger*' (picks) were 'fuckers', and anything else 'cunts'. This mutual understanding did not always exist with the officers, strutting about with their swords and boots. One Aoki Chui broke a driver's arm for nothing at all, and stood a working party in the sun for ten hours. On the other hand another lieutenant, Sato, spoke excellent English and was a partner in one of our major rackets – petrol (the other being cement); the Chinese were third parties in this operation.

I first met with Nip corruptibility early on, when coming out of the golf clubhouse with a looted case of beer. A sentry had materialised and was regarding me quizzically. I put my finger to my lips, handed him a bottle and passed on. Experience was to prove that the further away they were from their officers, the better the guards behaved. They often seemed to hate them as much as we did, and it was the officers, not the men or NCOs, who did their best to humiliate their opposite numbers.

Yet a Nip commander could express tender feelings – on paper:

During I am the Orderly Officer I will conduct the evening roll call with solemnity.
(1) When the review is going under the command 'Attention!', all of the ranks must not move, smoke, laugh, talk, even smile.

(2) The remainder in the camp (example sickness) must keep quiet for they never destroy the authority of roll call.

(3) The soldiers who are free from roll call by duty, if they see Nipponese Orderly Officer they should salute him privately.

(4) For officers I admit the absence to keep their dignity. But the sacred roll call is not a show. So if there is any officer sitting in the chair and seeing the sight of roll call, I feel serious displeasure.

If there are soldiers who oppose the above-mentioned, whatever it may be, I will return them with furious training.

Lieut Fukuda

Soon after our arrival at Sime Road camp a pep talk ended by exhorting us to work hard, and promising that the war would soon be over and the happy day of our repatriation would come. It was a depressing example of crowd psychology that the troops, deaf to the implication behind these cheerful words, clapped enthusiastically.

(The reference to repatriation figured regularly in Japanese speeches until mid-1943, when it was dropped in favour of more serviceable admonitions: 'You will work until you die for the Japanese!', or 'the railway must be built even at the cost of fifty per cent of the prisoners and fifty per cent of the Nippon engineers!' And we were told not to complain of sickness as we should be thankful that the noble Japanese had spared our lives at the fall of Singapore, when we were too cowardly to commit *hara-kiri*. It was not until 1945 that references to 'the happy day of repatriation' recurred, but then with an altered significance.)

At the beginning of October 1942 our hosts were still in magnanimous mood. For them the Rising Sun bathed the Island of Shonan in its refulgent beams, and the liberated peoples of the Greater East Asian Co-prosperity Sphere basked in its glory. A general thanksgiving was decreed, and its climax was the opening of the Shonan Jinjya War Memorial on Bukit Timah Hill, and of the Shinto shrine we had helped to build. Besides the officers in their best uniforms, clanking in and out of beflagged Studebakers, we saw civilians for the first time. Bespectacled correspondents were distinguished from the military by their long hair, and tubby nurses and highly made-up wives stared at us curiously. Cameras clicked. The War Memorial consisted of a large obelisk (to the Japanese) and a small one (to the Allies). Our senior officers were invited to attend and then share a feast and a cinema show. Their views, in the form of essays, on Nippon culture were requested, and they were given to understand that having completed our period of six months' punishment for presuming to resist the might of the Imperial Japanese Army we could look forward to more favourable treatment.

Our Shinto shrine looked pleasingly unmilitary with its airy Buddhist archways and 'lacquered red sacred bridge' leading through the landscaped grounds of the golf club to the wigwam-shaped sanctuary and oratory. 'Here,' in the words of the magazine *Sakura – formerly Home Life*:

> was neither ostentatious display intended to hoodwink the gullible nor various artifices intended to overawe the masses. Here was only solemnity, an atmosphere of sublimity that entered deep into the people's souls. . . . The construction of the Shonan Shrine and its dedication to Amaterasu Omikami, the Sun Goddess, was an expression on the one hand of the deepest reverence to the Divine Ancestral Goddess whose gracious will led to the founding of the Empire of Nippon. On the other hand, the great spirit of the Divine Ancestral Goddess was also spread by the construction of the Shonan Shrine to the South and was a manifestation of the lofty ideals of the Nippon race. Needless to state, this is the spirit being shown by the people of Nippon in waging the Greater East Asian War to a successful conclusion whereby the sinister and imperialistic Anglo-American designs in the Orient will be crushed for ever and an ideal Greater East Asian Co-Prosperity Sphere be established.

Once the tumult and the shouting had died, our guards were replaced by trouble-making Sikhs of the Indian National Army and by Koreans (*heikos*) who, being given hell themselves as non-ranking auxiliaries of the IJA (Imperial Japanese Army), took great pleasure in passing on that hell to us. Our freedom was severely curtailed and walks outside the camp were no longer possible.

It was unsettling, just when we were getting used to sparse rations and local cooking methods, to receive some Red Cross supplies from South Africa; and not only food but tropical clothing. We felt suddenly back on the edge of civilisation after resigning ourselves – as a forgotten and disgraced army – to keeping a very low profile indeed. And if not exactly fighting fit we were at least healthy and no longer hungry. Was that ocean between us and Colombo still uncrossable? The locals showed no signs whatever of taking the Japanese at their word; should we not get down to learning Malay and take our chance in the jungle? Suppose we made for the north, what was happening up there? Some funny things, according to *Sakura*:

Up until the 19th century continuous rivalry existed and constant battles were fought between two great racial flows, namely the Annamese representing the northern family, who were the inheritors of Chinese civilisation, and the Thais, who were affected by Indian culture. It was indeed a most regrettable tragedy for the people of the Indo-China peninsula that two races, both Orientals, should have continuously fought each other. Finally, the people of Indo-China, divided by this racial rivalry, had to entrust the administration of their state to the French. Today, however, Nippon has shown to all the peoples of Asia the path of advancing toward a common goal. On September 23 of the 15th year of Showa (1940), with the friendly consent of the French authorities, Nippon troops advanced into French Indo-China and were everywhere given a warm welcome by the people. Following the founding of Manchokuo, a sacred war has been fought under Nippon's leadership to expel Anglo-Saxon aggression from all Asia. Both Thailand and Burma have today awakened to the new day that has dawned for the Orient. The cry of the liberation of all Asia has today penetrated into Indo-China also. In this we are convinced that the cultural contribution made by France to Indo-China is destined to flower to its full perfection in the new atmosphere of Asia's renaissance.

Well! 'The lucky Alphonse is always in the middle!' But the news from Burma sounded horribly familiar: muddles, army leaders who thought they knew better than teak-wallahs, inter-service rivalry, strategic withdrawals, the premature blowing of the Sittang bridge, lack of air cover, and finally the stampede to beat the monsoon back to India. We got the gist of it, if not the details. It all added up to a mixture of feelings: of guilt for having landed the poor buggers in Burma in the shit, and of relief of the pull-up-the-ladder-Jack-I'm-all-right sort; our share in the general mess was over and now it was someone else's turn. However, though physically comfortable enough, we began to feel the walls closing in round us. So when rumours of a move to Thailand began to circulate we were not altogether sorry. John Beckett and Corporal Rogers turned to the problem of transporting our radio. Precious bully beef tins were eviscerated, refilled with condensers, valves and resistances, and re-soldered, and in that form the makings of a portable wireless were to reach Thailand safely.

Most of us had never heard of 'Thailand', though Siam with its mythical associations had been familiar to many a schoolboy. We were all too ready to think of it as a Shangri La aloof from the imperialist ambitions of East and West. We happily swallowed stories of 'hill stations' (where our health would cause the Nips less anxiety), of greater freedom (the locals had no colonial ties with us), and of better food (independent of imports).

My own knowledge of Siam was hazy. I knew that on the authority of Sam Johnson Siamese envoys had waited on Louis XIV; that Prince Bira raced a Bugatti; that the Siamese national anthem, according to an advertisement hoarding in Bristol featuring a donkey, was 'Oh whatana Siam!'; that the King of Siam had been thrown out in a revolution, the country renamed Muang Thai, 'Land of the Free', and an attack made on French Indo-China (with Japanese help); and that a great deal of rice was grown there. Perhaps from this last circumstance we could believe Nip assurances. Moreover, we were to travel by rail – and were not Malayan Railways, with their grand airy stations, renowned for comfort?

13

Not The David Lean Bridge

"Good God!" cried a major of the 5th Suffolks, staring at the cattle trucks drawn up at Singapore station, "they can't do this to British officers!" He was wrong. The trucks were about half the size of the '30 *hommes* – 10 *chevaux*' ones of World War I, and were made of steel, with sliding doors at the centre; and the sun beat down upon the roofs. Thirty of us were crammed with our kit into each truck, and for five days and five nights we sat, stood or squatted there as we moved slowly and with frequent stops the nine hundred odd miles (one thousand four hundred and forty kilometres describes its slow length more vividly) to Ban Pong. As we crawled over the Causeway we noted with gloom how little repair it had needed, and many bridges after that had been shored up with rickety-looking timber.

Apart from the overcrowding, the Nips treated us reasonably well. Frequent stops permitted emptying of bowels, filling of water bottles and distribution of rice, while some Red Cross bully beef remained to relieve our hunger. One unfortunate (no names, no pack drill) was stricken with dysentery, and had to be held out of the sliding doors as we moved along. All one night, calls on the support of David Cherry and Michael Cory-Wright – "Greater love hath no man, m'dear chap!" – were made every twenty minutes or so. Often they had all three scarcely squeezed back among the close-packed humanity when the gripes struck yet again: "So sorry, m'dears, still one up the spout! Thought I'd emptied both barrels."

That journey has remained with me always as both a nightmare and a relief from nightmare. The claustrophobia of it made it unforgettable and yet there were blessed moments when, in spite of the foetid atmosphere and cramped position, I felt myself drifting off to sleep to the accompaniment of the quickening click-click of the bogies and the breath of fresh air as the train accelerated slowly away from one of our interminable stops. At such moments it seemed that the acceleration might go on and on until we were humming along, driven by a supernatural power bent on restoring the *status quo ante* man's inhumanity to man; that all the signs of our indignity – the Nip guards, the makeshift clothing, and even the evidence of physical distress on the sill of the door – would drop away into the jungle and we would glide, safe and sound, into the brightly lit platform of Bristol Temple Meads station.

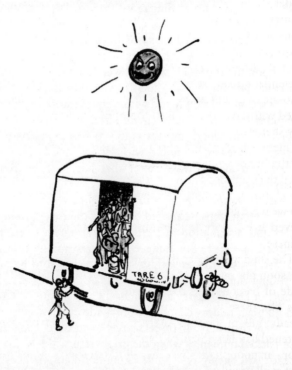

Room for one more inside.

Ever since then, into recurrent nightmares of the incomprehensible exam paper, the guns that won't fire, the flying that runs out of lift, the on-stage drying, the clothes that melt away, and the grave persons with unexpected sexual habits, the Japanese have often intruded. But I counter the grip of fear with the memory of that railway truck, pulling away from my persecutors – click-click, click-click, clickety-click, clickety-click! – in the happy knowledge that, yes, this time I shall glide safely into the heaven-haven of the bathroom and breakfast. The recipe seldom fails.

But it failed in November 1942, when we clanked and jerked after what seemed a lifetime into the squalors of Ban Pong. We had not been prepared for them by our first sight of Thailand. At the border station Stuart had remarked on a characteristic of the new country. On the Malayan side of the dividing wire an old ragged Tamil squatted on his haunches sweeping the platform in slow motion with a bunch of twigs; on the Thai side dozens of people strutted about, every one of them, down to the banana-seller, resplendent in uniform. After that, the *padi* fields stretched away in a mosaic of greens and yellows to outcrops of grey limestone hills, pitted with caves that seemed to promise refuge. Perhaps even now they sheltered *sakais* ready to shelter us – were we to jump train in the night – from future horrors. Not that these were yet apparent. On the bunds women walked gracefully in conical straw hats, and when the train stopped we were besieged by villagers clamouring to buy clothing, fountain-pens and watches. Many gave us 'V' signs and we were greatly taken by the girls, who appeared, at least to our starved eyes, more voluptuous and more forthcoming than the Chinese.

The staging camp at Ban Pong, already delapidated from much use, soon put this sort of nonsense out of our heads. The huts were made of bamboo and roofed with *attap* leaves. The condition of huts like these was to dominate our lives henceforth. Were they already full of vermin? Were the slats – sleeping platforms of flattened bamboo ('*bali-bali*' to the Malays) a couple of feet off the floor – in good shape? Was the *attap* watertight? Above all, did they exist at all or did we have to bivouac in the rain while we built them? And the latrines; were they already dug? Were they overflowing, and their maggots with them? At Ban Pong not only were the latrines flooded but so was the whole camp. The rotting huts leaned drunkenly into the water, the water came to within inches of the *bali-bali*, and makeshift catwalks led from hut to hut, from kitchen to hospital, and from hospital to underwater latrines. Few bums were carried that far and the floods, I fear, stood in for latrines for most of us. Yet, as the sun's reflections danced about the huts, from the stagnant and infected water a terrible Venice-like beauty was born.

"This camp is a disgrace!" said Toosey to the Major luckless enough to be in charge of it. "You ought to be ashamed of yourself, letting it get into this state!"

"But what could we do? The Japanese . . . "

"Nonsense! You threw in the sponge too early."

"It's very different from the set-up in Singapore."

"I can see that all too clearly."

"I've got no men to do anything with."

"Well, you should jolly well see that you get them."

"You don't know what the Japs are like here!"

"No, but it's up to you to get their respect and co-operation. It'll pay them in the end. They must see that."

"But, my dear man . . . "

"Don't you 'my dear man' me!" Toosey stamped an unwontedly tarnished boot and the two parted in mutual animosity, the one secure in the impossibility of his task and the other in the impossibility of showing a similar defeatism. Whether Toosey was right in his conviction we shall never know; he gladly accepted responsibilities and put many of his fellow colonels to shame by his confidence and vitality; and he saw to it that his reputation impressed the Nips to our advantage, if also to his own. His reputation was high among a disparate lot of men, and even the Aussies, so rough with Brigadier Duke, paid him their respects. "Colonel Toosey!" cried one as he passed a working party, "you're no shit-house bastard, you're a fucking gentleman!" The hospital camp he ran later was said to be the best of them all. But he was never in a real hell-camp; his infrastructure remained intact because he never left 'the egg belt', the lowland area where farm produce was available – money and access permitting.

At any rate his ingenuity was not put to the test in Ban Pong because we moved on thirty kilometres the next day – luckily by truck – to Kanburi, or more properly Kanchanaburi, the 'City of Gold'. It was a busy little town with an old gateway, a Buddhist monastery (our first experience of temples that looked like frolicking red and green dragons), a paper factory, an aerodrome and a prison. It stood at the junction of two rivers, the Kwa Noy, or little stream, and the Kwa Yai, or big stream. The Kwa Noy ('the Kwai') was navigable to barges in the monsoon almost as far as the Burmese border, and the railway which – as we now discovered – we were to build, would run more or less along its bank. We were also to build a concrete and steel bridge over the Kwa Yai, five kilometres beyond the end of the metalled road at Kanburi, near Tamarkham (Tha Ma Kharm, the 'Ferry of the Tamarind'). The camp was above flood level and had just been built by an advance party of Argylls and Gordons from Poodu gaol, Kuala Lumpur. There were five long *attap* huts, each holding – packed tight – three hundred men.

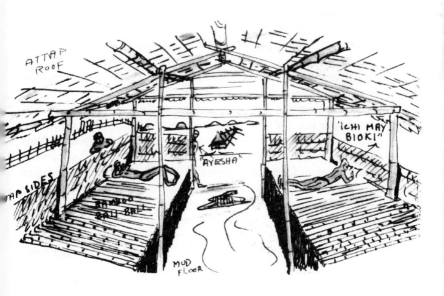

The Argylls, just as they had been veterans of jungle warfare, were, compared with us, veterans of the River Kwa Yai. They had worked well with their captors – Major Roberts even getting away with hitting a Korean guard in a moment of exasperation. Two subalterns, Kenny McLeod and Ian Primrose, were extrovert types who were viewed with wonder by our more uptight Territorials for their disdain of rank and for their chumminess with their men; they perfected a cabaret act of wrestling in mud to enliven the odd camp concert, and this provoked a mixture of hilarious laughter and misgivings of *lèse majesté*. As for their men, they too were not quite what we were used to. When I addressed one on a working party, he stared blankly at me as though I were speaking a foreign language; at my third repetition he was good enough to say in a pitying voice, "We only take orders from our own officers."

The Gordons were rather different and were variously referred to as the Gay Gordons and the Gordon Thailanders. The Nips liked the 'Scotlanders' because they worked hard. There was certainly no doubt about their Scottishness. One of the Gordons had a thumbnail extracted, and as he walked unsteadily back from the MO's hut, still under the influence of ether and remembering, perhaps, being held down by Sassenach orderlies, the ancient grudge surfaced and he cried out again and again, "Bannockburrn, ye buggerrs! Bannockburrn!"

We found that at Tamarkham we were to be closely controlled by the Japanese and, under them, the Korean guards. The camp was clean when we moved into it, with water supplied by mechanical pump, and firewood from woods not far away. There was just room beside the huts for a soccer ground, and then came the closely patrolled fence. For the first time we felt really caged in. Yet not far away the limestone hills reared up invitingly, seeming to say, 'Come unto me all ye that are weary and heavy laden'. The lure of those hills betrayed Stuart and Padre Robertson (or the 'Dizzard of Doulting', as he had been re-christened by Mike Cory-Wright and Seymour Dearden) into an indiscretion. Like me they had been reminded by them of happier times, and they were standing together one evening, feeding each other's nostalgia with their fancies.

"Look there," said the Padre, pointing to a long low outline with a deep fissure running down it. "That could be the Mendips from

Lower Milton, with Ebbor Rocks in the middle. We could be looking at it as we take a stroll in the evening in March, coming up from –"

"Evensong at the cathedral?"

"Well, to be honest, I was going to say from a martini at The Swan. Do you see the fissure there? That clump of trees over the bare rock looks like the viewpoint over Wookey Hole. D'you see?"

"Yes. But I'm reminded of Henley. If you look over there where the river bends round into the jungle and the ground rises to barer hills, doesn't that look rather like Remenham Hill from somewhere near Temple Island?"

"By Jove, I see what you mean. From that bend there – "

"*KORA! NANDA! SHOKO!*"

A furious guard leaped upon them, screaming and jabbing them with his bayonet. They were hustled across to the guardroom and poor Toosey and the interpreter, David Boyle, were summoned to explain why these two officers were discussing and pointing out escape routes from the camp.

"What exactly were you doing, Simmy?" asked Toosey, and gave a hollow laugh at the explanation. "My dear chap! How d'you expect us to explain the associations of Henley Regatta to the Nips?" He did his best but it was not good enough, and Stuart and Struan were subjected to the pain of being tipped up and down while kneeling on rolling bamboos and then put into 'ovens' for the night. Next morning Toosey managed to extricate them before the sun added to their plight.

Nearer to hand the scene was full of life and beauty. The Kwa Yai itself was pretty to look at; 'pom-poms' puttered busily up it, and huge rafts of bamboo floated down; little boys bathed buffaloes and brightly clad women washed clothes, their smiles – fortunately for our peace of mind – neutralised by mouthfuls of blood-red betel nut. Near the banks grew all kinds of exotic trees, some – like the tamarisk and kapok – new to us, and others obviously useful, like the coconut palms, mangoes, papaya, pommeloes and bananas, with beyond them fields of maize and tobacco. Two farms on the further bank were happy to sell all these things as well as biscuits and eggs. We were supposed to patronise the camp canteen but we used to slink off from working parties, when the heat was off, and bargain for the superior farm products. As we also had to slink off into the undergrowth for a quite legitimate '*benjo*', it was annoying some-times – just at the critical moment – to be hissed at by a hopeful trader from behind a banana leaf earmarked as toilet paper.

Now and then the Nips would have an anti-black-market blitz, and we would be lined up and searched as we came back into camp. There was one field day when I was bashed up by a Korean known as 'the Undertaker' and was only consoled by the sight of him going down the rigid line of men and confiscating all *their* little hoards as well. He may have been a bastard but he was no fool: his parting shot was to tap each man's hat, whence the hidden egg would flow down over motionless features.

My pay at Tamarkham reached thirty Japanese dollars a month, which went quite a long way. Eggs cost five cents, corn cobs three for five cents and quite good 'Battle Gong' cigarettes, made in the Thai BAT factory from Virginia tobacco, only twenty-five cents for twenty (their superior brand of 'Sheaves of Rice' was strictly for the Nips). By the end of the war eggs were thirty cents, corn cobs ten cents and cigarettes prohibitive; we had long switched by then to rolling our own from 'Sikh's Beard'. The Undertaker's real name was Kaneshiro and his boss, the Commandant, was Lieutenant Takasaki, alias 'the Frog'. As his nickname suggests, he was not one of the really vicious Japs but mild and studious in appearance, looking more like a bank manager than an army officer. Though strict he was on the whole fair and got on well with Toosey – until the Great Disillusion. We were kept firmly with our noses to the grindstone but the seriously sick were not as yet persecuted, and Toosey persuaded him to allow us to continue using English rather than Japanese words of command; Jap commands were introduced later upriver, and to start with were depressing beyond measure.

In Tamarkham there was no nonsense about senior officers being left free to construct racecourses or play endless games of bridge. The railway had to be built to schedule and everyone was needed. "If officers do not work hard," said the Frog, "they will be punished. I hope they will work!" Work lasted from eight in the morning to seven at night, except for a *yasumé* day each week or two. The *tenkos* were all too frequent and gave limitless scope for delays since the Nips, abacus or no abacus, always had trouble adding up, even when everything and everybody had been grouped in tens. Should the Nips require a *speedo* we might have to carry on working till two in the morning. No longer could we keep men in camp to do our own chores, and, as we were only allowed thirty men to work in a cookhouse and feed two thousand five hundred people, the menu each day was reduced to a very rough and ready rice and stew, once for the dawn breakfast, once cold from our mess tins on the job, and once when we got back – in the twilight (if we were lucky).

The work consisted of making the trace for the railway tracks for three kilometres each side of the river, and building first a temporary wooden bridge over the Kwa Yai and afterwards a steel bridge – with girders brought from Java – on eleven concrete piles a short distance upstream; then the sleepers and rails were laid, with a subsidiary line down the far bank towards Kanburi. This was done with sheer manpower, and the only tools were picks, *chunkeols*, shovels, baskets and stretchers (for carrying earth and sand and pebbles), axes and adzes, hand-trucks, hand pile-drivers, and later on concrete-mixers (made in Britain) and grabs.

The pile-driver for the piers of the wooden bridge was slung from a pulley in a wooden scaffolding between two barges and worked by about twenty ropes on each barge; a Nip engineer squatted in the rigging and chanted a little ditty on the theme of 'ONE and two and THREE four and THREE four!' or in musical terms:

Ich-i ni no san yo, no san yo

In time with this everyone pulled on the ropes with a short pull and a l-o-n-g pull and a l-o-n-g-e-r pull, CRASH! And the weight pounded down on the top of the pile. This went on for hour after hour, and the monotony of it and the primitive nature of the tools and the sheer numbers of men slaving away – some digging, some in long snaking queues carrying baskets of earth, some chaining sand and stones from the river bed – made for a positively biblical scene. We felt like the Israelites building a temple to Moloch. We were delighted when in December the river rose to an unprecedented height and swept the half-built bridge away. But our jubilation was short-lived for we only had to work all the harder to reinstate it when the floods receded.

Much the worst job – and we did our best to share and share it about – was unloading metal rails from barges. Iron pincers were used, each handle cradled by one man in his bent elbows, each rail requiring about ten sized-off pairs of men. The work was back-breaking. First we would have to heave up the rails into our bent arms and then manipulate them from the horizontal up the river bank. This at once shifted the balance and the pairs at the back might suddenly find themselves collapsing and the rail lashing about viciously. Inevitably there were malingerers who, instead of really supporting the rail, went through the motions with the loudest of grunts and groans. Mutual recrimination was never long in coming. I shared those agonising days with Wilkie, and all his Darlington aggression was put to good use. As we staggered under the load, his exhortations: "Come on, lads, altogether now – one, two three, HUP!" would gradually disintegrate into shouts from the others: "Up at the back!", "Down at the front!", "Keep it up, damn you!", "'kin 'ell!", "Cor, fuck the bloody bastard!", "Wish this was a bloody Nip!", "Oo, my fucking arms!" "Steady now, lads! Put it down then; now, once again – altogether, one, two, three, HUP! Keep it going there; up at the back! Up at the – hold on! Up at the – LOOK OUT!" And CRASH! the rear would drop, bouncing and whipping along to the front, which would follow it down, scattering men with grazed arms, bruised thighs and even broken shins, the least of the injuries likely to turn septic; and the Nip would jump down among us, screaming and lashing out with his stick of bamboo.

On tough jobs like this officers worked with the men (though I wouldn't swear that all did) partly because every little helped and partly because we would have felt ashamed or overtly 'wet' not to have done so. And on pile-driving jobs we often took a hand at the ropes out of mere boredom. But at work on the line itself we were

often forbidden by the Nips to work physically on the grounds that it was our job to see that the earth was levelled properly, the ballast laid firmly, the drains angled correctly; and we couldn't do this if we had our heads down at one particular spot. Above all, it was a question of delegation. It was easier for a Nip guard who wanted more *speedo* out of twenty or thirty men to harangue us and if necessary bash us up until *we* got it out of them, than to run around bashing the individual men. He therefore liked to have the officer in a prominent position – and easily reached. This made the officer's lot not a happy one. In the first place he suffered long periods of solitary boredom; he could walk up and down chatting to the more interesting men but not deflect them from their work for too long; similarly, at the end of his patrol he could hobnob with the officer in charge of the neighbouring gang, but only until the Nips took exception to their chatter. In the second place he was always on tenterhooks for that dreaded call: "*Oi! Shoko! Kora! Baka-yaro!*" And then he had to decide how far to brave the Nip's fury by standing up for the men – 'they were sick', 'had been working too long', 'needed a tea break' – and how far to risk the men's scorn as a 'Jap-happy bastard' by shouting orders to them. So he usually finished up by feeling the complete tom-noddy and saying things like "OK, chaps! Donald Duck is on the warpath. Says you can't go home until this section's finished, even if it takes all night. So can you put on a bit of a show? You may as well as they've nearly finished next door."

This situation was complicated by the varying attitudes of the men. Some were natural skivers, some felt themselves in honour bound to do as little Japanese war work as possible, and some simply could not do any work without taking some pride in it.

The question of war work was a tricky one. About the beginning of February we suddenly realised that the wooden bridge was actually finished, and to our incredulity the first train came over – and the bridge refrained from collapsing. We had never believed the railway would work, expecting vaguely that we would be free before it did or, if not, that the RAF would bomb it to bits. Yet now railcars were followed by genuine snorting wood-burning locomotives and our next job was to tackle the permanent steel bridge upstream. We could hardly laugh this off. The Burmese border suddenly came closer, and before we knew what we were doing we might find ourselves loading shells at Tamarkham to be whizzed up to the border of India to knock hell out of our own troops there. But by now the moral issues were quite dead. At every step our complaints had been blocked by the taunt that the Japanese had never signed the Hague Convention, and from our own experience and from tales brought back from upriver we knew there was only one thing to worry about: survival.

Toosey, of course, was at the sharp end of all this. On the one hand he had a lunatic fringe of senior officers who expected him to cover for them; and not only senior officers. In the early days, when we first found ourselves threatened with physical work, a Captain Hawley exclaimed indignantly: "I can't be seen swinging a *chunkeol*!

I've got to earn my living East of Suez after the war!" On the other hand Toosey could see that the Nips meant business and that their pace was quickening, just when our own demoralisation was beginning to set in and make our working practices questionable. To 'go slow' not only drove the Nips to a frenzy of beatings, longer hours and denial of *yasumés*; it also made the work more intolerable than if it had been tackled at a reasonable pace and with some responsibility, even pride, in its performance. The combination of Japanese exasperation and the men's low morale was clearly leading to disaster. As the work got more behindhand, the Nips dragged more sick out of camp to add to our number, which itself accelerated the rate of sickness. To break this fatal circle it was decided that Toosey should propose to the Frog and the Jap engineers that we should be given piece work and left to organize it ourselves. Whatever the morality of the arrangement, it was not quite so satisfactory in practice as it sounds because our targets were often impossible, or could only be reached by forced overtime. But it did ease things, and though there were dark accusations of 'Jap-happiness', it stopped the skivers from claiming to be more patriotic than their fellows, and ensured that everyone did their fair share. And those who had skills, such as the carpenters, need fear no longer to exercise them. We were also able to cut out some of the countings that had bedevilled our lives, as we now had more say over the numbers of men used, and implements issued, for the various jobs.

For the steel bridge piles were sunk in a different way. Doub: ring moulds of wood were sunk in the river bed and filled to make concrete shells. The centres were sucked out with pumps and grabs until the concrete casing had sunk fifteen feet. Then sand, pebbles and cement were poured in until the solid foundations were ready for the piles which were to carry the steel girders above. Shaped wooden moulds were then erected on the foundations, and a scaffolding built. At the top were platforms for the concrete-mixers, and up long ramps queues of men chained baskets and sacks of sand, pebbles and cement to feed them and fill the moulds. It was even more Cecil B. De Mille than the building of the wooden bridge because the scale was so much greater, with hundreds of cursing men and excited Nips milling around, barges pom-pomming up the river, tipper-trucks squeaking along narrow-gauge supply lines, and over all – in this dry season – the blinding glare of the sun above and the white sand below.

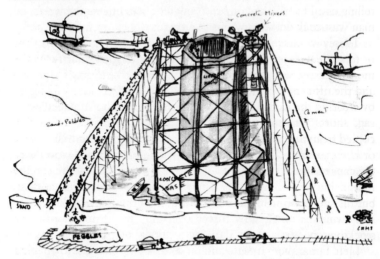

The Japs on my particular pier were quite a good crowd. We christened one Angelo, a corruption of *hanchau* or squad leader, because he spoke a bit of English and, being rather vain, was open to flattery. This could be useful. "Can you show us how to do this, Angelo?" And, after a useful rest while we watched him, we would shower him with admiration and then ask to go and buy *gula malacca* or perhaps some of those little spotted *pisang-orang* bananas that so seldom came into the canteen. His side-kick, the round-faced 'Jack Oakie', was a very good swimmer and could sometimes be prevailed upon to allow an extra swim before that blessed moment after work when everyone went in. The Nips, to my surprise in view of the communal bathing in Japan, used to hold one hand coyly over their private parts when swimming. This did not prevent badinage about those of their better-endowed guests: "Ah, OK soldier! Very good-*en-ah*, number one jig-i-jig!" And the old Thai women, squatting on the bank with bundles of bananas, would cackle and ostentatiously hide betel-dripping faces under high straw hats. It was Jack Oakie who one day spotted a chap relieving himself on his shovel which he then washed fastidiously in the river. He was hugely delighted, pelting him with pebbles and telling us all to look at 'the *benjo* soldier', a nickname the wretched man was stuck with for weeks afterwards.

Toosey would come out of camp to encourage our flagging spirits or to settle a dispute, and always took care to dress smartly. As the months passed we learned to conserve our disintegrating clothing – and the officers particularly their precious Herbert Johnson caps – by wearing the minimum to work. A head-dress *à l'Arabe*, a sweat rag, shorts removed for working purposes to reveal a G-string copied from the *fundoshi* loin-cloths of the Japanese, and flip-flops, or *klompen* as the Dutch called them, made from shaped wood with toe caps of tyre-rubber nailed across them, were all that the climate reasonably permitted. Even Toosey soon gave up wearing a shirt, but his shorts, sporting at the waistband a little tag with his crown and two pips on it, were always immaculately pressed, his long stockings spotlessly clean and his shoes brightly polished.

I left Tamarkham in May 1943 and so missed the grand opening of the bridge to traffic. But in one of the bloodier periods in the jungle upriver we met these same engineers again, and they were changed men. Even Angelo and Jack Oakie were bashing men right, left and centre in the frenzied urgency of getting the line through to the Burmese border.

To what extent Phil Toosey was the 'fucking gentleman' of the Aussies or the 'Jap-happy bastard' of some others was much discussed. Stuart had been closer to Toosey in the campaign, and still saw more of him than I did. He went on working parties with the drivers and reported back to Toosey on possible escape routes. (So to that extent the Nips had not been so far out in their suspicions, though they had been very far out in including the poor Dizzard of Doulting in them.) The local farmers told him escape was hopeless, not merely because of the jungle but because prisoners would be instantly recognised, unless perhaps one managed to pass himself off as a Buddhist monk. Nevertheless it was not long before Toosey's courage was tested further. The cool monsoon season, the idyllic nature of the river, the fertility of the surrounding farms, the friendliness of the people in them and, above all, the working parties that took us out of camp and sometimes as far as the huge and well-equipped Chungkai camp up the line on the Kwai Noy, inevitably encouraged fresh thoughts of escape.

Six people made a break for it at the same time. Four men of the East Surreys were away for ten days before recapture; they were taken off in a truck and never seen again. Two officers, an American journalist named Pomeroy and an anti-tank gunner named Howard, made for the Chinese border and were away a month. They were betrayed by Thai police, brought back roped together – I remember the sickening silence in the camp as they passed through – and thrown into the guardroom. Of course there was hell to pay. Toosey had covered for them all for three days, and then on a morning roll call a discrepancy was spotted. He confessed that six men had escaped and the Nips laughed heartily – until they realised he was serious. Thereafter a man only needed to drop his shaving brush through the fence and fish for it to be savagely beaten for attempting to escape. As for Toosey, he was made to stand to attention all day in front of the guardroom; he had betrayed the trust in him, and favours were no longer to be granted. Howard and Pomeroy were eventually taken out in a truck with shovels and picks and, as we afterwards heard from a Korean guard, bayonetted by the Undertaker. This form of execution was said to have been chosen 'so that shots should not disturb the prisoners'.

The scene was darkening everywhere. And perhaps it was just as well that we were ignorant of the reverses in Burma in the Arakhan Peninsula, or indeed of the unrealities still dogging military training in England, as recorded by Frances Partridge in her journal for 20th January 1943:

> Heywood Hill says that in the field where they do bayonet practice there are large notices saying 'Remember Singapore. How would YOU feel if a yellow man raped YOUR mother, sister, wife?'. . . . A feeble and neurotic ex-chemist was heard to say during parade: "Sergeant, may I fall out? I'm nothing but a bag of nerves!"

14

Going Dutch

As 1943 crawled slowly on we found that the beauty of our surroundings had seduced not only escapers but all of us; heavy work, malnutrition and chronic malaria began to take their toll. Deficiency diseases became rife: beri-beri, *tinea cruris*, pellagra, and the ringworm that ate into the men's tattoos. The tattoos were of great variety: 'SWEET' and 'SOUR' under each breast; dots round the throat with 'CUT ALONG THE DOTTED LINE' under them; 'MOTHER'; 'DEATH BEFORE DISHONOUR'; the crucifixion; and, outdoing all others, the fox hunt: bunching across the shoulders, horses and hounds strung out along the small of the back to pull down the fox by his tail – as he disappeared up the anus. Its possessor must have regretted his primacy as the Nips kept asking for private views. Tattoos were the object of official interest, too, and were included among personal details we were required to give in questionnaires; height, weight, pre-war jobs, technical qualifications, hobbies and (slipped in unobtrusively) influential relatives.

The sweet smell of squashed bedbugs had long become familiar, but it was some time before I realised that a maddening itching round the waist was due to little white creatures with dark insides that clung obstinately to clothing and could only be destroyed by cracking with the thumbnail: lice! In spite of periodic boilings, they were never long in re-appearing. Bedbugs could be roasted out of mosquito nets by spreading them in the sun, but lice were impervious to it. Bedbugs also lived in the bamboo slats, and though we would slide these out and lay them in the sun, the bugs would reoccupy them from the larger bamboos as soon as they were put back. Bugs and lice and crabs and worms had their less domesticated relations on the river. Leeches were familiar to us in the wet, but we had not been prepared for dry weather dangers. 'Turn but a stone and start a wing' was often the case when we were hacking about in the scrub or shifting logs for the bridge; and it was no 'many-splendoured thing' we disturbed, but scorpions and huge red centipedes, which could give very nasty wounds.

We tried in vain to be philosophic about our skin ailments. I had acquired Herbert Read's *The Knapsack*, and on the flyleaf was the name of the previous owner, 'J. G. Chamberlain, Cambridge, 13th October 1941'. Under the title he had written, 'The art of living is to be fully aware of one's personal existence – to become a privileged spectator – Llewellyn Powys'. This aphorism seemed particularly fatuous in our circumstances. The anthology was on the solemn side with a strong whiff of Fabianism, so it was a surprise to read in the 1939 preface that 'the love of glory, even in our materialistic age, is still the main source of virtue. The real good is not done by calculation nor defined by reason; it is an act of courage or of grace.' Read's choice was eclectic and no entry gave us more pleasure than the *Thirty-three Happy Moments* of Chin Shengt'an. And of those thirty-three happy moments none struck us with a more sweet and sour note than the nineteenth: 'To keep three or four spots of eczema in a private part of my body and now and then to scald or bathe it with hot water behind closed doors. Ah, is this not happiness?' In the months to come this little Moment was to become a kind of mad refrain against a background of pure carbolic, mercurochrome and sulphonamide, or of pus, maggots and amputation.

In February 1943 we were joined by the Dutch – or, rather, the Netherlands East Indies Army; most were Eurasians, many of them finely built. Notwithstanding a rough trip from Java, they had brought a lot of equipment with them. Their green uniforms were replete with accessories: jackboots, gaiters, cartridge cases, belts, swagger canes, trimmings of silver lace, peaked caps, forage-caps (fastening under the chin like those of the Boys' Brigade), and high wide-brimmed Rip van Winkle green straw hats. Some of their officers were old traders and enormously fat, with shaven polls like Frank Reynolds' World War I 'huns'; some of these were suspicious of us and there were dark mutterings of '*Sodemieter Engels!*' They were still waited upon by batmen and later cracked up very quickly in the jungle. Others shamed us with their knowledge of our own history and their facility with languages. Naturally we laughed at them, the Old Etonians mistaking their formal manners for servility. The men, too, were not slow to look for faults but were puzzled by products of inter-marriage so different from the only other colonial army they knew: that of India.

Nothing excited our mirth more than seeing the Dutch colonials walking to the latrines carrying bottles of water instead of toilet paper. But it was borne in upon us that quite apart from saving our books (or our pay in buying Thai toilet paper) Moslem ablutions cost nothing and were more suitable to the climate; after delicate experiment we were soon following their example and wondering why we hadn't thought of it months before. We also found that Dutch aluminium mess cans and water bottles were better than ours, and a brisk trade in them sprang up. I acquired an anti-gas ointment tin which had been engraved most cunningly by its owner. On top was a palm-fringed smallholding at Malang, Java, with Smeroe volcano in the background, on the bottom a hutted camp relieved – like ours – by hills on the skyline, and round the edge were flowers and fruit. Under the lid was a fully-rigged three-masted clipper under sail, with every detail picked out – jib, staysail, furled skysail and spanker. Inside the base the vendor obligingly added my name and regiment and the date '21 MARCH 1943 – SIAM'. It soon bore round the hinge the brown stains of the 'Sikh's Beard' tobacco which I carried in it up and down the river.

The Dutch knew more than we did about cooking rice, grinding peanut butter and making *sambal bajak* – peppery herbs fried in oil that provided vitamins and helped to down as much rice as one could get hold of. Similarly, their MOs knew more about tropical medicine than ours did, and, with the Australian doctors, added considerably to our expertise.

One Dutchman, 'Fritzie', neither an officer nor an Eurasian, also added immeasurably to our entertainment. He had a 120–base Hohner accordion, and his great stubby fingers ran up and down the treble keys and hopped in and out of the base buttons as if they had a life of their own. He played on this fancy by sometimes pretending that they had; he would look elsewhere and use a free hand to scratch his head or tuck his Tolstoyan beard under the bellows, or fetch it out for an airing. Later on he discarded more and more of his kit upcountry but always kept the accordion; he looked much thinner the last time I saw him.

The Dutch were more voluble than we were, their language more gutteral and their voices deeper. We learned to recognise a Dutch hut by the noise emanating from it, by the explosions of "*God Verdomme!*" or, worse, "*Sodemieter op!*", and by the names being bandied about at top volume: Telemaar, de Jong, Swartz, Eiswogel, van der Walt, Luis van Heist. But there was one character who really did surprise us and that was the beefy Eurasian Colonel Man Sel Beck, commonly known as 'the Brown Bomber' or 'One Minute to Midnight'. He surprised us by his authority and the awe in which he was held, and we were astounded when he laid into subordinates just as though he were a Japanese. But we were lucky to have this new Dutch dimension to our lives; it was at once a reviving window into Europe and an instructive one into Far Eastern habits and beliefs.

In early 1943 some family letters caught up with me at Tamarkham; they dated back to the capitulation and were written before a twenty-five-word limit was imposed. One was from David, my ICS brother in Government House, Lucknow. It began with the family propensity for jingles:

The other day a Moslem commentator wrote, 'The British government's confused and complicated new plan is neither fish, flesh nor good red herring.' This is my variation:

"The Mission offers nothing Fresh!
Their plan is neither fish nor flesh
Nor good red herring," critics growl.
By inference it must be foul.

I was greatly amazed when Putch Beloe accosted me outside church one Sunday morning. He said John Middleton-West had been killed in Burma.

My mind went back to this pleasant and no-nonsense chap at school, the only son of Colonel Middleton-West (retired) of the Indian Medical Service. John had joined the Indian Army as a regular and must have found relief in it from the claustrophic atmosphere at home. It was often said that when people in the services 'get God', by God they get Him! This was certainly true of the Middleton-Wests, who were for ever organizing coffee-squashes in Clifton. My parents, flattered to receive what they took to be a social invitation from the handsome Colonel and his wife, were not best pleased on their first visit to be offered only coffee, orange juice and prayers. If there were any prayers to be said, my father liked to be the one to say them – as he did every morning and evening with the family. My sisters were similarly courted by their classmate Mimi Middleton-West, and learned to avoid her extensions to their already intolerable Sunday exercises. John Middleton-West's probably glorious death made we ponder my own inglorious life. Burma suddenly seemed more real – and nearer.

But it did not seem nearer to some of those prisoners who had remained behind in Changi but were now sent up the Kwa Noy, leap-frogging people like us, to work far upriver near the Three Pagodas Pass. We watched them with pity – and perhaps a little smugness; their grand piano had been abandoned at Ban Pong and they staggered past, already caught in the dilemma of jettisoning kit – and missing it later – or struggling on and risking a fully-equipped collapse. It was not long before news filtered back of horrors in the camps further upriver. This, added to the fate of our own escapers, put a damper on my newly-awakened interest in Burma. The limestone hills that looked so welcoming from our perimeter were evidently not to be trusted; beyond them lay jungles and diseases we knew nothing about.

Soon we learned that even those who did know something about them should have thought twice before trying their luck. The escape attempts from our camp were echoed at Nikki on the very border of Burma and failed almost as miserably. The main protagonist in a party of eight, which included a local guide and an old Malaya hand, was Colonel Wilkinson of the Engineers, a stout, jolly man and just the chap for a tight corner. But he was not quite the figure to trek through the jungle, and was one of the first to succumb to disease. Food and kit were lost when a raft capsized, and – defeated by hunger, malaria, beri-beri and dysentery – three more died. When the rest at last came in sight of the Indian Ocean and the guide went to get food at a *kampong*, the headman betrayed him to the *Kempitai*. They were brought back to Nikki but, amazingly, Stanley Harris, the Camp Commander, managed to persuade the Jap Commandant that their crime was political rather than military and that they should be sent to Singapore for trial. Sentenced to ten years' hard labour, they became so weak that they were transferred to hospital and eventually recovered. So in fact they did fare better than many of those who stayed in Nikki. They had had no time to recover from the three hundred-kilometres march, with no camps after Takanun at two hundred and twenty kilometres to help with food and water. Pitched straight into work, they were in no condition to fight cholera when it hit them. Fewer than half returned to Changi six months later, a record only equalled by a party building a road to Mergui, which consisted initially of a thousand men.

In Tamarkham I read my other letters from the outside world. My father's, as usual, made me feel ashamed of my frivolous nature. Here was I, scrounging my way through camp life and thinking of myself first, last and all the time. And here was he, thinking of my contribution to others.

See how we cast our bread upon the waters! Almost we might as well have put our letter into a bottle and thrown it into the Severn at Clevedon! Margie being with us one warm delightful April day we walked from the Nautical Chapel, remembering all that we had enjoyed in past years, finding everywhere as beautiful as ever, and refusing to feel that hardships or thirst or want or sickness lay about the camps in Singapore!

Your last letter to us told of nearing Singapore, the tenor of which was ominous. . . .

Assuming that life and health are maintained amongst you one wonders what employment you can find, how escape ennui, how turn idleness to advantage. To learn Chinese, or any other tongue, would be laborious. One must believe in a world restored to the leadership and governance of England, and more Englishmen and army and civil servants abroad, so that the acquisition of a nation's speech could be a means to office. I can also imagine you turning what you know of anatomy and of cognate sciences to the advantage of your military hospital so short of hands.

Your mother and I have the house much to ourselves; it grows upon me and I am at home in it. We think sometimes that our family under other circumstances could have been about us. Our gate has followed the railings to the foundry; we have not replaced it yet. Bath received the Teuton's rage and Exeter.

We are trusting, dear boy, that not a hair of your head has perished either from plague or death.

Aunt Jane also wrote from the surgery. One of my father's Bible-crazed unmarried sisters, she worked in his dispensary and had no difficulty in finding the prescription for my ills.

. . . What a strange life! From what we hear not so exacting as was Joseph's in prison. But 'the Lord looseth the prisoners. He lifteth up those that are bound down. The Lord loveth the righteous'. Much love, dear boy.

Hugh wrote from a camp different from mine but not without its trials.

I am sitting in a breezy barn window; smells of cattle and sheep everywhere; there are two dozen boys here. The usual camp adventures – Sam Mogford was sick out of the barn door and a pig dashed up and lapped it up; four small boys were homesick after a rainy day at the beginning, so I let them go home; they looked so weepy. A boy nearly suffocated from being tied up in a kitbag and rolled about – so bad that I sent for Dr Trumper of Ivybridge – an old man who didn't get here till 11.30 p. m.

I went to Bude for Clifton Commem: a gorgeous sunny day. At the play – *The Apple Cart* – Duncan Forbes Mackintosh's little girl kept her eyes glued to one of the players, and in the

intervals his eyes were glued on her. We have been for a
five-day holiday at Stogumber; walked from Bicknoller Post
to Bagborough, quenching our thirst on wild strawberries and
wild raspberries in the valleys and wortleberries on the hilltops.

From Kumasi in the Gold Coast Bim wrote of other thirst-
quenchers:

> I gather from home that you have not yet been heard of; but
> Mother asks me to write in case you still exist; so letter
> herewith; though quite what one can say under the
> circumstances I do not know. You must just take every kind
> of good wish, commiseration, blessing, etc. as read. What a
> happy little war mine was compared with yours!
>
> I am, as you see, no longer in the army – was released to
> the civil dept. three months ago. Now on the one hand I live
> in a rational way, and in reasonable comfort; but on the other
> the work is just hellish; and the end of every day finds me with
> not a drop of virtue left, and the batteries needing vigorous
> recharging with quantities of beer and Beethoven. I wish I
> could post you my frig. and its delightful contents. I still think
> with little shudders of those dreadful Abyssinian days in the
> desert, when our tongues hung out of our mouths until six
> o'clock when we could afford to have a little drink of our
> precious water; and now my frig. is just full of beer and I can
> have a bottle whenever I want one.
>
> A belated list from East Africa includes my name among
> those 'mentioned'. I suppose old Blackden must have shoved
> it in out of charity; still, however it got there, a mention is a
> mention. One of my working principles was that the battalion
> commander should never be worried about the medical side
> of the business – that he should safely be able to take it all for
> granted; so, though my lack of many soldierly virtues must
> have been obvious enough to the old man, he may have
> appreciated that.
>
> God bless.

Finally there was a letter from Joan which in its way did more to stiffen my resolve to get home again than any ambitions to cure the world's evils.

My dear darling Stweevoogly,

Of course we have all been thinking of you so much that our heads have nearly burst. I went home in March and Aunt Beatrice came over from Bath. You can imagine what a flap she was in – as she came into the room she said, "Oh, I think it's simply ghastly. Of course it would be bad enough about Noel but *much* worse to think of Stephen, oh a hundred times worse!" Mother was looking a trifle ghastly, and D. A. was working hard and sleeping at the surgery. Margie came up here for Whit. I met her and we fought our way out of the station, squeezing past the ticket inspector like orange pips. Margie gave up her ticket and was pushed on, and then called out, 'Oh! Wrong half!' and had to force her way back. I am so jealous of Rachel about to have her third next month. In her last letter she said she'd been to a dance and danced three times and, when I think of her scorn and bitterness with other young matrons of our acquaintance in our youth, who danced in a similar condition, words fail me. . . . I am reading three plays of Tchekov, which is like walking on a map. . . .

They say we have to type letters to you, so I am doing my best with father-in-law's absolutely archaic machine at Kirkoswald. The wobbly leg is propped up by a toffee in a paper, flattened out in the middle and oozed out and hardened at the sides. I had a weekend with Bid in a lovely flat in Regents Park – everyone very gay and all parks and plays crowded. I saw John Gielgud in Congreve's *Love for Love* – perfect; bawdy but beautiful. The food in Soho excited me a lot; so did the life-belts hanging beside all the emergency water tanks! Then I went to Clifton; the new road through Queen Square is quite lovely, the Civic Building on College Green atrocious. Everyone talked about you and Robin, you are not in the least forgotten. Bim is at home now, looking absolutely the returned warrior. He came up here for a visit and enjoyed the country but I think found the goodness and kindness of the old folks a trifle oppressive. Biddy was here at midsummer for two weeks and had the only spell of summer weather. She gave a spirited account of her efforts (successful) to defend her virtue in London. She has had to keep two men forcibly out of her bed; on one occasion she was drunk, quite by mistake (she had three Pimms No.1 without knowing their power) and a very old friend – one whom she regarded as a brother – took unfair advantage. When she told Mary Fedden about it, she rolled on the floor with laughter and kept saying, "But that LITTLE man, Bids, that LITTLE man!"

Now that more letters had arrived we heard news of those who had been evacuated from Singapore by boat; or, more ominously, heard no news about them. It seemed probable that Bobby Greene's wife, with his dachsund puppy, had not survived. This gave the sole survivor of his family, Ludwig, an almost human part in Bobby's life, and Ludwig's welfare became a matter of concern to all of us. Bobby trained him to keep quiet when Nips were about, and we all helped carry him on long marches. When the hut was surrounded by guards for one of their searches, the little creature used to dive into Bobby's haversack and keep as quiet as a mouse, his nose appearing now and then to sniff the atmosphere. Sometimes the haversack was passed by sleight of hand from those who had not been searched to those who had; sometimes it was left hanging in such an obvious place that the Nips didn't bother to look in it. And once Bobby did have to open the haversack, but amazingly that particular guard's sense of the ridiculous saved the day.

One letter that reached Tamarkham was from Mrs Fisher. Fisher, a God-fearing man, led the choir in our church services. In civvy street he had worked at Huntley & Palmers and played the organ in his Reading church.

"Thank the Lord!" he cried over and over again. "I've had a letter from the wife. Now I'm content. It'll take more than the Japs to stop me getting home now!" He was right in a way. It took dysentery upriver and only a couple more months.

15

Kinsaiyok No O.K.

WE went upriver on 1st May 1943. I had been working so hard physically on the bridge and was so far removed from the news source in camp that both my interest in world news and my knowledge of it was hazy. Oddly enough, the Japs seemed not displeased by the German surrender at Stalingrad. Perhaps they welcomed the weakening of a nation they would have to eliminate sooner or later if they were to dominate the world. In Burma an unknown tribe called the Chindits seemed to be doing the sort of thing in the Japanese rear that I had so missed in Malaya; but evidently there were no spectacular results. In Tamarkham the bulk of the work on the bridges had been done, and Toosey stayed behind to command the camp in its new role as a hospital. We were split up into parties of two hundred, my own destination being Kinsaiyok, a hundred and seventeen kilometres away. I was in Granny Keane's party with Alan Haldenby (with me since Oswestry days), Philip Hay, Mike Cory-Wright and Wilkie. There were also a few officers from other regiments but we remained more or less in our Hertfordshire Yeomanry gang.

As before, the prospect of fresh woods and pastures new raised our spirits, in spite of the news that came back from them. I felt like poor Fisher, only more so. "I'll show the buggers!" I told myself, meaning not only the Nips but my own companions. And there was the whiff of freedom, of getting away from bureaucracy, from too many senior officers chasing camp sinecures, from *tenko* roll calls that were too big and never came out right and lasted for hours; in

the jungle there'd be less organisation and more room for manoeuvre.

But again we faced the problems of packing up. We had to carry
everything this time (except rice *kwalis* and cooking stuff which
went by barge): webbing for stringing together mess tin and water
bottle, and remnants of gas mask, map case, first-aid dressings,
puttees and holster, all cannibalised to serve new purposes; the
officer's valise, heavy and beginning to rot but still a useful hold-all
for bedding and mosquito net, not to mention forbidden things like
diaries that might escape searches better there than in a haversack;
a choice of books – the Bible or *The Knapsack* ('well, someone else
is sure to have a Bible'); shoes – should I march in brown *veldtschoen*, kept for the Victory Parade, or in Japanese rubber boots;
should I wear or pack the precious caste mark, the Herbert Johnson
cap? Then there were all those bits and pieces we had collected to
make our leisure hours more tolerable: padding for the *bali-bali*,
shaving mirror fragment, latrine bottle, ant-proof containers for
gula malacca, cloth for future G-strings and sweat-rags, *klompen*,
curved glass for sharpening razor blades, oil lamp tin, and paper
(hoarded now for writing not shitting). Which of all this personal
junk should be taken, and which left behind and scrounged at the
other end?

In the late afternoon we lined up for our last Tamarkham *tenko*
and boarded open railway trucks for the first part of the journey. A
few kilometres beyond the bridge we passed the big camp at
Chungkai (where John Beckett had reassembled his radio parts) and
an hour or so later entered the bush. Tangled woods and patches of
farmland were pierced by the railway line and broken here and there
by limestone rocks bathed in the sunset; hills, covered impenetrably
with trees (as were the river banks between the camps), stretched
away as far as the eye could see. As darkness fell we were caught in
a tropical downpour, a check to further illusions of escape through
Burma. We detrained, still soaked, at midnight near a camp christened Arrow Hill (from its Japanese name of Aruhiru) and slept
beside the line.

Next morning we started marching at eleven; the sun blazed
down and we were soon in trouble. We stumbled along the railway

track, varying the discomfort of jerking along on the sleepers, so that our packs bumped up and down on our shoulders, with crunching on the stones between them or serpentining up and down the sides of the trace. We crossed the Wampo Viaduct, a rickety curving affair skirting a deep gorge. We knew that it had cost lives to build, and it was a sinister spot.

As it was our first long march for five months our feet were soon in a bad state. We staggered under the mountains of kit we had not dared to discard. But bad as were the blistered feet, the aching back, the strangling shoulder straps, the scraping crotch, the sores beset by flies and the salt sweat soaking and congealing by turns, worse by far was the rasping thirst. It only took an hour or so to strike, and thereafter, once the water bottle was empty, it struck implacably in one long relentless torture.

We reached Tarsao at ten o'clock that night after marching twenty-five kilometres, and were unable to get water before bedding down in tents in the transit camp. But at least we were free of dysentery, the real killer on such a march. And in spite of my thirst and exhaustion I remember vividly the moment just before I dozed off.

The large working camp of Tarsao ('Landing Place by a Post') near our tents was commanded by Lt. Col. 'Knocker' Knights of the 4th Norfolks, a small hook-nosed and much respected figure. Though contact was officially forbidden between our staging camp and his working one, it was to Knocker that we owed the eggs that embellished our breakfast of rice and cucumber. But lying that night, looking at the tent ceiling and listening to the cicadas, I went over the distresses of the day – the blisters, the vertigo of the Wampo Viaduct, the aches and strains and sweat – and I felt the glorious relief of knowing that for the moment at least they were all gone and I could look forward to some hours of sleep. I was in that half state between waking and sleeping when bright images pass and repass as on a screen.

Kirkoswald vicarage from Joan's letter faded into the green of the jungle, the church tower dwarfed by vast trees; the trees had lianas trailing emptily as though awaiting some absent Tarzan; monkeys cried like lost souls, and nearer grunts and snuffles betrayed souls very much at home. I re-ran the march, surfacing now and again from the grim plod to awareness of scenes of great beauty: the river running quietly by white rocks and fountains of bamboo; orchids on tree stumps; butterflies moving as heavily as pigeons; the flash of a toucan amazingly graceful in flight. Then, like a blow, the obverse: the track fouled with huge betel-red faeces, harbingers of a dismaying Tamil camp; silent squattings and sidelong looks; the neat hut of some unfortunate MO or Malayan Volunteer; and, as evening fell, a jungle grown dark and menacing. The fantasies half-dreamed on the train to Ban Pong of a magic carpet to freedom stopped here. Nor, under this canopy, could we imagine white clouds black with Allied planes and a rain of parachutes. Anyhow, who were we to be rescued, and who would want to be landed with such a tatty, bug-ridden, worm-eaten, lousy, loose-reined lot as we were?

From the working camp came the quaver of the Last Post – 'De-da-ah, De-da-ah!' It cut through the heavy night like a beam of silver. 'De-da-ah, De-da-ah! De-dah-de-de-dah-de-dah-de-de-dah . . . !' The notes, at once martial and elfin, were transfixing, and as the silence surged back I heard the echo in it of voices in the field, going back through a long, long line of real and fictional campaigns: Robert Graves, Captain Stanhope, Rifleman Harris, Edward Waverley, Montrose, Samkin Aylward, the Black Prince, Alfred . . . They were by no means heroes all the time but they'd have had no truck with self-pity. As I dropped off to sleep their whispers sounded in my ear and they all said the same thing: "Get on with it!"

Reveille sounded in the dark and we started off again, leaving behind a dozen sick. These included my erstwhile batman, Bill Hunt. A knotty Roman-nosed hot-eyed little Cockney, Bill was a mine of half-digested Marxist philosophy, which had landed him in hot water before he was palmed off on me. Whenever I gave him an order he'd give me a quizzical look as though weighing up its pros and cons; would obedience compromise his commitment to the Final Solution? Then he'd give a little nod, as much as to say 'Why not? It'll make you happy and Won't Make Any Difference in the End'. In the early days in Changi, when the military chicken was still running round in circles with its head chopped off, batmen were solemnly allotted little jobs we would by then happily have done ourselves. They used to gather in the patio to polish boots or launder shirts as we sat reading and involuntarily listening to their chatter.

"Hey, Bill! What'll happen to your lot when the Nips reach the Old Kent Road? Harry Pollitt, Jimmy Maxton, all that crowd. Think they'll string 'em up? Or will your lot help the Nips string up the bourgeoisie first?"

"First? What d'you mean by 'first'?"

"When they've knocked out the bourgeoisie they'll start on you, won't they? Like they did in Manchuria."

"Dunno about that."

"And the Nazis in Germany."

"London ain't Germany."

"And what about the Ribbentrop Pact? Didn't you and your lot go AWOL then?"

"'Course we did."

"Why's that then?"

"Stands to reason. Couldn't have no revolution after the war without the Russians."

"Oh, so you'll hang us on the lamp posts then, soon as we've won the war for the Ruskies?"

"You're not bourgeoisie. You'll think the same as me when the war's over."

"What about my bloke then?"

"Lieutenant La-di-dah Hay? Ha ha! It'd be a very tall lamp post for him, eh?"

"And Captain Dearden?"

"Oh, no more fevver bedders for Deardy. No, my dear old chappie, it's us who'll be putting down the birdseed."

"So, what'll happen to your bloke, Bill, when you're Commissar Hunt?"

"My bloke? Well, I'll need a batman, won't I? Eh?"

The days had long passed when our batmen had gone through the motions of looking after us. But their presence helped to preserve a family feeling. I should miss Bill Hunt if he didn't catch us up again.

It was still cool when we set off from Tarsao, but the track was muddy and hilly. Then came the sun. One moment we were toiling along in the grey dawn, the next we were streaming with sweat in searing light, with the last swirls of mist scuttling into the treetops and the jungle bursting into hammer-strokes of insect life. The sun was still beating down when we reached Tonchan after nine kilometres, already frantic for water. We were able to wash down our lunch (rice and the dried fish that tasted as if smoked in excrement) with water from a stream. Refreshed, we marched on for another seven kilometres to overnight in a tented transit camp at Tampi. The next night, near Hintok ('Falling Rocks'), the party's MO, a tough Scot named Christison, developed malaria but decided to struggle on with us. The Nips would only let the sick stop off if they fainted or could display bloody feet. Those who lagged behind on the march were prodded with bayonets or bashed with rifle butts to keep them going. (It did keep them going on the march but five men died soon after it.) We had about ten kilometres to go along a fairly level track to our next night's stop at Upper Kanyu. In this Australian camp a Major Moon had contrived an ingenious system of bamboo piping to lay on water throughout the camp, and in one corner even showers with water from hot springs.

I was by now pretty well broken in, with feet effectively padded, and I appeared to be suffering from nothing worse than thirst and exhaustion. There had been much repacking at Tarsao; heavy volumes had been 'lent' with relief to friends, and most of us had dumped our valises in the hope that they might follow by pom-pom. A final day's march brought us to Kinsaiyok ('Banyan Tree') where we could at last shed our stinking clothes. We had a marvellous bathe in the river, which flowed slowly and deeply through a beautiful limestone gorge, and after the miseries of the march I felt as though I were in Shangri La.

The camp itself was not so welcoming. In place of the smart regimented huts of Tamarkham we found sagging and ramshackle ones with holes in the *attap* roofs. They had been left by a Dutch party in a filthy state, with pools of swill, rice and excrement under the *bali-bali*, and flies everywhere. I missed my valise as a protective layer, and when it did reach me two months later it was mouldy.

But I had little time to reflect on these shortcomings because the day after we arrived I had to take out a working party. Up here we had to work flat out all day; the Nips themselves did so, and woe betide anyone who did not. This was a *speedo* with a vengeance; we worked against the clock, often half way through the night, to blast cuttings through rock and erect a large wooden bridge and viaduct. With the pressure permanently on, the officer in charge of a working party was more than ever vulnerable – to the Nips for not getting the men to work harder and to the men for not getting the Nips to ease up; ever and anon would come that nerve-wracking cry, "*Kora! Oi! Shoko!*" and he would run up yet again to face some crisis, leading to a craven appeal to sick and bloody-minded men, or a bash in the face or worse.

I generally chose to work with the men, whether I was told to or not, partly to encourage them (or at least put on an act for the Nips' benefit that I was encouraging them), partly to keep out of the Nips' line of sight, and partly for company. There is no doubt that physically most men had to work harder than most officers, and the take-your-pip-off-Mr-Beverley Aussies were not the only ones to resent it. On the other hand a Private Ward and Gunner Simpson, torpedoed by American submarines while being shipped to Japan from Singapore, were quoted as saying that 'the other ranks did not like to see officers working under the discipline of the Japanese guards'.

BLASTING A CUTTING.

Although we prided ourselves on learning by experience how the Nip mind worked, some crises almost called for the service of a trained psychiatrist for their solution. One day, when my party was excavating a bank to build up the railway trace, a man straightened up after filling his mate's basket and clutched his stomach, smitten by one of the spasms that plagued us between bouts of dysentery. "Oh!" he cried, "me fuckin' guts!" Whereupon the guard jumped down and started beating hell out of him. I joined them and made the usual gestures of tactful remonstrance.

"No goodena! Ingris solja velly bad man! Bugayero! Ingris solja speak puckin Dutch! No goodena! Puckin Dutch no!"

A linguistic confusion had made him do the wrong thing for the right reason. He thought the man was cursing the Dutchmen working with us, thus causing ill feeling which might jeopardise the efficiency of the gangs.

The jungle here was provokingly fine, with views of the Kwa Noy gorge nearby and the blue hills of Burma in the distance. And the lunch-breaks when we gathered round the great oil drums of stewed China tea were occasions of sybaritic relief. The rice and dried fish, or rice and veg or – as the case might often be – rice and rice was gobbled down or spun out as the spirit moved or the availability of canteen *gula malacca*, peanuts or bananas permitted. And then, with a careful disposal of red soldier-ants, centipedey logs and scorpion-friendly stones, I would clear a space for a few minutes of glorious siesta, drifting down, down out of the jungle and into the heather of Will's Neck on the Quantocks, perhaps, with the bees droning in the whortleberries, or onto the banks of Horner Water with the dragonflies glancing off the surface, or over the pebbles of Lilstock after a misty swim with the foghorns in the Channel crying to each other . . . boom-boom, boom-boom, boom . . . "*KORA! KORA! Orumay* come! *Yasumé* finish! *Baka yaro! Speedo! Oi, shoko*, come!"

As 1943 wore on, conditions worsened. Birds vanished and insects lost their sheen. Rain fell, and the darkening jungle seemed to spew out its own entrails. Paths turned to mud. Huts leaked. Latrines overflowed. Axes and shovels became blunt, baskets caked, dynamite damp. Brew-up fires were hard to light. Work got longer, *yasumés* shorter. We started to fade out. The Nips grew frantic. We were very sick. No one was excused work; dysentery cases with streaming legs, and ulcer cases with bandages exuding pus tottered about carrying rocks and baskets of earth.

I developed dysentery again, with its familiar griping pains. At night I would lie awake while they came and went; could I lie still and get away with it? Or must I fish about for my clogs and bottle of water and sweat rag to stumble down the hut between the *bali-bali* and ghostly mosquito nets, out into the rain and across the mud to the leaking latrine? Oh, God, yes I must! And out I would go, muttering inane exhortations . . . flip-flop, flip-flop . . . 'Nóbly, nóbly, Cápe St Víncent tó the Nórth-west díed away.' I would slip and slide resolutely, only to meet disaster on the way; and I would slink back to the hut, wet and dirty but relieved enough to go out like a light – until the next attack. Each morning the camp was covered with evidence of similar excursions by others. We were never dry; night after night we arrived back after dark soaked through, dried ourselves on damp towels, put on lousy shirts, climbed into bug-ridden blankets – only to climb out again, and again and again, during the night. Next morning we paraded before daylight in the same wet shorts and, if we still had them, the same clammy boots.

Cholera had begun upriver and we could no longer freshen up with a swim but only wash in a small feeder stream. Our rice was flavoured with the toilet-taste of dried fish, sometimes streaked with shoelace-like dried vegetables, and only on red-letter days dignified by a couple of ounces of meat. Canteen supplies tended to go at prohibitive prices to neighbouring Tamil coolies, who were paid more than we were but appeared to get even worse rations. They began to die at a terrible rate and were shovelled into graves ten at a time. I did some grave-digging myself, and was delighted to do it – as a cushy job that kept me off the line. It was while resting in a lean-to during one such job that I became aware of a sickly sweet smell and saw that the rolled-up straw mat I was leaning against contained not other mats, as I had supposed, but a corpse. At this time, when we had no secrets from each other, its silence seemed oddly enigmatic rather than involuntary. A yellow fluid oozed from the bottom of the mat and gaps revealed a tallowy skin.

The cholera hit Kinsaiyok in June; it was a Dutch doctor who diagnosed it. The Nips at first isolated the hut where the victim lay, and kept everyone else in it in quarantine. But they gave this up when cases broke out all over the camp, and thenceforward all men worked, sick or not, cholera-contacts or not. Often a man would start vomiting out on the line in the morning – that innocent-looking white vomit resembling under-cooked rice pudding – and be dead by the evening. One of my most painful recollections is of rocketing a bombardier for malingering on a working party one day – and burying him the next.

There was at this time a tricky incident at a sub-camp to which half our party had been sent. One Fuji Tai, in charge of the camp, ordered that the first hopeless cholera case be shot. Major Roberts (he who had clocked a Korean guard at Tamarkham and got away with it) and the Argyll mud-wrestler, Ian Primrose, who had by now learned some Japanese, were sent with a Korean guard to the man's isolation tent. The Korean revealed a Buddhist reluctance to shed blood and proposed – as in the days of Good King Thebaw of Burma with his clubs and velvet bags – that they should let the tent down and bash the man inside it to death invisibly. Dissuaded from this course, his hand shook helplessly – and the rifle with it. "Here," cried Primrose, "give me the bloody thing!" And on the Major's order he put the delirious patient out of his misery. Then the balloon went up. The senior Commandant, fearing trouble in high places when the affair leaked out, reported it to the Group Commander. Roberts and Primrose were taken off to Bangkok with Fuji to be tried for murder. After a few weeks they were acquitted, with a caution. The Nips, nothing if not punctilious at the wrong moment, produced medical evidence that the man had died before being shot.

Stick and carrot exhortations that had come down to us from on high in the English of interpreters rang very hollow now:

"You are all only a few remaining skeletons after the invasion of East Asia for the past four centuries and are pitiful victims . . . HM the Emperor has been deeply anxious about all War Prisoners . . . The Imperial thoughts are inestimable and the Imperial favours are infinite and as such you should weep with gratitude at the greatness of them . . . The hunter does not kill the wounded bird . . . We appreciate very much for what you have done by means of Nippon *bushido* (Spirit of Nippon Knighthood). At the same time regret to find seriousness in health matter. It is evident that there are various sources inevitable to this end, but to my opinion due mainly to the fact of absence of firm belief as Japanese 'Health follows will' and 'Ceases only when enemy is completely annihilated'.

"If there is one foolish man here who has at least one per cent of a chance of escape we shall make him to face the extreme penalty. He shall see big jungles towards the East which are absolutely impossible for communication. Towards the West he shall see a boundless ocean and, above all, in the main points of the South and North our Nippon Army is staying and guarding.

"Railway works to connect Thailand and Burma have started to the great interest of the world. . . . You shall have the honour to join in this great work. I shall expect all of you to work earnestly and confidently every day. In conclusion I say to you 'WORK CHEER-FULLY' and from henceforth you should be guided by this motto."

Our spirits were at a very low ebb. But to protests at his treatment of the sick, Commandant Sezuki reminded us that we were lucky to

"WORK CHEERFULLY"

have had our lives spared in Singapore; honourable men, he said, would have committed *hara kiri*, and his adjutant added with relish, "You will work until you die for the Nippon Army!" He explained that the line had to get through on schedule, even at the cost of half the Japanese engineers; and prisoners were much more dispensable. Not to be outdone, the sergeant added his recipe for success: "The best cure for dysentery is – WORK!"

It was at this time of deep dejection that I had an unexpected reunion on a jungle path. It ought not to have been such a shock, since he had been at Sennybridge and on the boat, but when I suddenly saw again the mischievous moonface of my Peterhouse gyp I felt a fearful jolt; it was – as the phrase has it – as though I had run into my mother in a whorehouse. In spite of his sorry state Harry Asplin still had traces of his old bounce. (My mother had thought him too full of it for a college servant. From my bedroom she observed him through the half-open door bounce across the sitting room, bounce open the lid of my cigarette box, pocket a handful of my 'special' cigarettes with the cross keys of St Peter stamped on them and bounce out again.)

"They was good days, sir," said Harry. I don't think the honorific would have sprung to his lips without the 'Pothouse' connection. "But they didn't do us much good, did they? I never thought I'd end up in this lot."

"I expect Pothouse'll still be there when we get back."

"I could do with one of Sergeant Cooper's omelettes now!"

"Ah! With whitebait to start and *crème brûlée* to finish!"

"Oh, don't, sir!"

"See you there anyway, Harry."

In July I cut my shin on a piece of bamboo. It was only a small cut and I at once treated it with iodine. But it blew up after ten days into a roaring jungle ulcer. My leg swelled up and the pain was excruciating. I used to go outside the hut so that I could whimper unheard – until the skin burst and the pressure was relieved. After that I would press it every hour or two, when the pain had built up again, and squeeze out jets of nauseous pus. But this was at least serious enough to keep me off work and the relief of that was almost enough to make the ulcer worth it. To be able to lie back in the morning when others went cursing out to work was an undreamed-of joy. So far, I felt with some shame, fate had been kind to me. To assuage my sense of guilt I hobbled over to the hospital hut to do some visiting. A joky Australian padre who had slept next to me not long before had been caught in that fatal pincer movement of malaria and dysentery; for malaria you needed to eat, for dysentery to take liquids only. I was shocked to find he had used the pages of his Bible as lavatory paper. He was the first person to show me that illness can change the character – any character – absolutely. He had no Christian resignation by this time and died shortly afterwards.

But I had chiefly gone to see Sergeant Barber of my own troop, a rather unmilitary-looking chap but an excellent No.1 on a gun. He had succumbed to an ulcer earlier on and his leg had turned gangrenous. I found him lying quietly under his blanket.

"How's it going?"

"Had the operation yesterday."

"What happened?"

"That's what I asked myself when I came round. Doc said he might be able to save it or he might have to take it off above the knee. I couldn't feel anything; just lay there wondering, 'Has he taken it off or hasn't he?' I didn't dare ask anyone; just lay there. Then after a bit I thought, 'This is no good; the longer I leave it the worse the suspense'. So I pulled off the blanket and propped myself up till I could look down at it. Ah-ah! Gone!"

Back in my own hut I indulged once more in the luxury of reading, a luxury even with *Gone with the Wind*; at least it carried me far away from Kinsaiyok. Long-winded women novelists seemed to have a common failing: they filled hundreds of pages of melodrama without a sentence, without a line, approaching the humorous. No wonder their historical romances were so flat! Even in our bitterest moments there was some humour left, or at least rueful or caustic wit. The Nips, and the Dutch too, never ceased to be amazed, out on the job, when, as it started to pour with rain and the trees dripped dismally and mud flowed everywhere, the British burst spontaneously into song. Up the line would spread such mellifluous classics as 'My eyes are dim, I cannot see, I have not brought my specs with me' or 'Bollocks! And the same to you!'.

As July wore on, the line-layers reached Kinsaiyok and we were told we were to march up to Konkuita, ninety kilometres further on. As I was still immobile I was evacuated with my ulcer by boat and train to the base camp at Kanburi. On arrival I had fearful cramps again and started to pass green liquid. At a routine cholera test, when the long-suffering Japanese orderlies pushed glass rods up our revolting arses, I was found to be cholera-positive and, as a 'cholera carrier', was banished to the base hospital nearby. There I slept on matting on the mud floor with other cholera cases shrieking and dying all round me; but in my extremity I had the consolation of feeling that fate had saved me from the march to Konkuita. I had been innoculated for cholera at Tamarkham, as we all had been, and can only assume that that was why I was in no worse a state. Pints and pints of green liquid left me hourly until I felt desperately weak and thirsty; but I did not vomit and was spared the saline drip of rock salt and distilled river water. I lay on the floor isolated in a huge mosquito net, with a handy bedpan in the corner of it; this, a kindly orderly would frequently empty, and as frequently bring me warm rice water to drink. I was determined not to let the family down by snuffing out after so much hard if ignoble work, but I felt myself drifting involuntarily away in that dim white wilderness. I was so very tired. Why wake up? Why not join them in my dreams and stay with them for ever? It would be summer at home now. They could be bicycling out over Clifton Suspension Bridge, checking the state of the tide by the river under it – yes, about two hours to high tide, by the look of it; say half an hour earlier at Clevedon Old Hill, if anyone felt like going in for a swim; just nice time for a pause at the Failand Inn for bread and cheese and a pint of Coates' cider, and then on over Cadbury Camp; or would it be nicer to go down through Clapton-in-Gordano and stop at the Black Horse? No, of course it must be August by now, or very near it; they would be in the Quantocks at Cross Farm, and bicycling down for a swim at Shurton Bars; up first from Over Stowey to Bincombe Green, down past Spinsters Roost at Nether Stowey, across the Minehead road, left into the drive of Fairfield House and right and left for Burton, with the smell of bread from the farm bakery; stop at the post office for some Five Boys chocolate (examining it for worms) and along the lane past the railway carriage bungalow (*Journey's End*) to the gate at the end; no red flag flying for target practice, so up the track over two false crests until at last, down there beyond the field, the sea; over on the right nothing but the red cliffs and chequered meadows swooping up and down and in and out towards Stert Flats, and out across the shining grey channel the outline of Steepholm and, as my father called it, 'Little Flattie' beyond; straight ahead the bright chimneys (or were they magic towers?) of Wales, looking, as always, sunnier than Somerset; and over on the left North Hill, lumbering like a great whale towards Lundy.

There it all was, laid out at my feet, the long-familiar Avalon for me to ride down to, push out into – why not just drop the bicycle there, stretch out the arms like a diver and lift off into the buoyant air? Float slowly over the beach and up, up higher, to gaze over North Hill at the curve of Porlock Bay and away to the left at Dunkery Beacon; then with a slow sweep round towards Mumbles, hover, feeling the cool air coming up beneath me from the sheen of the sea and the warm western wind from Ireland fingering my hair, gently, gently, and float on the air weightless, thoughtless, bathed in light, dreamlessly asleep in flight:

> Sleep is a death; O make me try,
> By sleeping, what it is to die;
> And as gently lay my head
> On my grave, as now my bed –

"HELLO, ALEXANDER, CAN I COME IN?" And through the mosquito curtain bounced a large, ruddy-faced Gunner Captain. "You look very snug in here. We haven't met; my name's Harold Cassel and I'm doing some hospital visiting. I saw you were in Toosey's lot, so I thought I'd pop in and see you. How are you getting on?"

"What?" I said querulously, wrenching myself back to mundane things. "What? Oh, oh fine! Fine! At any rate the ulcer on my leg seems to have cleared up."

"Yes, they often do, when you get something worse. There seems to be a kind of Gresham's Law in matters of health as well as of money."

He was a cheerful character with a fruity voice, well suited, as I found out later, to his civvy street occupation of barrister. Although I had not met him before, he knew others in the regiment and brought me gossip about them, and I felt that if I couldn't hear of my real family at least I was once again in contact with my army one. I was immensely cheered, and though I never saw him again, I have never forgotten his inspiriting, perhaps vital, visit.

"By the way," he said as he left, "I almost forgot what I really came for. I've got a letter for you – or, rather, one of these wretched twenty-five-word regulation postcards. Here it is."

It ran as follows:

DO NOT COUNT TIME LOST. PAUL HAD HIS ARABIA, MOSES HIS DESERT. WISE WITHOUT BOOKS, RESERVE YOUR STRENGTH. SPRING IN FAILAND. ALL WELL. LOVE – FATHER.

16

Konkuita

AFTER three weeks of bum-stabbing I obliged with three negative tests and was shifted from my isolation 'ward' to the officers' hut of the hospital camp. I was ravenous; I ate two mess tins of rice at every meal for a month, and my rice belly was disgraceful. There was peace and quiet in the hut – we rarely saw a Jap – and with no duties we could just lie back and read; it was heaven. I devoured *The Forsyte Saga*, *The Works of Oscar Wilde* (skipping more the more I read), *War and Peace* and *What is Art?* Even the company of some elderly and blimpish Dutchmen failed to spoil my feeling of happy relief. The hierarchical structure of the Netherlands East Indies Army was more rigid than our Indian Army's and, even with men of all shades in higher and lower ranks, there seemed little love lost between them.

I enjoyed talking to Willie Tosh of a Dundee jute family, who had been at school with my eldest brother. He had been cut off in Finland earlier in the war. On his way home via Norway he had been a passenger in several destroyers, all on the lookout for trouble, and after being sunk in two of them had finally set off again in a trawler. He awoke the first morning out to find the trawler sailing alone in the North Sea. When he asked what had happened to the convoy, the skipper said complacently, "We give 'em the slip last night. Bloody convoys only attract attention!"

My neighbour on one side was Guy Coles of the Lanarkshire Yeomanry, an old World War I soldier. He talked about his cello-playing days and lent me *The Musical Companion*. To my surprise I found it exciting reading, like drinking after a long thirst, yet I had never before read books about music or even reviews of concerts. I began to understand the music lover who never went to concerts or listened to records because he preferred to read the scores and hear the music perfectly played in his mind. Next to Guy was a tall, heavy-browed major in the Gunners, with one arm bent horizontally at shoulder height and supported on an L-shaped bracket. This curious splint, Guy explained, was for a 'frozen shoulder', which might sound anomalous in a climate like ours but was no joke for Jim Swanton, otherwise known as 'The Church's One Foundation' from his hospital work and propensity to hold services at the drop of a hat. Before the war Jim had been a keen cricketer and cricket correspondent for the *Daily Telegraph*, but now he was leaning towards ordination, and the shoulder might decide the issue. His memory of great performers was as sharp as Guy's, and with Wisden as his alternative Bible, Hobbs and Sutcliffe could boost his morale as much as Paul and Moses. At school I had been so bored by cricket, and so bad at it, that I had switched to rowing (boring, too, but not so long-lasting), and I wondered which saints he would turn to in his last hour. I like to think that the consolation Guy received from Bach and Beethoven was the strongest of all, for six months later, mourned by many, he died of cancer.

On my other side was a man who had been an insurance agent in Bangkok. He said there was a tree of fecundity in the 'Venice of the East' on which barren women hung painted models of their husbands' phalluses. He also claimed that in the Siamese and Indo-Chinese War in 1940, when one of the Siamese Navy's two gunboats was sunk, the survivors retrieved her name plate, fixed it to cover that of her sister gunboat and sailed her triumphantly up the Menam Chao Phraya amidst general rejoicing. Then they sailed her out again, removed the name plate and left her crew to sail her back under her own name for another triumphal entry.

At the beginning of September my convalescence was judged complete and I was moved across to the working camp on the aerodrome in Kanburi. It was commanded by a Captain Renwick, commonly known as Renemoto from his Jap-happiness. After a sports meeting he had called for three cheers for Major Cheda, the Jap Commandant. The Japs favoured jollifications of this sort when they judged the moment ripe for making a gesture. Afterwards, with much ceremony they would present the winners with prizes such as bunches of bananas, packets of dried fish, or Red Cross tins of fruit. At Tamarkham we had had a terrific parade one day, with Jap boots gleaming and Jap swords flashing, to receive prizes from a general for being 'the best working camp in Thailand'. Philip Toosey received fifty cents and the prize squad of fifty men fifty cents between them. "The General," we were told, "is a very poor man. It is the spirit of *bushido* behind the gift that matters, not the gift itself."

On the anniversary of the invasion of Malaya a ceremonial parade was held to celebrate it. Much bowing and hissing heralded the presentation in an ornate casket of the Emperor's Proclamation, which was read out and followed by loud '*banseyes*'. In the evening the Japs processed in a circle – like van Gogh's prisoners exercising – chanting prayers, and concluded the ceremony with a Great Victory March; notwithstanding the mixture of Western and Asiatic modes, it was a stirring sight. They were also punctilious in bowing to the rising and setting sun, to the accompaniment of a communal prayer. Hanging on little chains from their waistbands were copies of this prayer; to these they attached small dolls, like cracker-fillers, remainders and reminders of their Red Cross comforts which seemed to consist mostly of balloons, paper streamers and small Japanese flags. We thought them cold comfort for a fighting man and when, in the following year, our only consignment of Red Cross food arrived, the guards opened their eyes in astonishment.

I was only in Kanburi working camp for three days before I was again detailed for a party going upriver. We were to rejoin the party I had left at Kinsaiyok, which was now up at Konkuita near the Burmese border. The other inmates watched us with a mixture of commiseration and relief. Some of them had made themselves indispensable, working in the cookhouse, pumping water, or digging latrines – or, more agreeably, graves. Others demonstrated palpable hindrances to being sent upcountry again; necks went numb and needed support; knees jammed with water; backs seized up (at least in the daytime). The real experts developed into a fine art Chin Shengt'an's advice on the cultivation of 'three or four spots of eczema in a private part'. As I was packing for the upcountry march, a subaltern I had known in Changi came limping along with a mess tin of *gula malacca* and some tapioca cakes from the canteen. The bandage on one leg had obviously done a fair mileage and he looked hefty enough, though pallid as if an airing in the sun wouldn't do him any harm. Heaving himself onto the *bali-bali* with an ostentatious groan, he put the tin down and reached for his copy of *Crime and Punishment*. Then, settling himself against his pack, he opened the book with one hand, dipped a tapioca cake into the *gula malacca* with the other, and took a lip-smacking bite as his eye ran happily down the page. I swore as a strap broke, and he looked up irritably.

"When are you off?"

"Tonight, worse luck!"

"My dear Stephen, I do envy you! You don't know how fortunate you are to enjoy good health!"

"Well, I'm not so sure about that – " I said, but his attention had already slipped back to his nice long book.

My second trip upcountry started more tolerably than the first, though I no longer had illusions about what lay ahead. Merely leaving the perimeter of a wired-in camp gave a feeling of freedom, and the changing scenery and fresh air of the jungle raised our spirits as we bowled up the line, feeling that we were getting value for our labour at last. And we were travelling lighter now, for experience had taught us what we could do without – bad books, 'battle-bowlers', bedding-bags, big bottles, webbing belts, broken boots. And we had become more adept at avoiding risks to our health – and misunderstandings with the Japanese and Koreans.

I found I had three interests in common with another Gunner in the party. Bill Atkinson had been taught at Radley by my brother-in-law, had been at Hertford with my brother, and was a nephew of my headmaster, Norman Whatley.

Whatley was on the austere side, and his want of charisma was reflected in his nickname 'the Cod'. A good classicist who chose his staff well, he was eased out after a row with the governors. I had first heard of it when I called one day on my tutor, the distinguished but dry mathematician John Burkill, and found him closeted with the charismatic history don, Bertie Hallward, who was to succeed the Cod. I stood there with my ears flapping, shocked to hear unworldly academics (as I supposed them to be) talking about salaries and inducements and the influence of the Master, Field Marshal Lord Birdwood. They noticed me ("Ah, Alexander, shan't keep you a minute!") just as things were getting interesting.

Gossip of this sort carried us back to our pre-war position of privilege and the assumption that we would one day resume it. Lately we had not cared to test this assumption against our actual condition. Now, again and again, we began with a bang of happy memories only to end with a whimper of their expiry in our cattle truck.

We spent the night at Tarsao, and the next day we reached Brankassi, a hundred and fifty kilometres above Kanburi. Here we spent three wet but restful days with Bill Peacock and others of the regiment, who were there on a rail-laying party. It was pleasant to meet my military family again, and intriguing to see how familiar figures had changed: which profiles stood higher and which lower. But from now on the tendency grew stronger to choose companions for their compatability, wherever they might come from, rather than clinging to the memories of shared experience with members of the same regiment. As regimentation broke down under the strain of life and death on the river, it was a relief to be able to drop the mask worn in a hierarchical group, and behave naturally. Certainly this was the case at the bottom of the heap; frozen artificially into his rank at the capitulation, the subaltern (a second lieutenant for three years and then a lieutenant indefinitely) remained a subaltern to his seniors in his own regiment, and constraints to easy friendship persisted. With strangers, rank was irrelevant and shared interests took over.

We entrained again for another ten kilometres to Takanun, where we halted for three days. Dha Khanun, or 'Landing Place by the Jackfruit Tree', was the base camp for the Officer's Working Battalion, consisting largely of Indian Army officers bereft of their troops. They had worked in 'coolie gangs' like other ranks and had suffered many casualties, dispelling any master-race idea such as the one propounded by a British colonel, when a Netherlands East Indies Army colonel succumbed, that 'white colonels don't get cholera!', or that only the lower classes suffered from the more ignoble diseases. Many of these officers looked like Paul Muni as Dreyfus on Devil's Island, and were covered in ringworm.

In my tent was a cello player from Leicester who had lost his gramophone and records on the way up, and now had only an HMV catalogue to remind him of his treasured past. As soon as he came in from work he would seize it and turn over yet again its greasy pages to recapture from the tiny print the magic of the music. Also there, as luck would have it, was Lieutenant P. K. Laing. 'Peaky' was the taciturn subaltern who had met me in the mess when I first reported, wet behind the ears from my OCTU, at Holt, and had allowed me to mistake his two pips and regimental hart for two pips and a crown, and address him as 'sir'. Irked by the absence of any apology, I had considered we were on non-speaking terms ever since, and had managed, as we were in different batteries, to avoid any contact that might have revived my embarrassment. I was not going to lose face by being the first to speak now. We ignored each other successfully for two days, but on the third, Peaky's reserve broke; like Kinglake in the Egyptian desert, he nodded as he entered the tent, and then unbent enough to ask if I had news of the regiment.

From Takanun we rode twenty-six kilometres to the railhead at Tamuron Part, and started marching. It was only about twenty kilometres to Konkuita but they were very nasty ones. We floundered in deep mud over steep hills for three days. The path was often lost in the jungle and the many false trails were just as confusing to our two Korean guards as to us. At one point we slogged up to a summit only to find ourselves blocked except for a dubious escape down the side of a cliff to the river. We were too exhausted to do anything but curse, until Alan Lewis, of the Cambridgeshires, nobly volunteered to go down without his pack and see how the land lay. We all, including our guards, rested thankfully while he hacked his way down. He found there was no way across the river unless we swam. To us in our desperate state this seemed an excellent idea, but it came to nothing when one of the guards confessed he couldn't swim. Back down the mountain we had to go to seek another track.

At Konkuita I found some familiar faces from the regiment, still

under the resilient Granny Keane. But some I did not find. My batman, Bill Hunt, who had joined them again at Kinsaiyok, had not survived the second march; he had been caught on it, as I might so easily have been, by cholera. I felt diminished by his death, as though I had lost a limb, a small and aching one perhaps, but a limb nevertheless. We would never again eavesdrop on one of his Marxist homilies. He had been a deckhand on a Greek coal steamer at one time, which had helped to fuel his wide but undigested experience of life. In Cape Town he'd come back to the ship with an expensive work on Van Gogh. When Carl Moser made some patronising remark about it, Bill had turned on him, confounding him with knowledge, and comparing this edition with others published in Germany and France. How far his cultural interests were dictated by political ones I did not know. His failing had been drink, which he was powerless to resist.

I was also shocked to hear that George Roberts of the Gordons had succumbed to cerebral malaria. He had been a Scottish rugger international; if such a mentally and physically tough nut could be cracked by such a disease, then luck or fate had more to do with survival than personal qualities.

We slept in overcrowded tents at Konkuita; they were airless at night and unbearably hot by day, though we were rarely in them then. The camp, like others, had a beguiling name – 'Waiting Place at the Foot of the Paper-making Tree' – and was beautifully sited on a slope from which we watched sunrises and sunsets sweeping dramatically over the mountains. But it was an evil camp. The ground round about – host to many Tamils – was covered with red faeces, and crime among prisoners was rampant. The chief racket was pinching rations and blankets to sell to the Tamils. And the food was the worst we ever had. Breakfast consisted of 'porridge', in other words plain 'pap' rice (and we were so hungry that we would consume a quart of it and go out to work still feeling mere leaky vessels), lunch of rice and chillies (and tears are a poor substitute for taste), and supper of rice, dried vegetables and two ounces of fresh meat from thin cattle or aged buffaloes. The meat did not always materialise, nor did supplies for the canteen, because the river at this point was seasonally too shallow for the sampans.

In charge of what meat on the hoof we had was Pharaoh Adams, an RASC subaltern well qualified for the job as the son of a Kidderminster butcher. Fair-haired and blue-eyed, he had the mischievous air of an overgrown cherub; a competent and bolshie character, he spoke with the Brummie lift that ends sentences on a note of innuendo. He had courage and a market-place shrewdness that went down well with the Japanese, but had a very poor view of authority in general and senior officers in particular, except for one or two like Toosey whom he greatly admired. His *bêtes noires* were senior officers who nursed little ailments to get off work. Two such malingerers had long been accustomed to settle back comfortably in their tent after performing their minimal 'sick list' duties while we trudged out to work. It was understood that muscular atrophy of some sort, for they had no visible symptoms, impeded movement and made it impossible for them to join working parties. They limped heavily about on bamboo crutches, lowered themselves gingerly to the ground, and only got up again to the accompaniment of heart-rending groans. One morning Pharaoh and his men were driving steers through the camp when he decided that, where medicine had failed, a little healthy exercise might cure the patients. With whoops and whacks the animals were stampeded through their tent – and the inmates shot out like bullets and sprinted for the nearest tree.

"And do you know, Steve," said Pharaoh later, as he brought his sledge hammer down squarely on the skull of a steer, "I'd been longing to do that for days and days! The selfish bastards! What do the men think of us? I don't mind telling you that if I had them tethered here like this, I'd as soon bash their silly brains out as do it to these poor bloody animals."

The work at Konkuita was similar to that at Kinsaiyok – blasting cuttings through the rocks, building embankments, unloading supplies – until on 10th December 1943 the line at last got through to us. Thereafter we built ourselves huts and, from the felled trees dragged to us by elephants, cut firewood for the railway engines. These had a fine Wells-Fargo-ish look about them, with big cow-catchers in front, and were a striking change from the diesel road-rail trucks used at earlier stages. It seemed incredible that these snorting metropolitan monsters could actually be supported by our grudgingly-laid line. As soon as the final link was made, near the Three Pagodas Pass, three hundred kilometres from Ban Pong, with the hundred and seventy-kilometre Burmese line from Moulmein, there was an opening ceremony with the usual Nippon pomp and circumstance; the only spin-off to us in Konkuita was a day's *yasumé*. However, the work slackened off and, though the completion of the line meant that we watched – with some dismay – troops and supplies going up to the Burma Front, we felt that the traffic would not long be all one way.

I had become used to history lessons from the Nips or Koreans when out on working parties. During slack moments the guard would draw maps in the dust. "This-*ah*-Biruma, this-India, Nippon-boom-boom, Biruma-finish, Nippon-boom-boom, India-finish, this-*ah*-Aflica, Nippon-boom-boom, Aflica-finish, this-*ah*-Alema-*ah*-Thjamony, Nippon-boom-boom, Thjamony-finish, this-Englan,

Nippon-boom-boom, Oru-Englan-Churchiu-finish, this-Lussia, Nippon-boom-boom, Stalin-finish; Japan number one."

"And America?"

"Amelica? *Wakarimasen.* I-don'-know."

However, one day, high in the sky there was a noisy black speck and my guard looked at me quizzically as he pointed to it. "*Oi, shoko,* *ah*-one-Churchiu-ailoplane; *ah*-come-look-see-go-back-speak!" And later on as Christmas approached another was very disapproving. "Yesterday," he said, "um-yesterday-yesterday-yester-day-your-Curisamasu-man-say-war-no-good. Why-you-vloody-fight-*ah*?"

And so, as lines of communication stretched towards us, we began to feel more cheerful. Then came a tragic break in one of them. It was the reason why Hawley of BAT, who had made such a fuss about being seen swinging a *chunkeol*, did not have to earn his living East of Suez after the war. At Kanburi two wireless leads were discovered sticking out of a bamboo pole in one of the huts. The whole place was taken apart, and a wireless was found in a water bottle. All hell broke loose up and down the line, with sudden searches at all hours. At Brankassi a great fuss was made, the Japanese declaring that they had heard radio morse being transmitted; this was eventually tracked down to a woodpecker. But at Kanburi affairs ended on an altogether more sombre note. Officers were thrown into gaol and beaten up, and two were picked out, it was believed erroneously, as the chief culprits. One was a gentle Irishman named Stanley Armitage and the other was Hawley. Set upon before witnesses, they were beaten insensible by Koreans, revived with buckets of water and beaten insensible again. Finally their bodies, whether dead or alive was uncertain, were thrown down a latrine. A dozen other officers were sent to Singapore, to suffer from scabies and beri-beri on rice and water in solitary confinement. After this, several radios were destroyed, leaving only half a dozen, used thereafter with more stringent safeguards than ever.

Considering our peripatetic existence it is surprising that more Japanese searches were not successful. John Beckett had brought the radio parts from Sime Road camp safely to Chungkai, where he found the expert he needed in Tom Douglas, a Signals lieutenant and former BBC engineer. Douglas used his bits and pieces to make portable battery sets capable of receiving transmissions on the 19–and 25–metre bands; Beckett's was in a water bottle, which hung nonchalantly from a false bamboo hut-support beneath the aerial, a wire from which his mosquito net hung at night, and socks and a towel by day. Inside the hollowed bamboo were twenty torch batteries, while the speaker, the sawn-off ear-piece of a telephone, lived in the toe of a spare boot. The radio was taken as far as Takanun and its use limited to one weekly reception at eleven at night. It only took five minutes to twist wires together and operate the set while others kept watch outside. The radio survived several searches by the Kempitai, and this was sometimes thanks to warnings by the camp guards, who had no love for their military police. On one search the water bottle was actually seized and shaken but fortunately emitted no rattle. The batteries were bought on official shopping expeditions with a circumspect bravado by Jack Masefield, an old Malayan hand, and hidden by the quartermaster in sacks of rice. These were prodded with steel rods in Kempitai searches but to no effect.

At the end of 1943 the upriver camps were evacuated except for small specialist groups, and maintenance was left to civilian labour. Beckett returned to Chungkai base camp where he handed over his radio to the redoubtable Webber brothers – Max in the Loyals and Donald in the Federal Malay States Volunteer Force; it remained operational to the end.

It was just before Christmas that we left the Tamils at Konkuita to maintain the line, and moved sixty-five kilometres down it to Hindato, twenty-five kilometres above Kinsaiyok of evil memory. Here we joined Bill Peacock and the rail-laying gang, and most of us, though we were not to know it for some time, and were still to suffer some bad moments, were over the hump. The work was much lighter than at Konkuita, consisting largely of line maintenance, tree-felling for the engines and improvement of Japanese quarters.

Our imprisonment, for those who spent most of it in Thailand, fell into three phases: the spiritual malaise (and physical hunger) in Singapore; the increasing horror of railway construction upriver in Thailand; and the easing of the physical – though not psychological

– suffering in Thai base camps. The frenzy was now over; so was the direst shortage of food. The Nips became nervous as their advance in Burma faltered and naval setbacks in the Pacific multiplied, and though on occasions this made them more trigger-happy than ever, they began to take thought for the morrow and a bit more care over our treatment. The Thais, always friendly, became more overtly so, and once we got down into the 'egg belt' again we could buy more sugar, fruit, eggs, peanuts and tobacco with our miserable 'earnings'. Those of us detailed off for special parties sometimes had a better time; sometimes – like our Konkuita MO, 'Killer' Caley, who was to find himself even nearer the action in Burma – a far worse one.

1943 was the most memorable of all my Christmasses. The camp at Hindato ('the Waterfall'), set among noble jungle trees, was tidied up, de-scorpioned and de-leeched; the river was innocent of cholera; the weather was cool and dry. Work had slackened off and hope was in the air. If we felt that to bear goodwill towards the Nips was carrying Christian charity a bit far, at least they had the grace to keep themselves to themselves for a few days and leave us to celebrate on our own. The Dutch, ever more experienced than we were at living off the land, brewed an effective beer from rice, fruit and yeast, and by our standards we had a terrific Christmas dinner. On Christmas Eve some of us processed round the camp singing carols and carrying coconut oil lamps and torches of pitch. The light leaped up into the shadows of the trees, playing on the lianas and dancing in counterpoint to our voices. Alan Lewis took the solo parts in an ethereal baritone. 'In the bleak midwinter' and 'amid the winter snow' of that tropical night we felt an unearthly happiness. Our magi's journey still seemed endless but if it was better to travel hopefully than to arrive, then the worse the journey the more vivid was the hope.

Were not the artful and archaic simplicities of Christina Rossetti the counterpoint to the artful and archaic simplicities of war? We may not have felt in the mood for her affecting conceits before, but in Hindato they hit the spot.

17

The Egg Belt

ONE reason why the Nips were in a good mood that Christmas was no doubt the convenient siting of a nearby Japanese brothel. The 'comfort girls' were very friendly to those of us sent to tidy up the area, and though I received no more than a conspiratorial smile, others were given cigarettes and even money. I was shocked at such a travesty of love, and so close to the horrors of our camps; it was one thing to ply for hire on the sunny side of Jermyn Street but quite another to be set up in the middle of the jungle as a kind of target for machine-gun sex.

As far as we were concerned, however, our hard labour and poor diet had so far confined our interest in comfort girls to the academic, and sex had rarely raised its head. At Tamarkham, it is true, we had felt upstaged by a handsome Cypriot in the Norfolks, who had fathered a child on a Thai girl, and at Nong Pladuk several men from a small outlying camp had reported to the MO with clap. And there was a sombre story of a man upcountry who had contracted syphilis; after being beaten up by the Nips he had run away and been found on the railway line with his head smashed in.

At Hindato, notionally at least, our interest in the fair sex began to revive. Vivid reminiscences were exchanged in the hut after lights out between Bill Comyn of the Garhwalis and Pharaoh Adams, 'the Kid from Kidderminster'. Just as at Oswestry I had lain in the dark mingling my thoughts with grunts on one side and whispers from Mike Hamilton's radio on the other, and as in Sime Road I had learned about Malayan maladministration from Henry Royle in the far corner of the hut, so here I heard about 'life' in cantonments in

158

India – and in butchers' delivery vans in Kidderminster. Like the two Norfolks on the *Mount Vernon*, these two inspired each other to flights of fancy rarely heard from either singly, and formed a kind of music hall act which took on a life of its own. It was as though the circumstances of time and place were more important than the people concerned, for the couple could scarcely have had less in common. Bill was very much the Raj in voice, but jumpy and sardonic in character. He had distanced himself from Indian Army colleagues and, as if to accentuate his independence, had grown a bushy black beard and eschewed anything remotely like a uniform; he wore a native straw hat and his shorts were long trousers torn off raggedly above the knee. At night we could hear his staccato tones exploding with tales of ballrooms in Bangalore or bricks dropped in Delhi, or feeding lines to Pharaoh's singsong replay of seductions in the blood-spattered rear of the Adams & Sons delivery van.

Bill's favourite story was of an ill-fated Indian romance which I never did get the hang of. I only remember the punch line, which was, 'Well, take your shoes off, then, and call me "Sahib"!' This phrase seemed to delight him hugely and one would hear him during the day bursting out with it all by himself and chortling away into his big black beard. Bill's and Pharaoh's unlikely partnership was not destined to last for Pharaoh, in an evil hour, went with a working party to Japan.

Any festive feelings and stirrings of concupiscence were dispelled early in 1944 by a virulent type of malaria which caused a week of headaches and vomiting. So we were not sorry in March to be sent further downriver, in fact right down below Tamarkham to the very start of the line at Nong Pladuk and well within the 'egg belt'. Here, again, the move proved fortunate for me. Shortly before leaving Hindato, I had been sitting at a bamboo table on the edge of a ravine running down to the gorge; after clearing out my mess tin I leaned my arms on the table to admire the view and the sharp edge of a bamboo slat cut into my left elbow. It seemed a very small wound but on the way down to Nong Pladuk it blew up into a poisoned arm that kept me off work for three months. Once again the pus poured out in pints, and this time a Dutch surgeon named de Jong, mercifully with a whiff of chloroform, lanced it four times. (Down there medical supplies could be bought locally, with contributions from officers of fifteen dollars a month. Known only to the few, money and drugs were also beginning to come through from the expatriate 'V' organisation in Bangkok.)

Here, in my longest period off work, I found that a large base camp provided plenty of scope for bureaucracy, corruption and gossip. At this time pay for other ranks, provided they were working, ran from twenty-five cents a day for privates to forty for warrant officers. Officers theoretically received eighty-five dollars a month, charged to their pay in England, but received only thirty, as forty were deducted for 'board and lodging', with the balance allegedly placed in a Bangkok bank for release after the war. It was a profitable racket for Jap camp commandants to put officers onto men's jobs and apply for pay of the equivalent number of other ranks, which they pocketed themselves.

The admirable Chinese trader Boon Pong made his presence felt more effectively as the war turned in our favour, and cashed IOUs at face value for redemption after the war. Until then people had agreed to the most outrageous terms to get their hands on a few *baht*. A colonel at Nacom Pathom had bought pound notes for six dollars apiece, and sold them through a contact with the Thais for thirty. With the profits he cashed cheques for his brother officers at the rate of one dollar to the pound. Naturally he was disliked for his sharp practices and for the delicacies they enabled him to buy. He would pay high prices for these, and when a Javanese Dutchman, claiming to have close relations with Thai villagers, offered to procure a whole chicken the sky was the limit. The treat was duly delivered, topped and tailed, cooked in spices and nestling in a bed of rice and sweet potatoes. He found it very hard going for a chicken – but that's not what it was. It was a creature more accustomed to carrion than corn.

Life could be trying for redundant senior officers. A colonel, for instance, who had no camp or regiment to command, had to decide whether to remain with his own kind or become one of the boys. The former solution required a communal job like cutting wood, manning a pump, pounding peanuts into butter or digging latrines.

To go out on working parties or to do the nastier camp jobs with junior officers and other ranks required a flexibility many did not have. Those who could not be included in the communal jobs and were too windy to join general working parties tended to seek niches in which to ensconce themselves or, if the worst came to the worst, nurse some recurrent ailment. The niches would consist of hospital visiting, 'keeping records' – a useful catch-all – or a sudden vocation for Christian mission.

It was inevitable that gossip about senior officers, like the story of the sweet-toothed colonel in Changi, should go the rounds now that there was a new audience for them. One colonel greeted philosophically the news of a friend's loss of his first finger from a tropical ulcer: "But it's all right, he doesn't shoot!" Another left his hut one night to slosh across to the latrines but almost ran into a fellow-prisoner vomiting just outside. His deafness and a very nervous disposition led him to think he had run into an angry Nip guard.

"*Benjo*, OK-*kah?*" he cried, bowing in the darkness. "*Ichi-may-shoko, benjo*; *speedo-speedo*; OK-*kah?*"

"Wa-a-a-h!"

Another lavatory story involved a colonel caught in a blitz on illicit hooch, of which he had a water bottle full. As the Nips entered the hut he left it, carrying the bottle as though on his way to the latrine. A Nip eyed him suspiciously.

"Me go *benjo*, OK?"

The Nip said nothing, but as the colonel edged away he followed him closely. The camp was large and enjoyed the luxury of a special latrine for officers of field rank, chastely screened by an *attap* fence. Over this the Nip poked his nose and his rifle, as the colonel lowered his shorts and squatted on the planks.

"*Shoko*-pinish?"

"Yes, *shoko* finish!"

"You-*ah*-water-OK?"

"Oh dear! Yes."

"You-*ah*-use-*ah*-water?"

"Yes, yes!"

Bowing to the inevitable, and with the expertise borne of long practice, the colonel flicked the precious liquid onto the regulation area, suppressing a cry as it stung the wrong end of his digestion.

One of the colonels with a niche in the hospital was fond of the sound of his own voice and after holding forth one day was questioned by a victim.

"And what do you think will happen in England after the war?"

"What do you think I am, a prophet?"

"No," came a distant voice, "a dead loss!"

Another hospital visitor was relentlessly cheerful.

"Good morning to you! How are you today?"

"Not too good, sir. Got the shits good and proper!"

"Lucky not to have malaria as well. Stay on liquids and you'll be all right. And what about you, how's that leg of yours? Jungle ulcer, is it?"

"Yessir. Hurts like blue murder!"

"Good! Good! Always a good sign! It's when it doesn't hurt that you can start to worry. Going to put maggots on it, are they?"

"Do what?"

"Put – oh, never mind. Got something to read?"

"No, sir."

"I've got one or two books here. How about this one, *Point Counter Point* by Aldous Huxley? Never read him myself, but he's a well-known writer. Like me to leave it here?"

"Not really, sir. I'm not much of a reader."

"Good, good! I'll get on then. Hallo there! Fancy a book to read now?"

"Not with this head! Can't shake off the malaria. And these ulcers won't dry up. And there's me stools."

"Good! Good! Keep at it! I'll have a word with your colonel. If he's here, that is."

"Oh, he is."

"Who is it?"

"You!"

Our oddities were not all colonels. A bemused congregation was berated by a Catholic padre for its sins; he had been examining the washing hanging out to dry and it was clear to him that sodomy was going on. Someone who might have been interested in this news was

162

a colonel nicknamed La-de-dah. He and a namesake nicknamed Changi, although notably unlike in their tastes, took to each other and became our Tweedledum and Tweedledee of work-evasion. They were famous for one of their salutes to the dawn.

"Time to get up, Changi!"

"Up what, La-de-dah?"

"Up my fucking arse!"

Colonel Peanut McKellar, on the other hand, was all too active. His nickname came from his size ("Napoleon," he used to say, "was a small man too!") and he made up for his lack of height by tricking himself out with much spit and polish. Stuart, carrying a message to his HQ just after the capitulation, found his officers in sombre mood – if not in such depths as their CO. "There, gentlemen, go all our chances of promotion and decoration! I'm not brilliant, I know, but I'm steady. At tactics I am sound. And of my rank in the British Army I consider I am quite the best!" In Changi he was a distinctive figure. Long after other senior officers had begun to loosen up, his turn-out remained immaculate and he would strut about, swagger-cane in hand and eye cocked for any junior officer who might throw him up a salute. It only took someone within thirty yards to raise a hand to scratch or light a cigarette for Peanut to react, and one of our amusements was to see who could extract a premature acknowledgment with the minimum movement. A member of his regiment composed a ditty in his honour.

> I salute on the 'rears',
> I've had twenty-five years
> Of intensive military training;
> I'm Peanut McKellar, a helluva feller,
> All discipline and spunk.
> Of Peanut McKellar it's said that he's yeller
> But that, I assure you, is bunk!
> They're a crowd of some standing,
> The crowd I'm commanding,
> But I swear – as sure as I live –
> I'd leave 'em all cold, if once I was told
> Of a chance to command a Div.

I've dignity, energy, guts and determination;
More colonels like me and we'd very soon be top nation.
Napoleon was good, but he's nothing on me!
I've a row of street-liners including 'TD' . . .
Kiotské! Yasumé! I command *Ju-Ichi Butai.*

Stuart was under Peanut's jungle command at Tonchan and found formalities rigorously observed for such chores as roll call. So predictable were these that, as Peanut strutted behind the Nip sergeant, a chant would rise from the ranks. "WE'RE NOT BRIL-LIANT, WE KNOW, BUT WE'RE STEADY. AND OF OUR RANKS IN OUR RESPECTIVE ARMIES WE ARE QUITE THE BEST!" The sergeant, suspicious of this chorus, was told it was a thanksgiving – rather like the Japanese sunset ceremony – for the day's work well done.

From some Indian Army officers at Nong Pladuk I had a poignant reminder of my bleak days at Catterick. Chalky White, the sergeant-instructor whose voice carried so many miles on the wind, had finished up in Malaya, and during the battle for Singapore he was commissioned in the field. Working with these Indian officers up in the jungle, Lieutenant White was on a railway truck when it jumped the rails into a deep ravine, and he was killed. Other stories were less gloomy. In Poodu gaol they had been locked in the cells and had to ask the guard every time they wanted to relieve themselves. Once, when he got tired of their shouts for the *benjo* and refused to let them out, they started to sing:

> Ten men want to go,
> Want to go to *benjo*;
> Ten men, nine men, eight men, seven men,
>   six men, five men, four men, three men,
>   two men, one man and his DOG
> Want to go to *benjo*!

The Nip was so tickled with this ditty that he kept asking for an encore. "All men sing *benjo* song! OK, very good-*en-ah!*" One of them had been surprised by special treatment when he ended up in a cell with a Tamil, a Chinese and a Malay. Their food was augmented by the remains of the sentry's mess tin, emptied onto the floor. However, he felt that the officer deserved better and spread toilet paper on the floor for his share of the *meshi*.

Ian Grimwood of the Frontier Force Regiment, who had been at Peterhouse with me, had a graphic story of how he found his way back through the Jap lines after being cut off in the retreat.

"I was skirting a Nip encampment in the best approved fashion, when I heard a challenge: 'Halt!' I flung myself down and lay as silent as the grave. Nothing happened. So after a bit I crept on. But I hadn't gone more than a few yards when it came again: 'Halt!', louder than before. Down I went again and lay still, listening. Nothing! Not a sound. Off I went once more but there it was again: 'Halt!' I dived down for a third time, and as I lay in the grass an enormous beetle beside my ear said loudly and distinctly: 'HALT!'"

Geoffrey Hulton, another raconteur, was a lieutenant of Marines who had been sunk in the *Repulse*. While he was treading water near a destroyer and hoping to board her, an AB leaning over the rail sang out, "Keep clear of the propellers, mate, we're moving!" He had to wait for another destroyer to pick him up.

The stories of his private life did not have quite the same bite. How he missed his 'sweetheart'! What a wonderful girl she was! When he had apologised to her for shouting at an obstructive driver and calling him a bugger, she had said "I think it's very manly of you, Geoffrey!" He used to write long letters to the wonderful girl, and as he was unable to send them he read them out to us instead. When at last we begged for mercy he read them to the Dutch, who were too polite to object. Great was our consternation when he announced that as it was clear that the Japanese were going to lose the war he had composed a Victory Ode and thought we would like to hear it. It began:

> Ring out those bells and spread the glad news
> Peace has arrived in our view.
> Our Island, our Empire, our Country, our Home
> Have weathered the storm and won through.

The awed silence that followed his six verses was broken by a gunner subaltern called Jack Stogumber:

"You've certainly given us something to think about, Geoffrey. I find it inspiring."

And the next day he slipped into my hand the fruit of his inspiration – a parody which ended:

> Ring out those bells! And Wop, Boche and Nip,
> To pay for your caddish endeavour,
> You'll take it in turns to sail round in his ship
> And listen to Geoffrey for ever!

My creative endeavours during this convalescence were devoted to nostalgic maps in pencil and crayon. At Hindato I had done one of Cambridge, concocted from my own memory aided by that of Phil Peachey, whose family farmed in the area. At Nong Pladuk, while my left arm was healing, I used the right to do a bigger and better one of Bristol, reinstating pubs destroyed in the 1940 bombing, and also ones of Bath and Somerset. Each took about ten days of absorbing work; a few months later they were confiscated by the Nips in one of their searches, and I mourned their loss.

Outside news had been steadily improving everywhere, except in the area that interested us most. Italy had long surrendered; the Russians pressed on at Novgorod, and the US in Dutch New Guinea. But the appointment of Mountbatten as Supreme Commander South-East Asia in August 1943 seemed to make little difference in Burma. Then in April the Nips told us that in Biruma there was a lot of bom-bom going on, with Churchu number ten and Nippon number one and India pinish and *oru may* (men) go home soon. For many weeks we anxiously balanced the Japanese news and the far from reassuring BBC versions of Kohima and Imphal, and then, at last, in June everything began to happen at once – landings in Normandy, the Japanese retreat from Imphal and the resignation of the smug little Tojo. Word from on high showed that these events affected even such worms as us, and it was clear that a move was in the air. The general optimism helped me to bear the loss of my maps more philosophically.

18

Little Bloomsbury-on-Kwai

A FTER we'd been at Nong Pladuk for six months – and as if to punctuate the news bulletins for us – the RAF flew over. Evidently their 'come-look-see' plane had reported that the camp alongside ours was full of Japanese, for two sticks of bombs fell on it. In fact Toosey was there with three thousand men. Unlike us, he had not been allowed to dig slit trenches; ninety prisoners were killed and hundreds wounded. It was a bitter-sweet feeling to find oneself, after three years of a very simple life and total neglect by the civilised world as one knew it, the object of its most sophisticated and powerful attention. In other raids there were five Allied casualties at Kanburi and seventy near the bridge at Tamarkham.

Bad as the raids were, we were almost more upset by the Nips ordering the shaving of our heads; with their own polls shaven, they gave short shrift to our objection to this manly and sanitary habit. Our resentment was mollified by a second release of Red Cross parcels – one to ten men – but we hardly had time to appreciate them before being moved forty kilometres upriver to Tamuang. Shortly before our move others had been shipped off to Japan, Pharaoh Adams among them. Such is the demoralising effect of constant irritation and unrelenting boredom that his party left Siam in the highest spirits.

We went to Tamuang by barge, and it was the first move I made where everything went smoothly and no one got bashed. Tamuang ('Landing Place by a Mango Tree') was a large, healthy camp, well designed to house and feed about seven thousand men. There was a camp farm and a flourishing brickworks, reputed to be profitable to the Japanese officers; and some of the Korean guards there, with an eye to the future, were beginning to retail news of the war – and even of the beginning of a Thai resistance movement. Our old friend Knocker Knights, who had sent us the precious eggs at Tarsao on our march to Kinsaiyok, had been there since June and explained the rift, often so confusing to us, between the Japanese camp staff and the much feared Kempitai military police. It was the latter who carried out the worst surprise searches and who blamed the other Japs for having failed to confiscate such miserable but forbidden comforts as they found: pencils, paper (my maps!) or tools of any sort. The British Commandant was warned that such things should be concealed more carefully from the Kempitai. But where? This was becoming more difficult day by day. Why not, suggested the Japanese interpreter, the camp office? That was never searched and was not suspected. Later on he even said that to avoid local papers being found in the camp he was prepared to give us 'true news'.

In spite of its better aspects Tamuang was an irritating camp for me because I found myself working under Nip privates on piddling little jobs like weeding paths. While others enjoyed outside working parties I seemed to be stuck with camp duties. On one of these we received another lesson in Japanese linguistics. We were to carry from a store some bamboo for building and it was important that we should take it from the correct – the old – pile. Pointing to the newly-cut unused bamboo and then to the old bamboo from dismantled buildings which was kept for re-use, the guard said, "OK-bamboo no good. No-good bamboo OK!" This kind of Nippon-lingo could be used in reverse, as when Stuart found himself in a party of six ('*roko*') officers ('*shoko*') clearing sewage out of the moat. The Indian Army Major in charge reported his party to the Nip Corporal – who punctiliously acknowledged it – as '*roko shoko* shovelling shit'.

From drudgery of this kind I escaped in a manner so frivolous as to be inconceivable in the previous year of horrors. A Nip sergeant promoted – and himself took part in – a series of touch-rugger games. I played in three of them against the Aussies, who soon dispensed with namby-pamby rules about touching and tackled with gusto on the rock-hard earth. I landed on my wrist, and our own

MO, Sidney Pitt, whom I had now rejoined, diagnosed a fractured scaphoid and put it into plaster for several weeks. So, feeling a bit of a fraud, I again retired to a hospital hut.

In Tamuang I had rejoined John Durnford for the first time since Sime Road days in Singapore, Stuart whom I had left at Tamarkham, and also Ian Watt and Guthrie Moir; we soon resumed the literary explorations started at the 'University of Changi'. In hospital I found two new recruits and we were to share our interests for the rest of our time in Siam. There was quite a good library in the camp, and my own by this time consisted of Boswell's *Johnson*, *Eothen*, *The Knapsack* (still), the *Golden Treasury*, *Letters to Malaya I* and *II* (and *III* in manuscript) and a tract of St John's gospel pressed upon me in Cape Town. Ian had the *Faber Book of Modern Verse*, Legouis and Cazamien's *History of English Literature*, some Dante, a selection of Yeats, an *Oxford Book of English Verse* and an issue of John Lehmann's *Modern Writing*. With this cultural armoury he still had the edge on us, and was referred to as the arbiter of taste. Increasingly, though, while we deferred to his knowledge we began to question the logic of his deductions and suspect him of over-solemnity, perhaps due to his French blood. But there is no doubt that in his dry way he was a patient inspiration to us.

My two fellow invalids were Terence Charley and Alex Hellawell (the latter, with a dislocated shoulder, a rugger casualty like me); they were in the Hong Kong and Singapore Royal Artillery and had enjoyed some of Singapore's palmy days before the Japs eclipsed them. It was at once clear from their conversation on one side of me that they were bookish rather than men of action. It was equally clear that my two neighbours on the other side were the opposite. Bob Stabb was a quiet Tasmanian, while his more ebullient cobber rejoiced in the name of John Chauncey Champion de Crespigny. They were pleasant neighbours and it was not long before we were exchanging confidences. De Crespigny showed me the book which was his favourite companion.

"Try it, Steve. It'll change your life."

He handed over *Wake Up and Live* by Dorothea Brand. It was a self-improvement manual, explaining how to better yourself by numbers until you were fit to be President of the United States. The salient points had clearly grown upon their reader. After a few pages a sentence or two was underlined, then three or four on a page. In the next chapter sentences were underlined doubly as well. Treble underlinings crept in halfway through the book, and by the end there were double lines in the margins as well.

Terence Charley rescued me from the rules of Dorothea Brand with the pragmatics of Housman in *Last Poems* and *More Poems*, *The Progress of Poetry*, art and history packaged by Van Loon, and *Teach Yourself Russian*, a good deal of which he *had* taught himself and was later to pass on to us. He sported a pale moustache but beneath it his appearance was perhaps more faun-like than military, and he soon disabused me of any claim to heroics on his part.

"The reason I'm in here is that I was out on a rail-carrying party with Ian Watt and he dropped a rail on my foot – thank goodness! It's a nice clean little break and I'm very comfortable here. My one aim over the last year and a half has been to prevent anyone sending me further up the line than Kanyu. That was quite high enough for me, thank you!"

"But what about your men?"

"I haven't got any men. They're probably in the Indian National Army by now. And if they are, they'll have found that they aren't as well treated as they were by me!"

Kanyu was south of Kinsaiyok and north of Tonchan, which was the highest John Durnford had been. Many of the people in these parties had enjoyed soft living in Malaya before the invasion, and one of the less militaristic of them was very put out when the bristly SOE Marines Colonel, Alan Warren, barked at him, "What about you? Ever thought of making a break for it, eh, have you?" It was understandable that Warren had escape on his mind, for he had given up his place in an official escape boat from Padang in Sumatra to restore order among the stragglers ashore. John Durnford, too, talked with Mo de Mier in Tonchan of a second attempt at escaping, but conditions deteriorated and he found himself wandering about, giving his clothes away, impelled either – as he claimed – by a messianic impulse or – as others thought – a nervous breakdown.

Like many only children, both John and Terence were happy to talk about themselves once they were given encouragement. Terence's father, in the Jamaica police, had been drowned when Terence was three, and he had been brought back by his Creole mother to live with paternal relations in Belfast. Here, before going to school in England, he quickly absorbed local lessons in hygiene ("Come out of that water now; it's full of wee Popes!") and history ("Little Tim, the blessed angel, was struck down by fatal disease, and at the end he sat up in his bed, beat on his little drum, cried, 'Death to the Pope', and fell back into the arms of Jesus.")

As with Stuart, Terence had gone straight into a bank from school. Alex Hellawell, a Stoic, went into the family cotton business in Manchester. Alex was an odd mixture of diffidence and urbanity and particularly affected the diffidence when coming out with a quotation of unnerving erudition. It was possibly because these two had missed university that they were more assiduous and curious in their reading than I was. Alex seemed equally attracted to the philosophers and the romantics, and put his ideas into verse:

> When asked if I write poetry I reply
> With this good reason why I seldom try.
> The teeming thoughts that occupy my head
> On paper seem far better left unsaid;
> That which *in situ* seems quite intellectual
> When written down is trite and ineffectual;
> Those close compactnesses, which should contain all
> The metaphysic meat, in print are banal.

This struck a chord in all of us – including Stuart who used to drop into our little Bloomsbury from time to time as a change from the barrack room arguments of healthier huts – but we nevertheless resolved to persevere; rather than make lists of the do's and don'ts advocated by Dorothea Brand, we dived straight into a course of Teach Yourself Poetry. With the bit between his teeth Alex, in 'Epicurus Admonet', admonished us to:

> Open the shutters of the mind,
> · Let in the purifying air.
> Shun not the sun which you shall find
> Will cleanse the cobwebs of despair.

Let the thick dust of prejudice
Over your life no longer lie,
Since toleration breeds a bliss
That sour contempt cannot deny.

Harvest experience far and wide,
Nor hesitate, nor fail to dare
With lasting beauty as your guide
To taste perfection everywhere.

Terence protested that it was pretty difficult to 'taste perfection *everywhere*'; *we only had to look around us.*

And the sun, said Stuart, might have 'cleansed the cobwebs of despair' in the chapel at Stowe but it didn't when he had to stand in it for three hours because one of his party had flogged a shovel to a Thai farmer.

Ian was such a stern critic of our verse that we challenged him to show us a poem of his own; we were chagrined by its elegance but amused that it was so derivative of you-know-W. . . H. . . O. . .

> *Song of a POW*
> Oh, the amazing elegance
> And the painted faces,
> The surrealist extravagance
> Of pre-war places!
>
> From our escalator time
> We glimpsed Edwardian graces
> And now the garden suburbs
> Vanish from our gazes.
>
> What doctrinaire ascetics
> Will shape our future phases,
> With pitiless economics
> Exterminate the lazy?
>
> There is no time like the present:
> None, sure, that's like the past;
> At the grimaces of the future
> The Idler stands aghast.

We expected something of this sort also from Stuart, coolly detached, we thought, as he was, and with a strong streak of irony in his make-up. So we were nonplussed by the directness of his trochaic love song called 'Musing':

> Of the muses Terpsichóre
> Seems to me the loveliest;
> She refuses always more
> Than one dance at my request.

"Ah!" exclaimed Guthrie, when he had read this far. "Terpsichóre! The stressed omicron, I see!"

> Underneath a Grecian moon
> See her whirl and pirouette;
> Underneath a sky of pearl
> Hear the Dionysian tune;
> Spellbound watch her silhouette,
> Like a living cypress tree
> Slim and dark across the lawn
> As she dances down to me.
>
> I am torn between the chances
> Of a turn between the trees,
> And the wish to pause and hearken
> To a whisper on the breeze.
> Whence it wanders – that I know not
> But it whispers strong to me:
> Seize her! Seize her!
> Seize the Goddess
> Round her slender,
> Tender hips;
> Mouth to mouth now, kiss the coral
> Of these more than mortal lips.
>
> Now I dare not
> Bow and swing her
> To the piping of the tune,
> On the grasses

Glistening, dew-tipped
Underneath a stately moon.
For I know that in the passes
Of some old immortal dance,
I shall listen
To those voices,
Turn and seize the other chance.

We liked the swing of the thing but questioned Stuart's logic. Why shouldn't he 'turn and seize the other chance'? We took it to mean seizing her and kissing her lips, etc., etc. What was wrong with that?

"They're more than mortal. I'd be turned into a stone or something."

But Terpsichore didn't go in for that sort of thing.

"Maybe she didn't; I can't honestly remember. But she *rhymes*, that's the important thing. As you know, I believe all poetry is fifty per cent contingent on chance."

In reaction to Terpsichorean pirouettes, we tried our hand at disdainful triolets. I went first:

> Poets who have spotty faces
>   Sing the tumult of the soul;
> But 'tis seldom beauty chases
> Poets who have spotty faces.
> I, whom God gave all the graces,
>   Let a girl my heart control –
> Poets who have spotty faces
>   Sing the tumult of the soul.

I was accused of poetic licence, since at the moment we all had spotty faces, and spotty everything else too. Moreover, I had failed to use different emphases in the second and the last lines. Jack Stogumber's triolet fulfilled this condition.

> Don't flash your Odol smile at me.
>   Do *I* desire your lips?
> If wedlock be your only fee
> Don't flash your Odol smile at me.

> Or, if you think in chastity
>> To launch a thousand ships,
> Don't flash your Odol smile at me –
>> Do I desire your *lips*?

This was approved, except for Alex muttering something about John Keats's porridge and Calverley's Bacon and the perils of using ephemeral brand names in poetry. There was no danger of this, said Terence, in his love poem, which was old-fashioned and – like all great poetry – perfectly clear. It was an attempt to distil his feelings on the barge journey downriver from Tamarkham to Tamuang: the hugger-mugger of sampans, giant rafts loaded with bamboo and teak, and pom-poms darting between high banks of deep terracotta, with here and there purple bougainvillea cascading over the edge; tamarisk trees silhouetted against the sky like fine green filigree; the foothills of the Tennasserim range sweeping up on the right, and on the left crazy flights of steps running down the cliffside from a monastery, which peeped from among the trees like a huge red and green bird; a lagoon with clouds and sky reflected in the water, studded with lotuses in bloom and, splashing beside a large flower, a little boy who grinned and waved to him:

> I am home, the war is over –
>> Nothing now to trouble me.
> I suck a stalk of English clover
>> In the land where men are free!

> Yet softly, softly, through the grasses,
>> Breathing on me where I lie,
> The warm wind whispers as it passes:-
>> '*Muang Thai*'.

This struck a chord in all of us, though Ian doubted if it would do much for Terence's post-war image as a tortured hero of the Burma-Siam railway, and Stuart complained that Terence was very circumspect about what exactly the warm wind whispered, whereas he had had no such inhibitions about Terpsichore. But he was right about 'Muang Thai' (Thailand); it would have made a hell of a difference if we'd been in a country with unpleasant people round us. The Thais had really been very good to us, and they looked good, too.

We thought about that in our various ways, though as the Nips were getting jumpier, herding us into bigger concentrations, with stricter controls over perimeters and outside working parties, we were actually having less contact with the locals. But they had indeed enhanced the landscape – the saffron-robed monks with their gentle air of escape from the world's ills, and the straw-crowned women swishing along with baskets balanced across their shoulders, or reaching up langorously and rhythmically as they punted sampans on the river. Yet in the *kampongs* the women could look very different, squatting among the pots and pans and spitting betel nut all over the floor through toothless gums, aged – it seemed – almost overnight with their long black hair now cropped like a Girton don's – to commemorate, according to Stuart, an ancient battle in which the women had fought as men. All this had inspired Jack to write a Siamese lullaby a good deal longer than Terence's:

> She smiled: I felt the Buddha's frown
>> That men are wise to shun,
> But silken was her skin and brown
>> With centuries of sun.
>
> She moved, and in her easy grace
>> There ran a liquid fire;
> She had no need to paint her face
>> To set alight desire.
>
> Her eyes as deep as surging seas,
>> Her hair as warm as night,
> She led me to a mango tree's
>> Cool cavern of delight.
>
> The river eddied gently past;
>> My heart remembers how
> We whispered that our love would last –
>> And pledged our faith in *lao*.

But in her nearby *attap* hut
    A crone, with champing jaws
And dribbling blood-red betel nut,
    Was squatting at her chores.

She combed with gnarled and knotted thumbs
    A straggling Eton crop;
She spat a quid from toothless gums –
    And let her bodice drop.

That pickled form that looked at least
    An ill-preserved four-score
Had all the glory of the East
    But fifteen years before.

Then what avails a native grace
    That fades away so soon?
The dawn that lights a dusky face
    Foretells a dusty noon.

The fruit that ripens early sours,
    The sweetest cake grows stale,
Before his appetite devours
    The European male.

So once he leaves his northern shore
    'Tis dangerous to kiss
The God of Asian love and war
    Who knows no armistice.

And often in the leaves I hear
    The murmur '*Muang Thai*',
As dark tormenting eyes appear
    Against the changing sky!

We could have gone on indefinitely, to the wonder of Bob Stabb who must have thought us an incorrigible bunch of Pommie pansies, while John Chauncey Champion de Crespigny thumbed through Dorothy Brand to see how best to hold his own against us. But one day Sydney Pitt came in and found us all with our forbidden bits of paper, nuzzling away at our lines like slugs in a strawberry bed.

"Now then, you fellows, I prescribe a bit of exercise for you. It's time you got out into the sun and made yourselves useful. Get down to the cookhouse and chop a bit of wood. There's plenty of work to be done!"

So, feeling ashamed of ourselves, we emerged blinking into the sun and began to lose our hospital pallor. Not long afterwards Sidney cut off my plaster cast and, back in circulation again, I found that Tamuang, for all its healthy situation, still provided alarms and excursions. On New Year's Day 1945 a man was shot dead near the fence, after climbing back in – some said, from a nocturnal dalliance, others, from collecting information. On another night a sergeant had his teeth knocked out and a rib broken by a rifle butt for not attending a midnight roll call; the Nip thought he had escaped, when in fact he was deaf and had slept through it. Guards sometimes came through our huts three or four times a night, either counting us or hot on the scent of the wireless. Yet pamphlets did reach us from outside, foretelling a Thai rising, and inside the camp more money materialised from the mysterious 'V' people in Bangkok. We heard on our wireless that some of our men who had left for Japan in early 1944 had been sunk and picked up by the Royal Navy.

One of the victims of the tightening of security was my own regiment's prince of operators, RQMS Beech. He had for long been established in a small party working and living on its own by the railway, loading supplies going up the line. Having squared the Korean guard, he made a very good thing out of selling Japanese equipment to the Thais. It was no rare occurrence for a perfectly good lorry, after standing in a siding for a couple of days, to continue its journey to Burma as little more than a body and chassis; the Thais were paying two thousand *baht* for tyres alone.

It was Mr Beech who had broken the news to us at Nong Pladuk of the long-awaited invasion of France.

"There's been a big landing. It's at the mouth of a river. Let's see now, it was the river – er – Seeny; yes, the Seeny. Somewhere in Italy, is it?"

But there was nothing vague about Mr Beech's own domestic

arrangements. He hired coolies as his personal servants and had the forbidden English-language *Bangkok Chronicle* delivered to him regularly. And it was that which finally landed him in the soup, for the Kempitai found his name one day in the list of subscribers. He was hauled in and court-martialled for 'illegally obtaining the *Bangkok Chronicle*'; and (which was worse) for reading it and (worse still) for passing on its information. And he was despatched to Changi gaol for a grim change in his standard of living.

In January 1945 the Japanese decided to separate officers and men. We liked to think that this was to prevent us rallying the troops for a great break-out. And the growing evidence of an imminent liberation movement, encouraged by British agents parachuted in, supported this theory. But another version had it that the Japanese were at last nervous of flouting international convention by not separating the officers and other ranks. At any rate, only the doctors among us now stayed with the men, who otherwise passed under the entirely competent command of warrant officers and sergeants, while we moved twelve kilometres upriver to Kanburi. We went by barge, which as usual gave us a tantalising illusion of freedom as we saw the life of the river going on. Alex Hellawell felt a Buddhist spirit of reincarnation stirring within him as he watched a white egret:

> Flying before the swift advancing night,
>   A bright and pure unblemished white he came,
> And with his beauty set the world alight
>   And squalor perished in his purging flame.
>
> His radiant ghost shall serve my storm-tossed soul
>   In future grief as gracious anodyne,
> And living memory of him console
>   My heart for ugliness my eyes have seen.

19

Officers Only

BEING separated from the other ranks, we did all our own camp servicing, as well as taking part in not very onerous outside working parties. As we no longer had to 'set an example to the men', the yin-yang of rank and responsibility was relaxed and civilian idiosyncracies began to surface again.

The food continued to improve, partly in basic rations and partly from canteen supplies for which Boon Pong's IOU cheques could be used. Kanburi, with its river, paper mill, Buddhist temple and shops, was a nice little place, and left alone we could have developed quite a hedonistic way of life there. But the Camp Commandant, Captain Noguchi, his assistant, Lieutenant Takasaki (the Frog from Tamarkham), and their henchman, the ferocious and syphilitic Sergeant Shimojo, saw to it that we didn't. Camp chores and enterprises such as the manufacture of paper, soap and bricks were supplemented by every kind of time-consuming and uncomfortable exercise; not the least irksome was catching a daily quota of flies, to be produced for inspection in a bottle. Failure to submit the required catch earned a bashing.

There remained plenty of free time but we were not allowed to enjoy it. Forbidden articles and activities included pencils and paper, reading or lying down between the hours of reveille and one in the afternoon and between three and six-thirty in the afternoon, smoking in the open air, lectures and – except for authorised concerts – music. Air raids were more frequent and the Nips first of all refused permission to dig trenches and then took a perverse delight in keeping us in them for hours whenever the warning went, even if it was obvious that the planes were nowhere near us. When Japan was first bombed we were confined to our huts for ten days. I think the Nips were seriously wondering if they could shoot us all and get away with it.

Not all our difficulties were of the Japs' making. The reunion of so many senior officers was not without its hazards and poor Toosey was to suffer from a constant pulling of rank. The Japs wanted him as Camp Commandant but he was by no means the senior of the hundred or so colonels, some of them jostling for the maximum of authority with the minimum of risk. So Toosey became in practice a liaison officer between the Japs and our own administration, and there were times when he found himself at odds as much with the latter as the former. The Webber brothers, for example, had brought in their radio and were running it under the cookhouse floor. Was it, as they and Toosey thought, vital to keep it going at any cost or, as the 'committee' feared, too much of a risk to run at this late stage? It was already being used with such circumspection that we knew only the barest international news and no details of the general election at home. And now, with freedom well in sight, we became doubly anxious not to put a foot wrong; the Nips often worked off their frustrations by trying to provoke us into acts that would justify some face-saving brutality. Shimojo, for example, broke one officer's arm with his sword for allegedly moving on parade. Two others were beaten up and put in a cell on rice and water for eight days, one for having an empty pipe in his mouth outside a hut and the other for moving his arms during roll call.

But the chief victim was Bill Drower who, having survived so many crises as interpreter in really squalid camps upriver, might have looked forward to a quieter life in Kanburi. However, Noguchi took against him and was on the look-out for an excuse for humiliation. The excuse came one day when officers on the pump refused to fill a bucket for a Nip medical orderly. This was justifiable, since he was supposed to use the Japanese pump, but tactless – particularly as the orderly was the boy-friend of a Jap Warrant Officer, who created a stink and started bashing right left and centre. Bill was summoned to sort things out, together with Noguchi and Takasaki, and in the course of the argument dared to say that British officers ought not to be beaten up or treated as servants for Japanese privates. Hardly were the words out of his mouth when the other two hurled themselves on him with shrieks of fury, kicked him on the ground, hit him over the head with sticks and split his ear drum; finally he was confined to a flooded air raid trench near the guardroom already occupied by drunken Koreans.

Next day the Japanese officers apologised, not for the fact that Bill had been bashed up but because they themselves had done the bashing rather than delegated it to underlings. Thereafter he was confined to a minute cell for nearly three months, and for the first seven weeks had only rice and water – albeit fortified with vitamins in the cookhouse. Malaria and blackwater fever added to his torture. On a working party one morning we saw him brought out to visit the latrine, a heavily-bearded skeleton tottering between his guards. They had told him that the whole camp was being punished for his arrogance, so when he saw us he just managed to croak out, "Awfully sorry, you chaps; please forgive me!" We felt sickened and, of course, ashamed. If we'd had any guts we'd have organised a strike or at least shouted some words of cheer. But we did nothing, except think, 'There, but for the grace of God, go I!'

That was one of the most demoralising reactions to punishment and torture: the herd instinct; pity giving way to revulsion, and the stricken deer driven from the herd. As far back as Tamarkham days, when a subaltern named Ralph May had struck a Korean and been made to stand outside the guardroom for a month, and many times up and down the river since then, I had felt this. First I identified fully with the victim and each day, as I shambled past, I disintegrated spiritually as he did physically; I grieved for the sunburn, beard and ulcers, the wasting, the increasing droop and dirt; I suffered with him. But gradually there came revulsion: for his inhuman condition, for the ugliness of the scene, for the upset to the natural order. In place of 'Man is a noble animal, splendid in ashes, and pompous in the grave' the allusion changed to:

> Seldom went such grotesqueness with such woe,
> I never saw a brute I hated so;
> He must be wicked to deserve such pain.

Some of the victims were, if not wicked, stupid or selfish, but all too often they truly were, like Bill Drower, 'noble animals'. We were the reeds bending with the wind, and with us, as in more glorious campaigns, it was often the unfittest who survived. In the convict Andaman Islands under the Japs the only literate and educated Indian was the doctor, and it was he who was tortured to death. In Kanburi, while Bill Drower suffered for his temerity on our behalf, we kept our profiles even further below the line of fire. Possibly if Toosey had had the confidence of sole authority he could have made a more effective protest. At least we had the consolation of knowing that even the most fire-breathing of all those senior officers were, on this issue, as circumspect as ourselves.

It is odd how differently moods affect the muse. Some of the saddest verse has been written by depressives – and some of the funniest; men sometimes sing in the rain – and sometimes expire in it. In the idle days of Changi, the mercurial adjutant of Terence's regiment, George Bartley-Dennis, had written a sombre and beautiful sonnet about Dozemany Pool:

> I watched the clouds glide in the pool below
> Like shadows of men restless nor ever still;
> I heard the wheeling gull's cry weird and shrill,
> As once they cried a thousand years ago,
> While in the evening of some autumn day
> The darkness filled this quiet battlefield,
> Shrouding each broken helm, each fallen shield,
> And some lone warrior bore his king away.
> Still the west wind sweeps cold across the lake,
> Shaking the slender rushes to and fro.
> Along the shore tonight the ripples break
> In gold, and still it seems the evening glow
> Shining o'er Camelot and her dead lord
> Flames on the jewelled hilt of Arthur's sword.

One of the Nips' favourite fatigues for us – since it was infinitely long-lasting, labour-intensive and demeaning – consisted of digging out with our bare hands from the moat that surrounded the camp the seepage from the latrines. It was hardly the sort of thing to make you whistle while you worked, but George, working beside me, was inspired to express his feelings in some of his more manic lines:

> In a ditch full of 'water' a bored *shoko* sat
> Singing 'Wallow, shit-wallow, shit-wallow!'
> And all that he wore was a string and a hat,
> Sing 'Wallow, shit-wallow, shit-wallow!'
> 'Is it weakness of intellect, *Shoko*?' I cried
> 'Or some *sambal bajak* that inflames the inside?'
> But shaking the shit from his hair he replied
> 'Oh wallow, shit-wallow, shit-wallow!
>
> Now watching that *Shoko* a bad *gunso* stood,
> Shouting '*Kora! oi Kora!! oi Kora!!!*'
> Adding 'All English *shoko* are no fucking good!'
> With a '*Kora! oi Kora!! oi Kora!!!*'
> 'Oh, bold Son of Heaven, pray tell me,' I cried,
> 'Why your sword is so long and your boots are so wide?'
> But clouting me hard on the ear he replied:-
> '*Kora! oi Kora!! oi Kora!!!*'

20

Poetic Licence

The unpleasant atmosphere of Kanburi officers' camp was compounded by lack of space. There was no room for football pitches or large-scale manufacturing enterprises in which to lose ourselves, though tucked away in one corner a space was found for a leper colony consisting of one Javanese private. Most of us were healthy in body if not in mind, and in the general upheaval were able to choose congenial neighbours on the *bali-bali*. As we were all officers and gentlemen now, I looked forward to sophisticated forms of entertainment.

I had left Changi before the 'university' got into its stride and had never been in a camp on the river where plays were feasible. But at Chungkai, I heard, these had been quite elaborate both in scenery and costumes – so much so that the actors began to identify all too closely with their roles. A camp favourite, with a fruity voice equally effective in dialogue or song, was the avuncular 'Fizzer' Pearson. His feelings towards his 'leading lady' extended to the morning after a performance of *The Circle*, when he made the remark much bandied about the camp: "I could have had Bobby last night, balls or no balls!"

Tales of such glamorous nights fired us at Kanburi to tackle more serious roles. We were encouraged in our theatrical leanings by the enthusiastic direction of Mike Curtis, whom Alex remembered as an authoritative Raina in *Arms and the Man* at Changi. His knowledge of history and literature and of their combination in Shakespeare's plays was inspiring, and we were easily persuaded to read parts for his *Richard II* at Kanburi. We made all the beginner's mistakes of over-emphasis and textual blunders, and Mike patiently showed us how it should be done. "I'm afraid this will be a bit ham," he would say and then, gathering his G-string round him like a regal cloak, transfix us with the deposition scene:

> Now mark me how I will undo myself.
> I give this heavy weight from off my head,
> And this unwieldy sceptre from my hand,
> The pride of kingly sway from out my heart;
> With mine own tears I wash away my balm.

We were just beginning to get the hang of things when the Nips intervened. They had interpreted the falling leaves in a pantomime of *Babes in the Wood* as paratroopers coming to the rescue of sleeping prisoners, and they began to be edgy about anything with dialogue in it. They did not warm to Ian Watt's assertion that 'gentlemen in England now a-bed shall think themselves accurs'd they were not here', and eventually decreed that in future only concerts and revues would be tolerated.

The concerts could be extraordinarily enjoyable, thanks to instruments hoarded in base camps and a few given by the Swiss Consul in Bangkok; and we had two musicians who seemed able to write out almost any score from memory. As we sat on the mud, keeping the mosquitoes at bay with our 'Sikh's Beard' and watching the fruit bats scuttering in and out of the improvised limelight, the plangent strains of Purcell and Handel would give way to thumping chunks of Grieg, 'The New World Symphony', 'Leonora' and *The Barber of Seville*. And as for 'Finlandia', I could positively see the Russians being swept away and feel, with a catch in the throat and smarting eyes, the snowflakes settling on my sweaty skin.

One night we had some excellent musical slapstick in a performance of 'The Hall of the Mountain King'; with a kind of Professor Strabismus conducting. The orchestra was always pretty odd, with an accordion acting as piano, saxophones as clarinets and tubas as French horns, but the Mad Professor added to the confusion by arranging for a succession of anomalies, such as left-handed or one-armed players; these he would spot in mid-cadenza and react to with increasing frenzy. His relief at approaching the finale was so strong that on the first long-drawn-out climactic chords he would turn to the audience with the lowest of self-congratulatory bows, the string hair from his wig flapping over his eyes, only to be brought up short by the orchestra continuing to play behind him. Spinning round, he would catch them up in time to repeat his bow after the next climax, and be caught out again in the same way – and, of course, yet again by the real ending when it came, which he had treated as a pause.

These antics reminded me poignantly of happier days at Clifton when the great Douglas Fox was Director of Music. His career as a concert pianist was ended by the loss of his right arm in World War I, but he had switched to the organ and learned to perform miracles with his left hand. It developed huge muscles and his feet great nimbleness, and as there were plenty of boys to pull out the stops for him, his listeners never suspected their organist had only one arm. When conducting the orchestra in Big School he made no concessions to his disability, turning out in white tie and tails, with the empty sleeve tucked into the right-hand pocket. But as the crescendos mounted they took their toll. The tie would work its way round to the back of his neck, watched by five hundred pairs of eyes, and the sleeve would slip its moorings and wave in ghastly imitation of the conducting left arm. His sense of the ridiculous, however, was not often at fault. The school song had been written by the revered Old Cliftonian, Henry Newbolt:

> For working days or holidays,
> And glad or melancholy days,
> They were great days and jolly days
> At the best school of all!

"And yet," remarked Douglas after a rehearsal, "he sent both his sons to Winchester!"

Music and revues were not the only means of letting off steam at Kanburi, and there was steam building up. Besides being healthier, we were more neurotic than we had been; although the end of the war grew obvious with the German defeat, our own end was still uncertain. The Koreans began to hedge their bets with friendly overtures ("Nippon boom-boom finish I go London you chauffeur

OK-*kah*?") but the Nips became ever more explosive and brutal. Having survived so long, we were not going to stick our necks out now, so anything remotely provocative such as a class or a talk had to be held surreptitiously.

Some of the talks were surreptitious not only because of the Nips but because they would scarcely have pleased our own senior officers. It was fine when Dan Blackater learned chunks of Macaulay's history by heart and reproduced them in the darkened hut to an audience of fellow Indian Army officers. But other people were seeking converts to their political views: there was Bertie Keane, for example, formerly of *Reynold's News*, a councillor for East Ham and prospective Labour candidate for Colchester. And there was scruffy, balding Norris Lindsay Emmerson, nurtured at Eton ('eaten and brought up' as we used to say wittily), academically brilliant and with a slight twitch ('the tic of King's' our fellow prisoner and his contemporary at Cambridge, Graham Hough, called it, adding disapprovingly, "he's so untidy, he uses a raw egg as a book mark!"). A leader-writer for the *Statesman of India* and a closet Communist, Emmerson had impressed Terence at 'Changi University' (after I had left for Sime Road) as a lecturer on philosophy. At least he had impressed him *at the time*; now all he could remember of his lectures on symbolic logic was the advice that it was a waste of time reading books on the subject because they were all similar in devoting the first few pages to the author's premises and all the rest to refuting every possible objection to them. At Kanburi, Emmerson lowered his sights a bit and, perhaps influenced by years of enforced intimacy with its army, made our flesh creep with subversive talks on Home Rule for India. Before going into details of the Nizam of Hyderabad driving his Rolls over the crunching bones of his adoring subjects, he would make a great to-do about screening his audience and exacting oaths of secrecy, thereby ensuring an atmosphere of privilege and awe. I had been honoured with the confidence of Emmerson through another new acquaintance, Ian Henderson.

As we were building the camp at Kanburi and more and more officers poured into it, there was a re-shuffling among the huts and we three from the Tamuang hospital ward found ourselves the nucleus of a new little Bloomsbury. Besides Terence Charley and

Alex Hellawell, there were John Durnford, Stuart Simmonds, Jack Stogumber, Ian Henderson and Smodger Smith (a dour Chelsea art student, not the Roger Smith who had the fall on the *Sobieski* and now spent every spare moment playing bridge with Graham Searles). There was also Bertie Keane, who crept in somehow under the lee of Terence Charley; I suppose somebody had to fill the role of Saki's 'Mrs Pentherby'. His cocksure simplicities freed me from any temptation to fall for socialist ideology or to believe anything I read in the papers – 'GANDHI COMING IN HIS LOIN CLOTH' was a headline that Bertie liked to repeat as an awful warning to pi sub-editors. He also taught us the value of insubordination. Turned down at his OCTU by a colonel who commented that a Labour Party official was scarcely officer material, he had got hold of Arthur Greenwood, who soon fixed the colonel for him. Perhaps, except to snobs like us, Bertie was the salt of the earth, but Terence had been enraged to find under his pillow an India paper anthology belonging to George Bartley-Dennis with half its pages torn out, long after most people had adopted Moslem rites. His bumptiousness particularly irked Jack Stogumber, to whom he showed signs of taking a shine. Jack retaliated with a triolet:

> Though our minds are dark and dirty
> Nature made us hard to please.
> Bumptious, sagging, shrewd and thirty –
> Though our minds are dark and dirty –
> Who could fancy poor old Bertie?
> Luckily for us he sees
> Though our minds are dark and dirty
> Nature made us hard to please.

Ian Henderson was probably more subversive at heart than Bertie but he was better looking and endowed with that Etonian air of genial assurance which covers a multitude of sins. His life had been glamorous, with spells at Oxford, Heidelberg and the Sorbonne, and early marriage to an actress. He combined a nodding acquaintance with the great with a relish for low life; the charm and confidence of his elitist upbringing had an anarchic edge to it. Perhaps that was why he was an actor – and not yet a successful one.

The only chance we got of judging his talent was his rendering at a camp concert of 'My Old Man Said Follow the Van'. He had won an MC in the campaign but never talked of it nor of his regiment, and seemed intent on exploring avenues as far removed from authority as possible. In this quest he took a proprietorial interest in his old school guru Emmerson, and did his best to bring us under his seedy spell. I found myself immune to this and chided him for whoring after false gods.

> Ian irreligious? Why,
>   He owns a blood-red God
> Who, when he lays his aura by,
>   Is bald and rather odd
> And has the nervous tic of Kings';
>   And Ian sits – poor sod! –
> With bated breath and glowing eye
>   And thinks Romantic Things.
>
> But if his God should doff his crown
>   And talk to you or me,
> The jealous Ian shouts us down
>   Before his deity.
> He knocks us all about a bit –
>   Oh, we are very out of it –
> But I don't mind it, not a bit,
>   For I am C of E!

We talked interminably about religion and politics, designing a brave new world where artists – modernists, of course, like Smodger – would set the design for living. Smodger himself, having had his semi-abstract drawings confiscated by the Nips, was driven nearly mad when they kept asking him to copy photos of their wives and children; a Christian Korean even asked him for a Virgin and Child.

"I don't know, Stephen," said Ian, "if you're being serious when you say you're C of E. But it won't get you far after the war."

Was I serious? I don't think any of us, except John Durnford, got much out of camp services. In my worst moments I prayed for a divine miracle, but Jesus seemed reluctant to 'bow hither out of heaven and see and save'. The padres had a hard time promoting a New Jerusalem in the waterlogged pox-ridden jungles, or a house of many mansions in the wired-in compounds of the egg belt. But the sonorities of the Prayer Book did remind me of bells across the rhynes and monuments in Quantock churches, and the hymns recalled motets in candlelit cathedrals. They in turn reminded me of the land and family that awaited me, and perhaps I went to services for this reassurance rather than in search of God. I should have found Him in the Bible, but the Old Testament was unsustaining, apart from offering comparisons with the Jews in captivity (and what a humourless lot they were compared to us!), while the New Testament was directed at settled communities living under a beneficent colonial rule (like ours!) which, with a mixture of academic nit-picking and irrational rhetoric, it seemed concerned to disturb. So how far had my faith been dependent on family and national solidarity? Were all faiths dependent on family and nation? Could any faith be truly international?

We talked about this, and the more we talked about it, the more inconsistencies we found in all religions: the simple grace of Malay mosques, the charm (if not too loud) of the call to prayer, and the ritual use of water, but also the dotty inhibitions about food and drink and about women; the informality and serenity of saffron-clad Buddhist monks in their pretty temples, but also the dirt around them and the sick or starving dogs that could never be put out of their misery; the flamboyance of Hindu temples, but also the dubious purpose there of the *lingam* and *yoni*, and the scumminess of the water tanks. As for the pleasant design and fine settings of Shinto shrines, they didn't make our guards behave any better towards us. Perhaps this was because Shinto was not a textual religion and the Japanese, springing directly from the Sun God, were not 'people of the book'. Other religions had their two elements, the moral and the mystic, the rational and the incantatory. In the dear old C of E these had polarised, on the one hand into sermonising, which was too often inhibiting and philistine, and on the other into ritual or music of the most rarified kind.

We didn't object to this last element, either in the C of E or any other religion. Wasn't that how everything worked? All education began with a form of ritual, learning by rote, whether in a mosque or a kindergarten. Army training began with ritual too; there was no difference between square-bashing and bashing heads in unison on a carpet. In England we were lucky that our form of ritual chanting had reached such sublime heights. But, as Stuart pointed out, religious ritual could lead to even more sublime heights in total silence, in meditation. So much so that, instead of coming to yourself with a bump as you did after listening to a Bach chorale, you simply became one with Surya and mingled with the beyond.

It was the preaching element in the C of E that I objected to, reacting to the 'said' psalms and long Low Church sermons I had been subjected to, until rescued by compulsory attendance at school chapel. What an opportunity had been missed in all those Sunday sermons! Here we all were, gathered together and in receptive mood and what did we get? The same Bible-babble week after week, and the British as the lost tribes of Israel. Why didn't we test the Christian message against others? Why didn't we read other texts from the lectern and talk about them from the pulpit? What were Joel, Habbakuk and Jude to us, when we could be listening to Huxley, Boswell and Aubrey, to Voltaire, Marco Polo and the *Thirty-three Happy Moments*? That would soon cure our imperial urge to convert people who were perfectly happy with their own religions?

"If you ask my opinion," said Terence, "which nobody ever does, which is why I give it without being asked, otherwise they'd never know what it was, which would be a pity as they'd be missing something, and even more of a pity for me because I'd feel I hadn't contributed my bit towards the welfare of mankind, and why nobody ever does ask my opinion I fail to understand, as I'm always asking them theirs – well, aren't I? – because I'm curious and interested in people's opinions, and why they aren't interested in mine is something that seems to me very curious, very curious indeed. . . . Where was I?"

Stuart, he was reminded, had said our soul could jump the wire and mingle with the beyond, while I had proposed mingling Bible-readings with the Upanishads.

"But if we're all to absorb each other's faiths and culture, we'll merely become wishy-washy Unitarians or, worse still, Theosophists."

"I didn't say that. Culture yes, faith no. Faith should be formulated into a practical state religion. It should suit the state and give it backbone but also give it tolerance, which is where the wisdom of the ages comes in. We need to know what other people think, not what they believe. Most people don't know what they believe anyway, but that doesn't invalidate what they write or compose or paint. Suppose the local church were a wireless set and every Sunday you switched on from habit and heard the same old stuff, you wouldn't go on paying the licence fee for long. Well, if the BBC has to vary its programme, why not the church?"

The idea was an appealing one, as each of us saw himself endowed with a divine authority to stand up and feed the hungry sheep with something *he* happened to know but they did not. Ian Watt would read the Gospel according to St Leavis, beginning with the chapter on Conrad; Alex the Dialogues of Plato (in translation), Terence *The Golden Bough*, Stuart 'Fishes' Heaven' by Rupert Brooke, Ian Henderson *Les Fleurs du Mal*, Jack *Candide*. I would read *John Inglesant*, and John Durnford *Cavalcade*.

These amusements took us away from the tricky subject of moral worth to the lighter ones of prosody and style. Guthrie's choice of Francis Thompson:

> Yea, in the night, my soul, my daughter,
> Cry, clinging Heaven by the hems;
> And lo, Christ walking on the water,
> Not of Gennesareth, but Thames!

sidetracked us into his reason for calling his soul his daughter. Was it a reference to the daughters of Jerusalem? Stuart thought it serendipitous. As he had said before, the exigencies of rhyming often brought more striking results than did more logical words that would not have rhymed. Which, said Ian Henderson, was why fully-inflected languages like French and Spanish often had such boring poetry; there were no happy accidents, just rhyming suffixes jogging along one behind the other. Though, warned Ian Watt, it cut both ways; rhymes were very limiting, and Wordsworth, for instance, was always rhyming 'flowers' with 'powers' and 'hours'. Once Thompson had plumped for 'water', he didn't leave himself much room for manoeuvre. Like the World War I author, said Alex, who wrote 'Wash me in the water that washed the Colonel's daughter, and I shall be whiter than the whitewash on the wall'.

"Obviously," said Jack, "great minds think alike:

> It's hard on my daughter, sir,
> Can't hold her water, sir,
> Whenever she laughs she pees.
> Look, there she goes, sir,
> All down her clothes, sir.
> Don't make her laugh, sir – please!"

As so often, we had descended from the sublime to the ridiculous, but I still stood by my theory. Of course there were snags in practice, but the details could be worked out easily enough. At least the C of E would be on the move instead of being dull as ditch water. As it was, people would stop going to church altogether as soon as there were better things to do on a Sunday.

"There are now, in Catholic countries," said Ian Henderson. "People nip in and out of mass as quickly as they can and go off to play *boules*. They don't want to spend hours in church listening to Voltaire. So don't waste your visions in the Church, Alexander. There are far too many visionaries there already. Use them in something better paid. The best place for you after the war is the British Council."

"The British Council? What's that?"

"A semi-official cultural hands-across-the-sea thing. Suit you down to the ground. You're wasting your time trying to tart up the Church. Parsons have always been philistine and suspicious of the arts."

Not all parsons, we protested. There was all that Morris dancing at Thaxted, and before that William Barnes, and Thomas Barham and Sydney Smith, and Herrick and Sterne and Swift, and what about the Laudians and the Tractarians?

"The Laudians? How long did they last? And I don't see the Anglo-Catholics keeping up their expensive habits after the war.

Anyhow, I don't believe in all this backward-looking business. To hell with tradition. Nineteen hundred is as far back as we ought to go. Stuart and Alex are quite right to be learning Empsonian tricks."

"I'm not sure about that," said Alex, "I was sitting on the *padang* the other evening with George Sully and Emmerson and found the conversation much too elevated. George talked knowingly about Eliot, whom he referred to as 'Old Tom', and I found I could take little part in it all. I was merely made to feel callow and uneducated."

Well, we others would show the Watts, the Moirs, the Sullys and the Emmersons that if we lacked their erudition, we could at least practice the craft of versification. However, while the rest of us struggled to imitate the modern masters, John Durnford would infuriate us by his facility with tried and trusted formulae. We would gaze into space, crossing out the few lines we had written on the set subject of, say, 'Nostalgia', while John would lie back on the *bali-bali*, say, "There you are!", and toss at us his:

POW Dream

> Last night I dreamed I was at home again.
> The blind cord on the window pane
> Tapped at the wind's suggestion, the last look
> Of the fire round the room, over my book
> Faltered and fell. Over the gravel ran
> The wind chasing the leaves; lights began
> Leaving the houses the opposite side
> Of the town. I opened the window wide,
> And put a hand down into the cool well
> Of the garden, and the light fell
> Over my shoulder on the lawn below.
> There was so little sound; the slow
> Gear-change betrayed the headlight
> Climbing up the hill, and out of sight
> The last dog barked; a bell rang late
> From a hidden steeple; past the front gate
> Some footsteps clattered home . . .
>   And here?

Here the moon pitiless patrols a clear
And unfamiliar sky; the over-shrill
Cicadas penetrate the close and still
Atmosphere. And in their huts are men
Waiting for sleep to take them home again.

We were fearfully jealous and accused John of being too derivative, particularly of Sassoon. And his sonnets were not innocent of
vaingloriousness:

Psalm 137

Be sure of this, no sufferings matched your own;
Egypt and Babylon fell long ago,
Be comforted you do not weep alone.
Complacent and indifferent worlds shall know
Sorrow like Israel's and a wilderness
(Such as those other children wandered in);
Whose sun destroyed the flesh made to caress,
And fevers sucked the blood beneath the skin;
Where if a yard was costly, lives were cheap,
And fear of company and want of rest
Made grown-up men cry as they turned to sleep
For the remoteness of another breast,
When by the bitter waters of disgrace
Sat down to weep another 'chosen race'.

But what upset us most was that John was so nearly a good poet.
If only he would take longer (like us) and write half as much twice
as well! But, alas, that is not how inspiration works, and though the
poems rolling off his production line were far better than ours, they
ended all too often in a dying fall.

These poetry games may not have been the most improving way
to pass our days but at least they passed them; it was at night that I
felt as lonely and bereft as John. The damp heat pressed down; the
body itched and shifted, setting off the sweet-sour smell of squashed
bedbugs; mosquitoes dive-bombed – outside the net or inside?
INSIDE, dammit! I try the water in the bottle; it is warm. 'I am
drinking on a winter's night, and suddenly note that the night has

turned extremely cold. I push open the window and see that snowflakes come down the size of a palm and there are already three or four inches of snow on the ground. Ah, is this not happiness?' Yes, my dear old Chin Shengt'an, it is; and you may well say so, with your obliging wife, gorgeous gardens, bobbing boats and pretty pictures. But we had none of these things. There was no snow here and, ah, at night this was not happiness.

Who knew what horrid phantoms of newsroom or council chamber haunted Bertram Keane? Or for Ian Henderson, what worries about his wife and her acting – and her acting up? Was Stuart missing the dear dead days at the bank in Southampton and the escapist glamour of the Territorials? Or wondering how much his father was missing him, or how much more his favourite younger son, John? And John? Was he a brigadier by now? Well, he'd throw him up a salute when they met and see if he had the nerve to take it seriously.

At least for Alex the doubts about following his forebears into the dark satanic mills vanished at night in the roseate glow of memory. When sleep eluded him he counted – like sheep jumping a fence – the mills where the yarns of T. Hellawell & Co. were spun, jogging his memory by linking the final and initial letters of their names; Durban mill to Nile, Nile to Elk, Elk to Knowles, Knowles to Sparth, Sparth to Holdsworth Bros, and Holdsworth to – heigh ho! – Hellawell, and he was away, tucking himself behind the last of his cotton flock to clear the fence and, with it, the boundary of sleep.

But it was at night that Terence felt at his most impotent and wondered if there would ever be an end to it all; the hours standing under the stars on 'pee picket', the high-pitched whirr of the cicadas, the futile croaking of frogs in the *padi*, the silent sentry pacing the perimeter in the moonlight, the crackling of the cookhouse fires at four o'clock in the morning as breakfast was prepared, the flashes of summer lightning in the distance; back in the hut the interminable whine of mosquitoes, the chirruping of *chichas* in the roof, and the faint rustle of a hundred men breathing in the dark; and, across the wide field separating the camp from the town, ordinary noises of people going about their affairs, a thrumming of drums, singing, the

notes of a pipe, a murmur of voices and sudden peals of laughter
that showed that some people at any rate found life amusing.

John Durnford was the only one of us to welcome the night as a
friend to his muse, and I would wake in the small hours to find 'the
factory' working overtime beside me.

> The Thailand night is hushed in slumber,
> Sleep the golden orioles.
> The sad pariahs howl and number
> Ours with their degraded souls.
> Kanburi tolls us hourly, hourly
> Nearer freedom, nearer death;
> The lively burdened *bali-bali*
> Creaks beneath our tortured breath.
> And I alone lie wakeful, watching
> *Attap* fret the flaccid moon –
> But, soft! I hear a furtive scratching,
> Can it be I spoke too soon?
> Yes, overtime, mosquito-netted,
> Where a vagrant moonbeam lights,
> The factory functions – silhouetted,
> Durnford writes!

21

Too Many Vitamins

DISTRESSING as our night thoughts were, they were as nothing to the fancies that took hold of us by day. With the nervy state of the camp, introspection flowered in unexpected corners.

One evening I was squatting outside the hut, cleaning my mess tin with earth from the drain and water from my all-purpose bottle. As I scraped away at the remnants of rice and dried fish, I sensed that I was not alone and, looking up, saw a chap I hadn't seen before watching me. He smiled and moved nearer.

"Hullo there! Can I talk to you a moment?"

Squatting beside me, he took out an anti-gas ointment tin, rolled a cigarette and offered me a fill of his Sikh's Beard tobacco. A little map of ringworm was spreading across his belly and I declined.

"We haven't met, but I think you can help me. You look the sort of chap who'd understand what I want to talk about. And I think you could keep a secret."

"Oh, it's hush-hush, is it?"

"Nothing to do with hidden radios, if that's what you mean. But it *is* in confidence. And I think I can trust you to keep it to yourself."

He launched into a long story beginning in the early days of Changi, when we'd had little to do but feel hungry. One of the ways to keep our minds off the subject of food, though I hadn't heard of it myself, had apparently been to start Old School societies – the schools, of course, being the snootier public schools. My new friend had been at Nottingham High, but in an evil moment had pretended he'd been at Marlborough. He'd been holed up under shot and shell with a garrulous Old Rugbeian from another brigade and, not expecting to see him again and not to be outdone in fashionable reminiscence, he had used a cousin's tales of Marlborough's prison architect and chapel and quaint masters to add verisimilitude to his claim. To his horror they had met again on a firewood fatigue in Changi. He was hailed as an Old Marlburian and introduced to a genuine Old Boy, who kept pressing him to join their society. To escape his tormentor, he had volunteered for the first party leaving Changi and had never seen him again. But now that all officers were converging on Kanburi, he dreaded another encounter.

"And, d'you know, I've actually been hoping that he died upriver. Isn't that awful? Well, that's my story, and it's really been giving me hell. But I was sure that if only I could talk to somebody, somebody sensitive," here he laid a hand not on my knee, because a squatting position is not conducive to it, but on the arm dangling over it, "I'd feel better! And of course someone who's been to a public school. I've heard you talking and assume you have."

"You should hear me sing," I said, and sang:

> The men that tanned the hide of us,
>   Our daily foes and friends,
> They shall not lose their pride of us,
>   Howe'er the journey ends.
>
> Their voice, to us who sing of it,
>   No more its message bears,
> But the round world shall ring of it
>   And all we are be theirs.

"I say! That's not Marlborough, is it?"

"No, Clifton."

"Oh, well, er . . . good! You don't know what a relief it is to have it out at last. What d'you think I ought to do if this chap does arrive here?"

"You'd better come clean. After what we've been through since then, who cares what anyone said in Changi three years ago?"

"You're right, you're absolutely right. And you will keep this quiet, won't you? It's just between us two. Isn't it?"

"Er – yes; well, I must be off. Another – er – hush-hush thing, as a matter of fact." Embarrassment made me effusive. "D'you know Emmerson? It's another of his talks on India. They're hilarious."

And that, I thought, was that. But soon I began to notice him hovering wordlessly on the fringes of the elect: Philip Hay (Harrow) playing piquet with Edward Douglas-Home (Eton), Harold Cassel (Stowe) refighting desperate battles of the courtroom, and Jim Swanton (Cranleigh) even more desperate ones of the cricket field. Then one day, during a tea break from a working party I saw him closeted with Ian Henderson.

"Ian, who was that chap . . . ?"

"No idea; never seen him before; didn't tell me his name."

"What were you talking about?"

"Mind your own bloody business!"

"Did he say that you looked sensitive and discreet? And make you promise not to tell anyone about Marlborough and Nottingham High?"

"He did!"

"And asked you what he ought to do?"

"He did."

"What did you tell him?"

"Told him to keep quiet. If the other fellow does see him again, the last thing he'll be thinking about by now will be his old school tie. I said he'd be absolutely dotty to bring the subject up himself and have a kind of Oxford Group thing over it."

"Oh? How did he take that?"

"Said I was absolutely right. And he was pathetically grateful; as a matter of fact I had a bit of a job getting away from him. And I didn't take to him one bit; not my type at all!"

"How did you manage it?"

"I said I had to go to one of Emmerson's Indian talks, which really were hush-hush. I said they were the genuine article, and if the Indian Army colonels knew about them they'd have his guts for garters. That shut him up all right. As a matter of fact he gave me quite a funny look."

After that our mutual friend gave us both a wide berth and he made no attempt to break into the charmed circle of Norris Emmerson. On the other hand we spotted him elsewhere many times talking apart to one bemused listener after another.

Was our penitent really seeking absolution from the fountainhead? Or was this his labyrinthine way of testing the wind in quite a different line of country? To my sharpened senses, hitherto unnoticed indicators did indeed seem to point in this direction, and I realised that the preoccupations of Fizzer Pearson on and off stage at Chungkai were now commonplace in Kanburi. Reviving physical vitality coupled with Nip constraints on mental exercise was bringing to the surface feelings long dormant. I was yarning one evening with Granville Keane and a matter-of-fact young farmer named Jim Flower, and gradually I found myself showing off and being unusually vital and amusing. I was obviously not doing it to impress dear old Granny, and I realised that what I was doing was – flirting. I saw that even Granny's eyes in the flickering light of the palm-oil lamp had an unusual gleam in them and that we were both behaving as if we were trying to impress a pretty barmaid in a pub. Increasingly, twosomes were starting to detach themselves from their fellows, and when I remarked on this phenomenon to Terence, expecting some deprecating words of wisdom, I was taken aback by the earthiness of his reply.

"Oh, yes, has it only hit you now? Many of us have been regressing to our schooldays ever since we hit the egg belt, and of course I've been in it longer than some of you. The better rations at Chungkai soon had me on the hop, and the stage shows didn't help my dreams a bit. But the female impersonators among the officers usually had their 'protectors', and when I felt the sparks flying with anyone in the ranks, I had to remember that even if I couldn't think like a gentleman, I had to act like an officer. As Schopenhauer says, 'to be alone is the fate of all great minds – a fate deplored at times, but still always chosen as the less grievous of two evils'. Needless to say, that wasn't the fate of this particular great mind for long. But the trouble was that there was nowhere you could *go*. However, I did eventually become hut commander in the hospital, where hierarchical distinctions were weaker. There was scope for a flutter or two there. But the slats of the *bali-bali* make neither the most comfortable nor the most discreet platform for venery."

Feeling properly abashed at our inexperience, we looked around us with new eyes, perhaps hoping to find relief from the boredom of our surroundings. One who remained impervious to the newly-charged atmosphere was Alex, who somehow fell prey to a shortage rather than a surfeit of vitamins. For some time he had felt more and more constricted, and now, with a woeful lack of sympathy from the hut, retired to be circumcised.

But the rest of us were not yet thus inhibited, and in our little Bloomsbury the muse became heavily infected. Jack Stogumber was very taken with a dim but affable marine named George, and chided us for sitting about arguing and splitting hairs. Stuart's immortal first line of Changi days – 'Eye upon chalk-line, hypnotised is hen' – was still bandied about, and inspired Jack's ridicule.

> I pity the poor intellectual
>> Whose body is ruled by his mind,
> Making joys of the flesh ineffectual
>> By leaving his instincts behind.
>
> Farewell to political fancies
>> And mathematising of Man,
> I'll revel in all the romances
>> And sin all the sins that I can.
>
> Farewell to you, Intelligentsia!
>> The chalk-lines – not chains – that you forge
> May hypnotise Stuart or Terence here;
>> I'm off to be happy with George.

Stuart himself was becoming more and more interested in mysticism and not least in its erotic aspects. Terpsichore could ask him to dance with her over and over again now, only to find his eyes straying to other chances further east. He had practised his Thai whenever he got the chance, and one can hardly exercise Thai with the lads and lassies in the fields and the boats and the jungle without exercising the imagination too.

> Climb the tall arepa palm
> Step the smooth and supple stem

Cut the hanging clusters down,
Stealing from the guarding green
The fruit full-grown:
And every one
An orange sun . . .
Lay the flesh in lips aside
With the cold bright blade,
Break the hidden nut apart
And uncover in its heart
This hanging tear. . .
And now you hear
The throbs and shiver of the single drum
That calls you, calls you – 'Come'.

He had found a Dutch scholar named de Casparis from whom
he learned about Sanskrit and its monuments, and he was moved by
some book illustrations to address the 'Artist who carved the ele-
phant relief in the King's Palace':

The elephants perpetual
Move in great stones along the wall
At Angkor Thom.

Was stone laid upon stone
In a dry wall
Waiting to feel the fall
Of your live chisel?

Or did a miracle
Raise up this wall
To meet the ready hand
That moulds your mind
Alive into the stone?

They are upgrown in one
Who lift their silent feet
In file along the wall;
Need leave no print to prove
This love, your use to build,

Is less ephemeral
Than love which moulds the child.

"This is rather exciting, Stuart," said Terence. "I must say I am relieved. I was beginning to worry about you in those Thai villages. In fact I composed a little ode to express my misgivings."

In a W. B. Yeats sing-song he recited the following ditty:

Little boys are running
Naked in the sand
Brown from too much sunning –
O, but so becoming!
Waiting for the poet –
Little do they know it –
Who will understand.

Little boys are cooing
Soft as any dove.
What is Surya doing?
Why (good Lord above!)
Poet's eyes are wooing,
Faint but still pursuing,
Poetry – not love.

Little boys are swathing
Body in sarong.
Some would say their bathing
Made the poet's song.
Others would be scathing?
Others would be wrong.

Looking back on this stage of our demoralisation, I can't help wondering what the Nips might have made of it. The news must have been stoking up their paranoia for months: Germany had let them down badly; Brussels, Warsaw and Italy abandoned, and in March Cologne surrendered. The grand design of *Germany-bom-bom-England* and then *Nippon-bom-bom-Germany* had misfired. Nearer home America, like a great dragon breathing a deadly fire, was consuming the Philippines, Iwo Jima and Okinawa, and in April, with Roosevelt *sleepo-no-good*, things were still no better. In May Rangoon fell and Germany surrendered, and the round faces in camp were very long indeed. Egged on by the unspeakable 'Old Nog', our captors were in no mood to be trifled with, devising ever worse humiliations that drove lesser mortals among us to paroxysms of effing and blinding, and even the courtly and aptly-named Jocelyn de Winton to exclaim: "It really is too bad of the Japanese!". And all this was done in the conviction that where two or three were gathered together trouble was brewing. Had they monitored our actual discussions, our strange allusive phrases would have alarmed them even more. 'The colonel's daughter', 'Odol smile', 'Egypt and Babylon', 'elephants perpetual', 'Gandhi coming in his loin cloth', 'shit-wallow, shit-wallow, shit-wallow'. Obviously no grown men, let alone those tall arrogant *ingresu-shoko* devils, would talk in such a way unless they were using a fiendishly complicated code.

22

Nacom Nyok

EVER more humiliations were no joke. Edicts went forth that we mustn't smoke when lying on the *bali-bali*; we mustn't wash before mid-day; we mustn't read or play games before six in the evening; we must not visit other people's huts. Just when the pace was quickening in the world outside, time in our miserable little corner seemed to stand still. Day after day, if we weren't out on a footling fatigue or working party, or lining up for yet another *tenko*, we would sit feeling sorry for ourselves in a kind of suspended and sweaty animation, all the stuffing knocked out of us for any more taxing physical or intellectual effort. The blazing midday sun bounced down onto the *attap* roofs and illuminated everything outside with a hard, dry brilliancy that, as Terence said, would almost break if you threw a stone into it. And in the distance came the ironic hoot of the siren from the paper factory. "Bloody thing," he complained. "You never know whether it's announcing the passing of the hours or another air raid." And all this time poor Bill Drower's fate hung like a cloud over us.

So it was with mixed feelings that in July we heard of another move, this time to Nacom Nyok, a hundred and eighty kilometres north-east of Bangkok. We would start by train and boat, but the journey would also involve a day's march of fifty kilometres carrying all our kit. Toosey elected to go with the advance party of four hundred under Lieutenant Takasaki, the Frog. Our own group left on Monday, August 6th, under Knocker Knights, with the attendance of Sergeant Shimojo, and other groups were to follow. News had filtered back that we were to build the new camp in virgin jungle but that all round it were concentrations of Nip troops and ammunition dumps which had been cut into the limestone hills by British other rank working parties. Helpful Koreans told us it was the officer bumping-off camp, and that the machine guns encircling it would shoot at the first hint of a Thai rising – which we had already heard was planned for August 18th. I assumed that with so many of our planes about, agents had been dropped to help with it, but I did not know some were already within thirty kilometres of Kanburi. David Greig, the new interpreter, was in a state of great anxiety, scarcely allayed by the Koreans assuring him that they would come over to us in our hour of need.

After the soft, yet uneasy, living in Kanburi, the prospect of the journey to Nacom Nyok revived memories of privations upriver. Yet the challenge in itself was welcome after the claustrophobia of our camp. Alex had to stay behind because he'd developed a corneal ulcer and his eyes were bandaged. Mike Curtis came to his rescue, partly from the goodness of his heart and partly to exercise the twin pleasures of reading aloud and educating someone. He read from G. Lowes Dickinson's *Modern Symposium*, but its pacifist message seemed to Alex like closing the stable door a very long time after the horse had bolted. Jim Swanton also came to his aid, but Alex was not converted, least of all in his then state, by the arguments of the book he had chosen, Arnold Lunn's *Now I See*.

Ian Henderson and John Durnford were staying too, and due to follow in a later party. I entrusted John with the secret of where I had hidden my diary: inside one of the bamboo struts of the hospital roof. There was a chance that his later party would be reprieved by an armistice, while there was a greater chance that I should be searched en route for the new camp or bumped off when I got there; so my immortal words seemed safer in Kanburi, which was also too public, I hoped, for pogroms.

We entrained at a level crossing at three thirty in the afternoon, with as much bullshit as we could muster, Shimojo clanking about with his curved sword swinging, corporals bowing and hissing and grooms steering ponies aboard. We sat till six thirty in open trucks getting very thirsty, then moved four hundred yards to Kanburi station, waited another two hours – and got our first rocket for trying to stretch our legs. At last we started rolling again, and went fifty kilometres down the line past our old rugger field at Tamuang, past that evil and involuntary Venice of the East, Ban Pong, to Nong Pladuk, where we spent the night warding off mosquitoes with Sikh's Beard, and trying to sleep.

We were jerked awake at four in the morning by planes going over, and scattered into the *ulu* (our preferred Malay word for bush or jungle). The Koreans disappeared and earned half an hour's haranguing from Shimojo. Back in the truck we settled down to our haversack breakfast: 'doovers' (from 'hors d'oeuvres', i.e. rice cakes flavoured with whatever was going – gravy, dried fish, dahl, or simply salt; the attraction was their crispness, from being moulded and then blackened on a rice *kwali*, which contrasted with the blandness of boiled rice); and 'pot-pourri' – the boiled rice dish with anything else available in it; and the ubiquitous but blessed peanuts. After breakfast we trundled on a few kilometres to Nacom Pathom with its orange stupa, serenely indifferent to the squalor round us, and shining high in the morning sun. Then we reached the Tha Chin, where a bombed bridge forced us to detrain and cross by ferry. The hand of God, we learned later, here struck down the Nip Warrant Officer, Mura, and his catamite who had caused the Drower disaster; they were swept away and drowned.

Beyond the river we sat in a coconut grove in the rain until dark, when we were packed into another train and found ourselves climbing over Japanese casualties from Burma. They had been told they were a disgrace to the Nippon Army and would have to look after themselves; their journey had already taken weeks and weeks and the stench was fearful; daylight revealed childlike shaven heads, punched with holes from which eyes stared out feverishly. The fit Japanese laughed at them, officers and men alike, and ridiculed us for giving them food and water. Some of the wounded were pathetically grateful; others showed no sign of life.

Our thirst would have been desperate by the time we reached the Menam Chao Phraya had it not been for the limes we were able to buy here and there. We detrained in the dark and transferred in a chaos of shouting and bashing to sampans, the tall Korean brute, the Undertaker, being in particularly fine fettle; there were fifty of us to each boat, lit up by great bonfires on the river bank. I was in the middle of a sampan and felt stifled after hours of alternate soaking and baking but dozed fitfully as we drifted down river. And then suddenly – WHOOSH! – a big junk came shearing out of the dark and only just missed us. I came to in a panic to find two of the Suffolks, Freddy Yorke and Guthrie Moir, tumbling on top of me. Fearful images flitted through my mind of being caught like the submariners in the *Thetis*, a picture graven on my memory since seeing the film at the age of twelve. (We Scouts had been taken to the cinema from a camp near Axminster, and my horror mounted as the trapped men watched the water rising round them, to build up pressure for the Davis Apparatus. Perhaps my memory was made the more vivid because at the most tense moment my dashing and admired scoutmaster, Martin Hardcastle, put a reassuring hand on my bare knee.)

But our Menam Chao Phraya *Thetis* was mercifully righted; we sorted ourselves out and by dawn disembarked about twelve kilo-metres downriver at some godowns near Bangkok. There we stayed two days, imprisoned in steel and concrete for the first time in three years, and were put to work shifting sand. On the second day a Thai threw a packet of cigarettes into the godown, with a note on it: 'More tomorrow'. Two chaps grabbed it but the Nips were on them like a flash and beat them savagely. On a day of extremes we had a marvellously refreshing bathe in a brackish pool, and back in the godown I enjoyed the incongruity of Fanny Burney's diary. Owing to rearrangements for the sick, I was split up from Terence and Stuart who were put in Shimojo's later party. In ours there were thirty-three to a truck with two Koreans. We were shunted about in Bangkok all day, passing our old friends the Japanese sick and wounded, and some bombed-out railway workshops. By the time darkness fell we had sweated gallons. The Koreans drank three bottles of hooch and bought us some cakes. I sucked limes to assuage my raging thirst, and we left Bangkok to travel north-east across gleaming *padi* fields.

We detrained somewhere near Prachit Buri at three in the morn-ing under a hysterical Nip sergeant and a heavy fall of rain. I drank half a pint of precious water and we started to march in the dark. The ground was level and I kept falling asleep on my feet, the only time I had done so since doing sentry duty at Oswestry. Sleep swirled up, I fought against it, stepping out more strongly; it enveloped me again, I fought it; and so the cycle went on, bringing me nearer and nearer to what I knew was the brink of a nebulous drop; at last I gave way, and for one blissful moment (of how many seconds or fractions of a second?) I hung, borne up weightlessly while my kit floated off on its own. Then, with a sickening lurch forward and a jolt as my knee jack-knifed, I was marching again with my pack hammering me into the ground.

After fifteen kilometres we halted in daylight for breakfast, a mess tin of 'pot-pourri' from the godown with a glorious pint of water. Back on the march my last lime was soon gone and the dry stabs of thirst grew sharper. Our first casualty, an apparently tough young Aussie, dropped out and was left, after much Korean screaming, to be collected by a truck. The old sweats among us were falling back, and when the truck came up they managed to put some kit on it. I felt completely exhausted by lunchtime, but we had three hours' rest and I used some chlorine tablets I had been hoarding since Singapore days, shaking them up with water from a murky pool. At supper time there were no murky pools, only hoof prints left by bullocks in the mud, filled with green scummy water, but, undaunted, I quaffed another chlorine cocktail. We marched on till dark, with the sick being prodded along and a good deal of kit being thrown away. 'Marched' was by now a euphemism, and our halts increased from ten minutes in the hour to ten minutes every half hour.

We left the main road about eleven that night and took to a track, often having to turn back from false trails. I was dreadfully tired again but hung grimly onto my kit – determined to be well turned out for that vaunted Victory Parade. The Koreans, having lined us up for *tenkos* all day, disappeared and left us to make our own time. I had volunteered for fatigues en route but decided to help the sick no longer; it was all I could do to help myself. Two of our remaining forty-four, out of a hundred, collapsed and were eventually retrieved on stretchers. At four in the morning, after a march and shamble of fifty-five kilometres in twenty hours, familiar smells greeted us – felled bamboo, cookhouse smoke, latrines – and we had arrived.

"Well done, chaps!" said Toosey, looking as if he'd just come off church parade, Herbert Johnson on head, knee-length socks freshly washed, and worn *veldtschoen* brightly polished. "Hallo Stephen! We've got some tea and a bun for each of you, and you'll be glad to hear we've even got a hut. A bit cramped; you'll have to double up and sleep on the floor for the moment, but it's better than nothing."

That day was a *yasumé* day; I washed my sweaty clothes and met more of the regiment who had come on the advance party: Alan Haldenby, Roger Smith and Wilkie, all looking peaked and once more covered with sores. A day later I joined them on the eleven-hour working parties carrying bamboo, and though the discomfort was extreme there was a pioneering spirit about the new camp that came as a relief after the more circumscribed life of Kanburi. Not, I fear, without a degree of smugness we watched later parties – Stuart, Terence and Jim Flower among them – come limping in after their march. We felt once more a very long way from civilisation; there were no elegant temples, no factory hooters, here. Nor was there time or inclination to talk about poetry – or even our brother-officers' physical characteristics. We were very hungry; the hard work and lack of protein made us scoff whole mess tins of plain rice to fill the void. And most of the time it poured with rain.

The dreaded Captain Noguchi rejoined us from Kanburi, and demonstrated his authority by punishing one Ben Mawer – I forget his crime – with the two who had been thrown cigarettes near the Bangkok godown, and a sick Dutchman who had collapsed on the march 'without the permission of the Imperial Japanese Army'. "You have behaved like beggars," said Old Nog, "and will be treated as beggars until the end of the war. This will be at Christmas as England will have surrendered by then." All four were kept in the guardroom at night and made to stand outside it by day.

One thing revived the fading hope of an Allied victory. This was the obvious change in the attitude of our Korean guards. It ran the whole gamut from turning a blind eye when we slacked (as soon as a Japanese was out of sight) to offering to be our butlers as well as our chauffeurs after 'Nippon finish'. So Nacom Nyok was a schizophrenic camp; in squalor and working conditions it was like going back to square one on the railway in the worst days of 1943, yet just around the corner was the road to freedom – or, of course, extermination.

Perhaps it was this sense of unreality that prompted George Bartley-Dennis to record the privations of our journey to Nacom Nyok in suitably unheroic verse. At Kanburi there had been a few animals about. A goat used to wander into the huts from time to time, and it reacted curiously to human company. If we blew tobacco smoke into its nostrils it wrinkled them in ecstacy, bared its teeth and widdled, and seemed able to go on doing so indefinitely. Another camp pet was a calf named, for obvious reasons, *Benjo*. This little creature for some reason inspired affection from the ferocious Sergeant Shimojo, which in turn inspired George's muse.

> The carriages rock on the rail to Bangkok
>> With Benjo, Shimojo and me.
> It's a pretty tight fit, with the kit and the shit
>> For Benjo, Shimojo and me.
>
> Soon after Bampong as we rattled along
>> A horrible sight did we see,
> For out of the rain came a great aeroplane
>> Straight for Benjo, Shimojo and me.
>
> So filled with dismay in the wagon we lay
>> And counted the bombs – one, two, three,
> Which sad to relate quite settled the fate
>> Of Benjo, Shimojo and me.
>
> When they came the next day to clear us away
>> We were all as mixed up as could be,
> And apart from the smell there was no way to tell
>> Which was Benjo, Shimojo or me.
>
> If you go to Japan you must stop – if you can –
>> At the Japanese Shrine at Ise,
> For one box there contains all the mortal remains
>> Of Benjo, Shimojo and me.

23

The Friendly Bomb

THURSDAY August 16th began like any other day: up in darkness at seven o'clock Nip time (five o'clock Thai time); breakfast of rice pap; *tenko* at eight o'clock; then out to transport bamboos. As we marched out, the four were still standing outside the guardroom. Ben Mawer had been forty-eight hours without (officially) food or water and was looking rough. I made three journeys and met some other ranks marching back to their camp.

"Where are you off to?"

"Home! The war's over."

"Ha ha!"

"You'll see."

By lunchtime Noguchi had discharged the four at the guardroom. "We are all officers," he had said, "though we are enemies. In future you must obey Japanese orders." In the afternoon a road-building party was suddenly sent back to camp. We began to indulge our fancies yet again but at the same time stuck conscientiously to our routine, as if to protect ourselves against one more disillusionment. But surely something really was up this time? Several Thais gave me the 'V' sign and a farmer was reported to have mimed 'Tokyo hands up 10.8.45'. Then at half past four our Korean guard announced that we were to return to camp after one more trip. Another, drunk on Thai hooch, shouted: "War finish – understand – *kah*?" and reeled about, vowing vengeance on Shimojo. Back in camp the Nips were clearly nervous, and several Koreans were tipsy. A guard beat someone up for laughing. Another, known as Hatchet Face, who would normally have joined in with gusto, looked sheepish and pulled him away. Rumours were rife and hopes were high, particularly as we knew Russia had declared war on Japan on August 7th. Toosey said he believed the Nips had capitulated but he had been told nothing officially, except that the next day all work on Nip huts would cease and only work on our own camp would continue.

Next morning I was off on the bamboo party again. There was a Sabbath atmosphere, and trucks passed full of very quiet Nips who looked at us curiously as though for the first time. Back in camp for lunch, we found an almost forgotten ceremony being performed: Red Cross supplies were being dished out – with parcels dated April 1942 and, ironically, enough medical supplies to last for years. And there were books from America, including among much dross *The Golden Bough*, *Decline and Fall of the Roman Empire*, *Elizabethan Plays* and Bury's *History of Greece*. I appropriated a fat *Familiar Quotations* by John Bartlett (1943), which was stamped inside, 'War Prisoners Aid World's Committee, YMCA, Geneva, Switzerland' and 'U. S. Censorship examined by 539'. Thank you, 539, for my first and last Red Cross book! The food supplies, from Britain, worked out at one parcel between five. The packing was inferior to that of the American parcels of eighteen months before, but the food tasted better.

The mail accompanying these parcels brought a shock to Stuart: the death of his brother John near Tunis on Easter Day 1943. The news came from John's housemaster at St Edward's, Oxford, for whom he had been a golden boy. The delay in such news was unnerving and left me wondering how Noel was and whether my much larger family had had casualties. But none was announced in the few twenty-five-word postcards that came for me.

That evening Takasaki summoned Toosey for the last time and told him the war was over. We were to carry on until further orders were received. I had heard nothing significant about the atom bombs. Both had fallen during our last journey, when we had no radio contact with the outer world. A Korean guard told me of much bombing in Japan, but I was more interested in his other news – that Russia had declared war. After reaching Nacom Nyok, we had had no chance to pump Toosey or David Boyle for news, because the camp was still disorganised and we spent all our time on working parties. Now that details of the bombing began to come through, I felt unease at the scale of destruction but relief that it had been large enough to stop the Japanese in their tracks. Having seen their inhuman pertinacity over the railway, I had resigned myself to an inch-by-inch resistance all over Asia.

But now it was over. I had the same feeling of weightlessness as in that split second of relief when falling asleep on the march. But the burden had gone for ever, and now I floated in ecstacy until the sights and sounds of camp intruded and I looked about for ballast to give me steerage way again. I had no control over my thoughts. The imminence of freedom was too unsettling for rational plans. What about the Nips in this extermination camp? Should I set about exterminating *them*, or at least smash their screaming flat faces in? I didn't feel like it. Not even monsters like Noguchi and Shimojo? Well, yes, maybe them. Or Tojo Number One? Oh yes, I trusted that he and his morning-suited henchmen would hang high – and not too quickly. But I knew I never wanted to see any of them again. As for their troops, however down and out they seemed now, they would always trigger feelings of degradation, and the fear that their ant-like activity could be diverted but never stopped. Meanwhile – poor little sods! – it was their turn for a bit of brutality and isolation and hunger.

I remembered one of the several Koreans nicknamed 'Donald Duck' complaining at a slack moment on a Konkuita working party that Nippon was "no good", *meshi* "no good", Thai "no good", and the heat "no pucking good". But Korea was "very good", his *wifu* "very good", and his home "very good". He longed for the snow, and mimed its fall and its effects – getting the animals in, sitting out the snowstorms and maintaining a lifeline. If I understood him, this consisted of tying a rope to a tree and carrying the other end into the house. When waking up to find yourself snowed in, you shook the rope and made an escape tunnel. Where did I live? What was it like? The only equally graphic thing I could think of was Clifton Suspension Bridge, so I mimed its height above the river and how, when things were 'no good' – no *wifu*, no *meshi*, no *yasumé* – people jumped off it. But sometimes women floated down, their skirts acting as parachutes. I'm not sure that I got this point over, because

Korean women wore trousers, but I hoped that he, for one, would return safely to his snowdrifts.

Out here neither the Koreans nor the Nips seemed to have much fun, by our standards. A bit of basketball seemed about the limit of their sporting interests, they played no musical instruments, enjoyed no concerts, and instead of leave had comfort girls. In the evenings they would squat in little groups, their voices bubbling and fizzing and clicking – rather like restless hens in a henhouse – as the drinks went round and the complaints mounted: the *wifu* – if *wifu* there was – not seen for years, the bashings from the sergeant, the insect bites, the rotten food, the no-good Thais, the pox, the *buggerayo* no work Churchiu Number Ten *ingresu*. Perhaps for them the discomforts of prison would not be all that greater than contributing to the Greater East Asian Co-Prosperity Sphere. But at last their amazing driving force would be gone. And when they did get home no bands would play for them.

All this time, as I drifted about more conscious of what I felt within me than saw outside, I became aware of others with the same absent air, the same beatific or just plain half-baked expression on their faces. We were all in the never-never-land between past squalors and future duties. As we passed we would grin and mutter absurdities.

"Home, James, and don't spare the horses!"

"More work for the Undertaker!"

"Tojo Number Ten!"

"Ah, is this not happiness?"

Why, yes! 'I wake up in the morning and seem to hear someone in the house sighing and saying that last night someone died. I immediately ask to find out who it is, and learn that it is the sharpest, most calculating fellow in town. Ah, is this not happiness?'

Then the implications started to sink in. Could such tatterdemalions as we were become a fighting and working community again? Had I hoarded enough status symbols for the occasion? What sort of figure would I cut on paved streets? And that family of mine, so long suffused in the golden haze of memory, was coming into focus and awaited me – perhaps not so admiringly as I had dreamed, perhaps even censorious about the ignominy of my war. I in my turn might find them grey and parochial after my colourful *kampongs* and untamed jungles.

Toosey gave a pep talk, saying that camp discipline must continue exactly as before and that we should not go out foraging for food – nor for women; we were surrounded by Jap fighting troops dug in for the expected push from Burma, and they were dangerous to us not only in themselves but – until he could get medical supplies flown in – in their effect on the local women. I was pained that in our moment of exaltation we should be credited with base thoughts. Not so others. "The sooner we get at the women the better," said someone, "another few months of this and we'd be a heaving mass of queers!"

There was a thanksgiving service and we sang the British, Dutch and American national anthems and the doxology, but this was a formal rather than an emotional bow towards established religion. There was a pricking at the back of the eyes, but we didn't roar our hearts out in the name of the Lord or of King George. Who did we really have to thank for our salvation? Not, now, Mountbatten and his boys, we learned, but some impersonal and sinister American invention. So a sense of anti-climax persisted as we sought the same old bug-ridden bed spaces as usual. But in the night the tenseness of expectation fell away. The cicadas, the tree frogs, the mosquitoes were at their usual tricks. Men murmured and snored, and Wilkie suddenly shouted angrily in his sleep:

"But he's committed a murder!"

"What are you going to do about it?" I asked.

"Put him on a charge!" said Wilkie, and turned over. And lying there thinking, with no dawn working party under the Nips awaiting me, I began at last to feel – well – free. Next morning dear old Reggie Lees, a moustachioed major in the Gordons, talked to us about being British and recovering our sense of decorum and showing respect for senior officers, and my spirits sank with a bump at this reminder of the army life that still lay between me and England, home and beauty.

On Saturday August 18th we cleaned up the camp and washed our clothes – with enough soap for once; I used the tablet of 'Asepso' I had hoarded superstitiously ever since Singapore, as a magic remedy for gangrenous infection. The Nips withdrew behind their lines and there were no incidents, except for some Koreans and ourselves 'looting' a shoe store. National flags on bamboo poles appeared from nowhere, and a Korean obligingly cut out stars for an American one. I had three more cards from the family and a letter dated 1942. To my parents I wrote that we were feeling jealous of those more fortunately situated on the other side of Bangkok:

> Nacom Nyok, Thailand
> 30th August 1945
> Lieut. S. C. Alexander
> 135 Field Regiment RA

My dear Mother and Father,

At last I can answer your letters but not, alas, at length nor with much certainty of mine reaching you.

I have had about sixty letters or cards altogether, mostly from Mother but several from David, Joan, Hugh, Father, Bim and Aunt Jane.

We are stuck in a squalid half-built camp seventy miles NW of Bangkok feeling very neglected, and jealous of those more fortunately situated at the other end. I cannot begin to describe our existence under the Nips in this scribble. Perhaps even more infuriating than their bestiality was their efficiency in mental torture. They suppressed all cultural efforts; thus we received no books (until three days ago!!) and have been forbidden to use pencil or paper, all diaries, note books, lecture notes, language exercises, etc. being confiscated. The pencil I am using I have kept inside the lining of my fly-buttons and it is therefore inconveniently small for writing.

I have heard nothing of Robin [Noel] since I came up here in 1942 but gather the food in Singapore has been appalling, and can only hope he is all right. If so I hope to contact him and David on the way home, probably via Rangoon and Bangalore or Ceylon (though I should like to see as much of the world as I can now I am out here, and may for that reason come via Australia).

We are all very well now and frantically trying to remember what we wrote in our diaries so that we can shock admiring relatives and create boundless sympathy. . . . We have lost in Thailand about twenty-five per cent since 1942.

I can still scarcely think coherently of my future but, unless anything else offers, hope I might go back to Peterhouse to read English for either journalism or the Colonial Civil Service . . . I have forgotten Estate Management so that I may as well read something in which I have become interested.

The thought of you two and the family at home has always sustained me, and I have never appreciated so much the interest we Alexanders take in each other.

Love to all.

Stephen

Our 'dicky bird', which had been smuggled into the camp in Noguchi's personal kit by his British batman, remained obstinately mute all day, so David Boyle asked the Nips for some batteries.

"What for?"

"For our wireless."

"WIRELESS – *KAH!!!*"

Next day there was a race meeting with the Nip ponies. Someone had found some silk shawls in the Korean quarters, so the jockeys wore colours. Herky Ross, a bookie in civvy street, and Mike Silley, who had trained racehorses in Malaya, ran the tote, and Peter Ligertwood acted as judge from a vantage point on a buffalo cart. There were four races of two laps each. The Nips watched from behind their fence. The Dutch spurned them because it was Sunday.

The wireless burst into life with disappointing news of Nips still fighting in Burma and filtering into Thailand. Even more disappointing was the emergence, from under the stones where they had been hiding while there were Nips to be dealt with, of senior colonels to jockey for position in the getaway queue, or for prestigious commands. One of their decisions was that subalterns should continue to salute Noguchi; a Colonel Carpenter said that in that case he would make all his subalterns temporary captains. The three journalists, Bertie Keane, Mark Quinn and Roland Revett, began arguing over ways and means of getting their story out. On August 20th news came that Bill Drower was safe but weak. His conditions had been improved once Noguchi had left Kanburi, and he had emerged from his delirium. As the other ranks were no longer being paid, it was suggested that officers get a flat rate with the differences pooled for the other ranks. Knocker Knights thought this "smacked of soviet practice" and wanted to give full pay and then call for voluntary contributions, a suggestion received with some cynicism. I worked all day on hut-building and felt caged-in. I longed to climb the hill behind the camp and get away from people. My impatience with our encirclement grew when a bearded French priest with bare feet visited us from a church over the hill. He seemed unaware of the sensation his appearance caused.

Colonel Warren fed our impatience by posting busily to Bangkok and back with news and views. While twenty-seven senior officers gas-bagged in conferences and our food remained vile, the other ranks had already got bullocks for their camp from the local farmers, pledging the government's promise to pay. I went a little way up the hill with a chap called Colchester to collect stones for flooring, and we sat looking at the view below us. He enthused on its beauty, on the buffaloes ploughing and the *padi* fields stretching away in chequered greens and yellows. But I was feeling gloomy and said it was a primitive, precarious scene and looked as though a few thunderstorms would blot it out. Yet I admitted its earthy self-sufficiency compared with the commercialised life of Singapore and Cape Town – or even England to which we must now return. Two years ago all we had wanted was a peaceful life at home; now we were unsettled by doubts and wanderlust. After supper they were aired and shared till three in the morning, lubricated rather than clarified by *lao*, the rice wine now freely available.

Guthrie Moir, Peter Bruckmann and I discussed the prospects of returning to Peterhouse to complete or improve our degrees. The thought of sitting in lecture rooms, of punting up to Byron's pool with girls just out of school or, especially, of bicycling in freezing East Anglian winds seemed quite unreal. Would anyone employ us if we didn't go back? Peter's Dutch friend, Kamper, was translating a file from the Nip office, dated after Beech's trial and describing the national traits of the prisoners. 'The British,' it ran, 'are proud and insolent. They think themselves number one in science, art and culture. They are well disciplined. They are convinced they will win the war. The Australians are hard workers and uneducated. They have great affection for the mother country. The Dutch after six hundred years in Asia are more internationally minded. They are great teachers. They act very independently among themselves. The Thais feel more and more pro-Allies, as they think they will win. Therefore no communication must be allowed between POWs and Thais.' Well, this was all water under the bridge; how much would the British count East of Suez from now on?

We were not the only ones to indulge in a mild debauch that night. Ian Grimwood cooked himself a fourteen-egg omelette – and ceremonially ate it. Toosey, Lilley and Knocker Knights celebrated their last night in camp before leaving to join the other ranks – the bulk of our own regiment being now at Ubon, near the Indo-Chinese border. Toosey had made one or two over-optimistic speeches when he left Kanburi on the advance party, and had blotted his copybook with his faithful adjutant, Malcolm Northcote. Restricted in numbers, he had been forced to leave behind one of three people: David Boyle the interpreter, Malcolm, or his batman Osborne; he had left Malcolm. Now, late at night, Malcolm-less but immaculate, he was in fine voice.

"I tell you one thing, you chaps, I won't forget you! And I promise you this – if I don't get you out of this camp within three days my name's not Toosey!"

"Then your name's not Toosey!" came a morose voice.

We drank to that, nevertheless, and eventually Peter and I went woozily to sleep, while Guthrie wandered about all night, parking himself here and there for meditative spells, and was found still wandering and full of affable greetings the next morning. Our three colonels, attended – amazing sight! – by a bowing Shimojo, left next day after trying to deal with the Koreans, who had been disarmed by the Japs, stripped of spare clothes and watches, given twenty dollars each, made to sign a renunciation of Japanese responsibility for their welfare, and dismissed. Toosey advised them to stay in a hut at Nacom Nyok while two of their number went to Bangkok to ask the Swiss Consul to send them home. So passed out of our lives the guards, whose non-combatant status neither excused nor alleviated brutality often quite as bad as that of the Japanese. At the going down of the sun and in the morning we will remember them: the Goat, the Kanu Kid, the Bombay Duck, the Singing Master, the Black Prince, the Mad Mongrel, the Silver Bullet, the White Slug and Doctor Death.

I flogged my service trousers for twenty dollars. Mark Quinn offered me a five pound cheque for my brown shoes, and a cable home via the Vatican for a pound, but I declined both offers. (In fact, I had hoarded two pound notes, by then equivalent to two thousand *baht* or one bullock.) On August 23rd I finally went right up the hill, first through dark jungle, then up a stream bed, then through young bamboo to *lalang* grass and rocks and, at the summit, open sunlight. My spirits, which had risen steadily with the climb, brimmed over on seeing the view below. Our camp looked tiny, with 'POW' ground strips showing up well, and a laterite road running off past the other ranks' camp – running off to where? As my eyes followed it I felt monarch of all I surveyed. 'Do not count time lost,' my father had written. 'Paul had his Arabia, Moses his desert.' What had this land been to me? In this high place and in this unwonted solitude I felt uplifted, detached, godlike. Yet, even as I absorbed the prospect, instinct told me to leave it at its most memorable moment, that to prolong the feeling would be to weaken it beyond the power of recall. I retraced my steps down through the rocks, the *lalang*, the bamboo, the stream and the jungle to the mundane world and immediate appetites of camp life. Arrangements had been made to buy meat on credit, half a kilo per man per day, and vegetables and sweet potatoes and two eggs, and a weekly quarter-*kati* of tobacco.

Next day a plane flew over low enough to see us and we waved white towels. Parties of two hundred and fifty men were to start moving to Bangkok; meanwhile we continued desultory camp work such as cutting *lalang* for the ponies. The Nip troops round us were mostly cavalry and looked very young and underfed; some turned out to be shanghaied Chinese. I re-read *England, their England*, finding in it a reflection of my bolshie mood, and *Pride and Prejudice*, with its potent brew of intense emotions and vapid actions. With what assurance, I thought, were we left to imagine a whole world of off-stage activity to make the characters tolerable to each other! For all I could see, the men couldn't as much as shave themselves, or the women boil an egg. A spot of the Kwai would have done them no harm!

We heard stories of Peter Heath and the civilian 'V' Organisation in Bangkok, who had been responsible for the mysterious money and supplies smuggled in via Boon Pong, and of four hundred parachutists dropping near Kanburi to aid the Thai uprising. But a wise-cracking American, one Lieutenant Bush, who came to see us on August 30th, knew little of all this; he had been dropped two months before with two other Americans, a Thai and a radio set, and had been living fifty kilometres away, training local guerrillas. When we asked rather smugly what he thought of our condition, expecting compliments on our morale and physique, he said that we "smelt bad". Our feelings of frustration were not improved by news of high jinks in Kanburi, where the villagers were putting down the red carpet for those lucky enough to have stayed behind there. The knife was turned in the wound when we learned that at Pratchai Colonel Lilley was offered a young virgin by the Thai C-in-C but pleaded the incapacity of age. Some younger officers had drawn lots and one Robinson had been lucky; he said it was "MARVELLOUS".

24

Satu Ampat Jalan

THE Dutch were leaving to concentrate elsewhere. We had learned much from their experience of life in the East, not least from their touch in the kitchens. As the days passed, with tales of gracious living in Kanburi and radio reports of our counterparts from Germany sitting their finals for degrees-by-correspondence, our cooks grew as bolshie as the rest of us, and their handling of our new rations reverted to good old British Army standards. We would also miss Dutch expertise in arts and languages – German, French, Malay, Arabic, even Sanskrit. In Kanburi I'd seen old Asian hands like the soft-spoken planter Bill Bangs ('Haji' because of his Moslem conversion) and Noel Ross, a South African Catholic in the Malayan Civil Service, communing cross-legged in corners with Dutch egg-heads and *Indisches jongens*. In Chungkai they had introduced John Coast to dances from Java and Amboyna, and to shadow plays and drumming and chanting. John had felt magically transported thousands of miles away, and began to study Indonesian dancing seriously. The physical excitement, as the *jongens* whirled and stamped in the lamplight, was heightened by a conspiratorial atmosphere of nationalist aspirations. Some of us who were delighted by one aspect were nervous of the other – and vice versa.

We argued about an East Asian Co-Prosperity Sphere without the Japanese – and sooner or later, we supposed, without us. In Malaya, and even in India, everything was still more or less black and white and we supposed would stay so until power passed, to Emmerson's joy, from one to the other by a sort of gentlemen's agreement. But the Dutch and Indonesians were already thoroughly mixed up, with quite different brews in hundreds of islands, and these troops weren't going to go back and wait for a gentlemen's agreement. Those who had opted for Dutch privileges and Dutch military service were not able to own land, and politically the situation was explosive. Meanwhile, their departure would diminish us spiritually as well as physically. Here we still were at the end of August and feeling more disoriented than ever. In a way we were reluctant to abandon a lifestyle whose simplicities had become so familiar. Without the Japs, what an idyllic existence we could lead now that we had learned the secrets of a rice economy! And those visions of home that had sustained us through feverish dripping nights in the jungle, would they survive the peace? Would we, with our G-string mentality, our squatting posture and our Moslem habits of hygiene, fit in at home?

As the *lao*-and-limes went down beneath our furled mosquito nets we grew maudlin over our isolation. No more *botteldoppers* who had taught us those Moslem habits; no more green gaiters, green tunics and great green straw hats ("Green!" cried Stuart, "Not arid khaki like ours, but green – the colour of life!"). The camp would be strangely quiet without their gutteral oaths – "*GOD VERDAMME! SODAMIETER OP!*"

Jack confided in us that George had taken up with an *Indische jongen* called Lodewijk, or Ludo for short. He had been jealous at first and had written a sonnet to annoy him.

> I little thought I'd live to see the day
> > My company – nay, love – would be required
> > And my most girlish gifts would be admired
> By those same men who used to scorn the way
> My fair hair curled. But now with languid play
> > Of satin skin on sunny curves, attired
> > In just enough to be the more desired,
> I hold a splendid – if vicarious – sway.
>
> "Good morning, George!" they say. I know a hand
> > Will rest upon my shoulder, soft, like this!
> Should others, growing bolder, understand
> > Too well my wishes and demand a kiss,

I love to quench those idle flames I fanned –
  They're mine to play with – till the armistice.

It had annoyed him, but not as much as the move to Nacom Nyok had. George was still in Kanburi, but Ludo had been detailed to come here. So on George's behalf he'd composed an ode to Bung Beauty.

Glory be to God for dimpled things –
  For skin of couple-colour, and the goofy cow –
Like goo-goo glance from tippling peepers all a-swim;
Loin-lean navel-nonsense; Jove – ah! – brings
  Schemes long-plotted success – Ludo, lusty on *lao*!
His smooth skin a-slide with muscle and slim!
Orgasmic, dark, aboriginal, bare, strange
Gollywog-gigolo, fecund folds me now
In sun-sweet salt-sweat; when a bloody prim
Old '*sodamieter*' sends him out of range –
  Sod him!

"I shan't show it to George, even if we do catch up with each other, because he wouldn't recognise it as a parody, and anyway I hope that by that time we shall have come to our senses and grown up again. When the bomb fell I thought, 'That's it, saved in the nick of time!' I meant, of course, from George. He's a nice enough chap but as dull as ditchwater. Could I be equally besotted with a girl who was just as dull? I hope not!"

We tried to visualise that forgotten creature – a W-H-I-T-E W-O-M-A-N. Was she like Hulton's 'sweetheart', and would we match up to her idea of manliness as we hurried to meet her in the close embrace of collar and tie, to the ring of leather on paving stones and the rustle of paper round our hothouse roses? And would she, however manly she thought us, banish our memory of 'the mango tree's cool cavern of delight'? The trouble was, as we now knew very well, we all had the *lingum* and the *yoni* in us, and it was only the cold climate of Europe that had denied us one or the other. The great *chedi* of Nacom Pathom and the friezes of Angkor Wat epitomised freedom from cold, from thick uniform, from work –

and from women; freedom to set out untrammelled upon the Great Way and seek the truths of Surya. The male element in us was created to be free to develop genius, while the female element was designed for utilitarian roles. It was up to us to get the balance right. Very true! But what about the balance in women?

"As Byron puts it, my dear Jack, 'there is a tide in the affairs of women, which, taken at the flood, leads – God knows where'."

"Wasn't Byron himself bisexual, handing out his used combs as mementoes to friends of both sexes?"

"The trouble is that if we want to behave like Byron we must be able to write poetry like Byron."

"Or like Wagner, compose like Wagner."

"Or like Lytton Strachey, write like Lytton Strachey."

Nevertheless, we saw ourselves as Byrons, one and all, our women tossed aside after each dalliance with Eros or each trial Agapemone.

But what if we turned out to be like Oscar Wilde and found we were not bisexual any longer? Then, said Stuart, we mustn't be afraid of following our inclinations. Here we were in Thailand. Providence had helped us escape from dreary old England with its sickly white people scurrying about the cold hard streets, and we had the chance to live in a green world of sun and trees and rivers, where people were still part of nature. Their intuition made them serve a supranational god and we must seize our chance, seize her, seize her, seize the Goddess!

"Yes, but how?"

"Well, for a start, how about joining the Malayan Civil Service?"

"Let's all join!"

"If we had any guts we'd get out of here now – commandeer a Nip truck and bamboozle our way down to Singapore."

Our heroics did not appeal to Terence. He had his mother to support and, whether he liked it or not, it'd have to be dear old Barclays's Dominion, Colonial and Overseas Bank for him. But we were in no mood for real mothers. Our thoughts were for earth mothers, muses, pantocrators, sun gods and goddesses and of the marvellous logic of Asian life; sun, the great aphrodisiac; women, slipping in and out of sarongs, cooking *nasi goreng*, and of course working in the fields and all that sort of thing as well. Men would always be bursting with sensibility and creative power, their love for men complementary, not alternative, to their feelings for women. Friends and lovers, what was the difference? What did Chin Shengt'an say?

I am drinking with some romantic friends on a spring night and am just half intoxicated, finding it difficult to stop drinking and equally difficult to go on. An understanding boy servant at the side suddenly brings in a package of fire-crackers, about a dozen in number, and I rise from the table and go and fire them off. The smell of sulphur assails my nostrils and enters my brain and I feel comfortable all over my body. Ah, is this not happiness?

The evening sun moved gently up the limestone hill behind the camp. Yes, friendship and love were one and the same. Under Surya we were born to live fully with men and with women while love burgeoned, art flourished, life was simple, time was timeless and death passed unnoticed. It was madness to kick against the pricks and pursue our mean sunless western lives like moles, working, working, working to consume our own weight every twenty-four hours in loveless pound notes. It was all blindingly clear as we sat in the lotus position with our *lao*-and-limes. The light faded suddenly to velvety darkness, mosquito nets blotched and speckled with blood turned into exotic hangings, geckoes scuttled companionably up and down the bamboo, cicadas chirruped their applause, and one by one coconut oil lamps began to glow and flicker round us. Across the camp came the notes of an accordion, and as the moon rose we joined in the plaintive chorus:

> *Terang bulan,*
> *Terang bulan di Kali,*
> *Boewanja timboel*
> *Katanja lah mati*
> *Djangang pertjatja*
> *Orang lelaki*
> *Brani soempi*
> *Dia takoet mati.*

But how would it sound as we walked down Piccadilly with ATS lieutenants on our arms? In the wintry blasts of England would we, like Terence, hear faraway the warm wind whisper, '*Muang Thai*'? And as we leaned over Waterloo Bridge would we think of another bridge over another river?

> Shine down, full moon.
> Shine down or dive
> And in the river shining still
> There stay alive with light to fill
> With life all creatures
> Dark would kill
> Shine on, full moon.
> Shine on us still.

25

At Sea

ON September 1st we were off. Out went all thoughts of *terang bulan*, together with haversacks, blankets, bottles, old clothes, flip-flops and mosquito nets, and sporting my Herbert Johnson cap, long socks and brown shoes I strode down the track I had staggered up three weeks earlier, with nothing to carry except *The Knapsack*, *Letters to Malaya* and my new *Dictionary of Quotations*. As though to make up for lost time, the military machine that had ground to a halt three and a half years before, swept us up onto its magic carpet, and (as far as Bangkok) onto Nip trucks. Children waved Union Jacks in the villages, and I remembered with unease the 'Poached Egg' flags that had materialised in Singapore on the very day of its capitulation. Nothing succeeds like success, but suddenly three and a half years seemed ominously brief. Would the next three and a half cause as complete change of heart? At the airfield wasp-waisted Thai Air Force officers were welcoming, and so was our first White Woman. Both she and her uniform were crisp as well as white, for she was Lady Mountbatten, evidently determined to be the first to greet us – and understandably so up here where she would find her cousin Harold Cassel, my cheerful visitor in Kanburi hospital. We were disconcerted by the 'news' in the popular press so thoughtfully laid out for us; there was no war news at all, only gossip about Hollywood film stars and naughty vicars, football results, and reports of Worthing town council's banning of bowls on Sundays and the award of a knighthood to A. P. Herbert.

"Now," said Lady Mountbatten, "have you got everything you want? We'll do whatever we can for you?"

"Well, there is one thing," said the stolid man lined up next to me, "these roobishy papers. Nowt about the war and what's going on in the world, like. It's all this socialism and the new government."

"But it's a very good government, isn't it, General?" Her attendant gave a ghastly smile as she flicked his red tabs. "However, we must get the gentleman the *Manchester Guardian* – AND the *Yorkshire Post*!"

Later, Peanut McKellar attended her and had expected to sit beside her when she left in the staff car. Ignoring the door he gallantly held open, she made for the front seat, and with a whisk of her skirt plumped herself down beside the smirking young driver. Peanut was left to sit whistling to the air in the back.

I flew to Rangoon with a cheerful crew handing out Wills' Gold Flake. When the Canadian pilot went to the heads the co-pilot waggled the plane about. We flew upriver over the mosaic of *padi* and jungle – three times the length of our desperate treks – in only two hours and twenty minutes. On landing, the pace quickened even more; in trucks to the WVS for food and MORE WOMEN (not quite white here, because prophylactic mepacrine for malaria had turned them yellow); on to the university, now a hospital, to sleep; Indian and African troops everywhere; jeeps (vehicles new to us), whizzing about, and in them shabby but workmanlike drivers in comfortable green kit. We were nonplussed at their attitude to each other ("You silly black bastard!" "Get fucked, man!"); was this the new democracy? At the hospital we saw 'proper' newspapers; in the *Times Weekly* General Slim likened the Japanese to 'the soldier ants of the tropics, with their strange inability to alter plans which had gone agley'. Yes, indeed, what a way to run a railway! He seemed to know his stuff, this general. Would the locals do better under him than they did under the Nips? As I sank into sleep in my fairytale bed, with soft pillow, white sheets and virgin mosquito net, I remembered the friendly locals I had left behind me. "Those good quiet Thais," I thought. "How grateful I am to them!"

Next day new impressions were piled on unexpected reunions in bewildering succession. I saw our gutsy little doctor from Konkuita, 'Killer' Caley ("Pure carbolic for you, my lad!"); he looked like a ghost after three months on the Mergui Road. Two hundred and fifty men (twenty-three from my regiment) out of a thousand had died, and two hundred and fifty were on the point of death. Killer said he'd reached that point himself and as near as dammit committed suicide; only a note from a paratrooper telling him to hang on for the Thai rising had kept him going. Then came tales of the celebrations at Kanburi. For me they were soured by a confession from John Durnford: he had retrieved my precious diary but left it on the floor of Bangkok aerodrome.

On the news front, Mark Quinn and Bertie Keane got themselves flown home to brief the British press (how would their audiences square their lurid tales with their look of rude health?), and we were given a film show only to find ourselves – whether by design or accident, I don't know – gulping at pictures of Belsen, crying with captured child-soldiers in Germany, and wincing at American rocket-ship attacks on Okinawa. Even *Henry V* brought tears of emotion.

Then we saw Mountbatten himself, 'El Supremo' – and he looked it. Undeterred by the battery of ribbons on his chest, he leaped lightly onto a box and his complexion under the Beatty-angle cap reminded me of George VI, heavily made up for inspecting our camp at Catterick. The atom bomb, he said, had baulked him of his prey and of the proof that the invincibility of the Imperial Japanese Army in the field was a myth. "But don't you worry, you fellows, we'll see that the Japs learn that soon enough! I know what you've been through and I'll personally see to it that those little yellow bastards are treated in the same way as they treated you!"

There was no applause. I was told afterwards that he said to his ADC, "Poor devils! They must be punch-drunk." In his diary he admits to such sentiments only with prisoners from Java in Singapore; of the Rangoon pep talks he writes in more characteristic vein:

> I had the most tumultuous reception I have ever experienced.
> It was almost impossible to start speaking when one first stood
> up on account of the excited condition of the men who went
> on cheering and clapping the moment one stood up.

How could he understand our state of mind? We had shared adversity with the Nips, albeit from different angles; we had all been on the receiving end of bad orders from 'scarlet majors at the base'. Some of the Nips had tried to soften those orders – even if more had not. Some of our own people had behaved despicably – even if more had not. But after three and a half years of jungle life together there was no question in our minds that, in the 'them' and 'us' division, we and our Japanese captors were 'us', having rubbed shoulders so long where nature was red in tooth and claw, while 'them' meant Tojo in his striped trousers and top hat and the well-laundered Mountbatten – and maybe all these people swanning around in jeeps as well.

But some of these people turned out to be not merely 'us', but from my own little pre-war world. They looked quite at home here, and the pips and crowns on their shoulders brought home one effect of our lost years. My cousin Martin Moynihan MC, a major in the Frontier Force Regiment, told me the British troops had fought with circumspection, were getting very bolshie and had booed Slim when told we would be repatriated before them. He said El Supremo was indeed an unabashed showman, but this had been just what was wanted, both to put heart into the troops and to flummox 'Vinegar Joe' Stilwell, the American general with the Chinese. And he had admired his courage at a rendezvous near the Chinese border when he had damaged an eye and was warned that unless he returned at once to base for an operation he might lose its sight. This he had refused to do until his job was done. (Luckily an operation later was successful.) Major Jack Valentine RAMC, a contemporary at school, also sought me out. He said many Japanese had committed *hara kiri*, but those captured were only too eager to talk. Fifteen of them hadn't been given the chance, being thrown out one by one from a plane by West Africans instead. One African medical unit in Chittagong, he said, had shot their CO. But it was Basil Pitt, Chaplain to the Forces, who told me of Noel's survival in Singapore. Basil, an Ivor Novello-ish Bristol neighbour, showed me the sights in his jeep. He thought the priests at the Shwe Dagon pagoda pro-Jap and, which was worse, bad types and, worse still, of loose morals. In the cloisters I bought a thousand 'Whackin' white cheroots' for fifty rupees.

Though I didn't know it at the time, Martyn Skinner was already celebrating Noel's survival in verse:

> Your letters tell me by their poise and sense
> You're little changed by your experience. . .
> And, seeking to express the faith I hold
> That man, though cancered, captive, bought and sold,
> Is still not finally by fate controlled
> What need I more have done to hint it true
> Than cited Changi, these last years and you?
> As starving, hope as well as rations short,
> Only your mind to turn to for support,
> You took the consequence from fortune's spite,
> And lived the poetry I strove to write.

On September 14th, the day after the Japanese surrender in Burma was signed, I boarded the *Corfu*. She was cosier than the *Mount Vernon* and now, by special dispensation, loaded with beer. At the last moment another old friend, Peter Prideaux, came aboard to see me, sporting a large black moustache which he said the mussulmen in his 4th Indian Field Regiment had made him grow. Compared with them the Yorks and Lancs and Berks and Worcesters were 'absolute shit'. He liked the Burmese and thought the country wonderful and ready to take off. There was a great opportunity there for running a transport company, so what about coming in on it?

In the morning, as we dropped down the estuary with the Schwe Dagon diminishing behind us, first to port then to starboard, a corvette hailed us. "Cheerio fellers! Happy voyage!" And so it proved to be – and no doubt a very therapeutic one, too. At three on the next afternoon we reached Colombo, a very different sight from poor ramshackle Rangoon; so were its Wrens from the WVS women. There was no mepacrine here to spoil their complexions, and one of them, looking as smart as paint, boarded us from a naval pinnace. She was Anne Popham, a painting friend of my artist sister, and as we stood talking, I found myself much sought after. Jim Swanton, whose prayer meeting below had been thinly attended, walked aft past us and then forward past us and finally hove to beside us. What was the news about going ashore? Stanley Hall breezed up and supposed we couldn't expect any more mail yet, could we? Guillermo de Mier wondered whether by any chance, my dear, there was a Coutts Bank in Colombo. Mike Curtis hoped Anne, as a local resident, might help him find some play scripts for a production on board, with Alan Lewis in the lead. When we did get ashore – to the sound of 'Bonny Dundee' on a Dogras band – all the Wrens in town seemed to have been detailed to help us cash cheques, buy semi-precious stones, and – because of the rationing – no less precious civvy suit material. But we were steered firmly back to the lighters from the Galle Face Hotel before we could get up to any mischief. "In any case," said Alan, "these Wrens mean nothing to me. There's only one woman in my life and that's my wife. I shall never forget that first night I slept with Marjorie in my arms. It was the most wonderful experience of my life."

As we sailed away, I had to make do with the hospitality of the Colonel OC troops (he lived aboard to liaise between the crew and whatever troops the ship was carrying). At one time he had been with West African troops, whose band used to play the 'Hausa Farewell' to vessels leaving port. But after playing it to the *Repulse* at Mombasa, the *Prince of Wales* at Durban and the *Hermes* at Cape Town, they thought they'd better not play it any more. When the West Africans found themselves in action against the Japanese they used the tactics that had proved effective against the Italians. Messages were dropped saying, 'We regret that we are so short of troops to defend the Empire that we must accept whatever volunteers we can get. You are now fighting opposite West African cannibals'. The *Corfu* had herself been used as an armed raider, with 6.8 inch guns and four planes, but her only excitement had been a collision with the *Hermes* off Dakar. However, others had not been so lucky and it appeared we were not the only people to have been bombed by our own air force. The Navy off Akyab in Burma had been bombed by the RAF for three days, and had fired back.

After Colombo we had a respite of eight days before suspense built up again at Abidjaya, a bleak depot near Suez. Our rival troopship, the *Monowai*, was leaving as we anchored, and the formalities of re-entering civilisation quickened. We had an hour ashore to draw winter kit (ugh!) and back on board there were visits from ENSA actor John Trevor, with his one-man *Merchant of Venice*, a classical pianist (soon bullied into playing jazz), and an official with Colonial Office application forms. A letter from my mother – full marks to the Army Post Office! – told me that Noel was on his way home. We went through the canal at night, with troops in Ismailia exchanging badinage, and on the morning of September 30th saw Port Said and the de Lesseps statue. We celebrated my twenty-sixth birthday on October 3rd, and next day we passed Gibraltar. It looked menacing in the evening gloom, and I wondered how long the Japs would have taken to swarm over it. Now only nine hours behind the *Monowai*, the *Corfu* seemed to relish the rough Atlantic seas, and on the 7th, seventeen hours ahead of schedule and comfortably ahead of the *Monowai*, we reached Southampton. As we came in past waving crowds and ships hooting the victory sign, my throat was dry with excitement. Yet I was uncomfortable in my bunchy battledress, such a thick unyielding barrier between my body and my natural surroundings, and I felt a very raw recruit, whether to a new-model army or a new-model civvy street. At the dockside the mayor's wooden speech and the platitudes of a Mr Latham, Under Secretary for War, delivered in pseudo-Churchillian periods, sounded as though concocted for the Boer War. But soon we were in buses, being carried in a daze through streets full of cheering people; we waved back, our faces frozen into smiles. This must be what the King and Queen felt like; no wonder they always waved in slow motion! We saw the odd American GI standing at the back, looking distinctly sour, but in front, waving frantically, blowing kisses and reaching out to us were girls, girls, girls.

From the transit camp I rang up my mother; we found ourselves breaking silences with inconsequential remarks about the family. Noel was not back yet, Hugh was a padre in Germany, Bim was home on leave from Africa, and my sisters couldn't wait to see me. I felt reaction setting in; there were no more unknown excitements to look forward to. Somehow I didn't feel quite ready for the front door to close behind me again. I would wait until Noel arrived, and we would share the family's expectations and pool our reactions to them.

We were put through a sausage machine of cursory medical tests and issues of pay, and despatched on leave. (The astute Bertie Keane, we heard, mindful of the scope for future disability claims, had declined to accept his A1 medical assessment.) I found myself on a train to London with Mike Curtis, who was anxious to establish links with the BBC. From the station we were given a lift to an officers' club in Mayfair by a Red Cross lady, who told us she had been a prisoner in France and knew exactly how we felt; I doubted that. Her driving was erratic but our cloud of euphoria bore us smoothly through the bangs and crashes and flashing lights of the enormous city. The moment of truth was upon us. 'A traveller returns home after a long journey, and he sees the old city gate and hears women and children on both banks of the river talking his own dialect. Ah, is this not happiness?'

The traffic had been moving so bewilderingly fast that I had yet to get my bearings. After claiming a bed and accepting a cup of tea from a motherly lady in uniform, I emerged and found myself quite at sea again.

"Excuse me!" I said to a passer-by.

"No English!"

I spotted a chap looking like an off-duty commissionaire.

"Can you tell me the way to Piccadilly?"

"Piccadilly?" He looked at me with amused contempt. "You're standing on it, buddy!"

26

Fallout

EVEN before Robin (Noel) and I converge on the family, their bush telegraph has been busy.

John Davis has seen Robin. Rachel says Martyn Skinner had a letter from him that was quite 'pre-war' in spirit. . . . About half past eight came a cable from Robin to Mary [our old retainer] saying he had arrived in Colombo and would soon be home.

(My mother to Margie)

On Tuesday afternoon letters from Robin in pencil began to arrive. He says if the house is crowded he can sleep on the box room floor, which will be luxury after his experiences. His ship, the *Tezelberg*, is due on the 12th at Liverpool. Friends may not meet Stephen's *Corfu*, due on Monday.

(*Ibid.*)

After tea came a telegram: 'Arrived Southampton expect me home soon. Stephen'. At a quarter past eight he rang up. He says he's very fit but won't be able to get home for a day or two. Joan rang up to say she heard on the wireless that the *Corfu* was in. Robin wrote that in 1942 someone smuggled him a letter from Stephen about Dakers' death at the fall of Singapore.

(*Ibid.*)

If I am away when you get home, you will find some medicine in the wine cellar. Go easy on it at first (especially Robin) and

give some to Mary. My horrors are nothing to yours but my
doctor has prescribed a few days' holiday in Llanthony to
recuperate from Africa's disgusting diseases.

(Bim to Stephen)

Over the telephone Robin said a few bright words about the
weather. He sounds just as I expected though I do hope he
won't try and be too jaunty and energetic . . . I feel he ought
to lie about on a sofa and eat most of the day, and not try and
talk. Thank goodness the fat and cheese ration is going up next
month. I thought they'd have to do something to pep up one's
spirits soon. I hope Mother has been able to get Stephen's and
Robin's double rations all right.

(Joan to Margie)

★   ★   ★

I hear that Noel is in Bristol, and journey down from London by
easy stages. Through the train window the fields of sheep are
blindingly beautiful. Rachel meets me at Abingdon station, but,
returning to the car, can't find her key. I tell her to try the turn-ups
of her trousers, and there it is.

"Not much wrong with your reflexes! But I suppose you had to
be pretty sharp to get through. Was there *any* day better than
others?"

"Yes. In 1943, the worst year, when I was pronounced too sick
to work and lay in the hut. I had time to think."

"What kept you alive?"

"Mother minding so much if I'd died, and the King and Queen
sitting on the throne of England!"

★   ★   ★

At last . . . Clifton: the ruins of All Saints; up the garden path (no
gate) to a rat-a-tat-tat on the door; dear old Mary in tears; my
mother with an unusually warm hug; my father lifting his pince-nez
off and on, pacing in and out of the room, hitching his pockets left
and right, and muttering to himself, "Robbie, dear boy! And
Stephen!"; Avery's Bristol Milk going round; and Robin, dear boy,

looking awful with only a screw left of one front tooth and his leg still indented, when pressed, from beri-beri.

★   ★   ★

Fresh air, walking with Robin over the Downs, speaking the same language; we look upriver to the Suspension Bridge ("Here when you need me!") and across the gorge over Abbots Leigh church to the Channel, the Mendips, the Quantocks, and not any more, thank God, back to Kinsaiyok; each euphoric return to the house loosens Nip strings a little more. But at night Nips intrude.

★   ★   ★

English food is tough and rice a travesty; chairs and lavatory seats are awkward, and I catch myself getting up and squatting on them; in the gap-toothed streets are grey elderly people. At a civic reception for returned POWs (Robin is not invited) the Lord Mayor of the 'Gateway to the West' – city of the Cabots, William Penn, Woodes Rogers, William Slim, Cary Grant and W. D. & H. O. Wills – presents me with a packet of twenty Gold Flake cigarettes.

★   ★   ★

With Robin I meet John Betjeman ("gentle, full of faith and very – perhaps too – charming"), and Martyn Skinner ("less austere than I expected; looks wet but epigrams sneak into the conversation with uninhibited guffaws; liked him immensely"). . . . We go to Mervyn Stockwood's church next to my father's surgery, where John Hayter, last seen at Sime Road, preaches badly . . . lunch at the Mauretania where Eric Walter White of CEMA reveals secrets of Mrs Shaw's will (to assist Irishmen to learn gentlemanly deportment) and Ronald Avery 'niggles at the last scraps of spinach and oysters as if he was as poor as a church mouse'. . . .

★   ★   ★

At Alderley Edge I hear that Peggy is qualified, engaged and elsewhere, but I see Fluffy Shelmerdine, back from the Wrens, and Sheila Burrows ("in bed looking English-rosey in pink negligé after being sat on by a horse; said she didn't like concerts").

*　　　*　　　*

Regimental reunion at Hitchin . . . Gaps from the long-ago battle (Ben Bolt, Lieutenant Raynor, Flo Stebbing and Colin Dakers) and from disease (BSM Murkin, Bill Hunt and many, many more) . . . Osmond Daltry and Sergeant Barber sporting new crutches . . . beaming pre-*Sobieski* faces: Colonel Hudson, Sergeant Tiplady and Brigadier Terence Sanders, (now a VIP tank-boffin) . . . We look over our shoulders for the Nips and over our McMullen's beers at each others' mufti: shiny demob suits with tight shoulders, mean linings and short arses or, like Toosey's, lovingly preserved single-stitching city jobs (Gunner McShane, fingering Michael Cory-Wright's faultless pre-war Savile Row jacket, "Demob suit, eh? So you're out now, are you, sir?") . . . We drink to Ailwyn De Ramsey's heir, born two weeks after the fall of Singapore, and to absent friends – Bill Drower, recuperating in Baghdad where his parents are living, and Henry Royle and Freddy Fitch, already picking up the pieces in Malaya.

*　　　*　　　*

Pharaoh Adams at Paddington station, talking of Japan after he'd left us in 1944: his zinc smelters jumping into tanks of water one minute out of four to prevent their clothes from burning; the camp butchers, in return for three bowls of rice, breaking bones to keep a man out of the mines; the Nagasaki camp run on gangster lines by four collaborationist Yanks. "I don't know how I got through it, Steve. Maybe it was because we didn't have any senior officers with us."

*　　　*　　　*

War trials and the hanging of Lieutenant Takasaki and Private Kaneshiro (the Frog and the Undertaker) for the murder of Howard and Pomeroy; Captain Komai and Sergeant Major Ejima for that of Hawley and Armitage; and Captain Noguchi (Old Nog) for the near murder of Drower and other sins. . . . I meet Stanley Armitage's lively fiancée (who plays jazz and drives a sky-blue Delahaye) and fend off her questions as best I can.

FALLOUT

* * *

Poor Percival's autobiographical postmortem: 'The news of my approaching departure for Singapore was too much for that brave woman (my mother) who, at the age of eighty-three, had stood up unflinchingly to many air raids. . . . Shenton Thomas was still there in his seventh year – a long time in that trying climate. . . . The Australian Imperial Force was always a little top-heavy and its senior officers had, so to speak, been out of harness for some years.' And of his first tour of duty in Singapore four years earlier he writes: 'Games were played with great keenness and with a high all-round standard of efficiency and, what is more important still, always in the right spirit. . . .'

* * *

Unfortunately, Yamashita had not played cricket, and – worse – before he is hanged he reveals that his capture of Singapore, where his forces were outnumbered by more than three to one, was a bluff; he had known that if he had had to fight long for the city he would have been beaten. Churchill had confided to his diary at that time: 'Our men cannot stand up to punishment. WE ARE NOT FIGHT-ING WELL. That is the sadness in my heart'; and Harold Nicolson to his: 'We intellectuals must feel that in all these years we have derided the principles of force upon which our Empire is built. We undermined confidence in our own formula.'

* * *

Inauspicious return to Peterhouse. To my amazement John Burkill does not fall over himself to have me back, but the magisterial Mr Barnes, the head porter, and the gyps ask after Harry Asplin. Also inauspicious are the efforts of Stuart Simmonds, John Durnford and Guthrie Moir to get their poems published, and of Stuart, John Coast and myself to get into the Malayan Civil Service. Oddly enough, considering his politics, Bertie Keane goes to South Africa. Jim Swanton goes to Pusey House in Oxford but becomes high priest (the qualifications evidently being much the same) of cricket, not Christ; Jack Stogumber and Smodger Smith vanish, and Stanley Hall joins the Iron and Steel Federation. Graham Searles returns to his Peruvian Railways, Alan Haldenby to his Derby solicitor's office, Alex Hellawell to the family firm in Manchester, Terence Charley to Barclays Bank, and Ian Watt to Cambridge (to gestate *The Rise of the Novel* and *Conrad*, volume I). Determined to avoid Terence's fate, Stuart tramps the quads of Oxford until Keble accepts him to read English. He reads it to good effect ("Write me a piece on Chaucer's women." "Right! Who shall I read?" "Read Chaucer."). Recalling Ian Henderson's casual advice at Kanburi, I go to the British Council, am offered a job in South America and, remembering Graham's adventures there, take it.

★   ★   ★

The odd man out in all this, John Durnford, on the rebound from a lost campaign and a lost love, announces a double engagement – to the regular army and to Paula. I think his temperament unsuited to the former and that he shares too few interests with the latter. I suspect that parental pressure has been applied and that he has found himself 'in a great big bag' before he knows what he is doing. Ian Henderson is the only one of us who *was* married, and his marriage is on the rocks. So why the unseemly haste? As the army has it: 'Time spent in reconnaissance is seldom wasted'.

★   ★   ★

A dance at Radley with Stuart. John appears in his new blues looking, like Captain Fred Burnaby in his scarlet and gold, dazzling. He dazzles Jean Shanks, a lively medical student who likes poetry. With her friends, John and I find ourselves in Mayfair at the Bagatelle, Milroy's and Queen Charlotte's Birthday Ball (where, in a ladies' excuse-me, I dance with a bosomy girl they say is Princess Elizabeth). But Bath Abbey beckons, and it is John and Paula who march out of the great west door under crossed swords.

★   ★   ★

I lunch with a tearful Jean at Quaglino's, and dine with a jaunty Ian Henderson at the Acropolis in Percy Street ("There's Stephen Spender. Who's he waiting for?"). We drink at the Salisbury, go to

This Way to the Tomb at the Mercury Theatre, and call on John Coast, in the Victoria Street office of something called the Union of Democratic Control. He plans to bring over some Javanese dancers. Ian takes me to a party in Old Church Street, Chelsea. I note 'two pansies dancing together and a sad foreign girl in love with one of them, several women looking like Lady Macbeth, couples lying about on the floor, and most of the men looking as if they've spent the war in the Ministry of Information or the BBC. To get a beer I had to push away a guardee with his mouth under the spigot. I liked the hostess, a scriptwriter named Barbara Tosswil.'

"Play the game, Alexander!" says Ian reprovingly, "Hardly fair on our host, is it?"

"Which was he?"

"Tall thin chap with specs. Looks as though he has a bad smell under his nose, but quite amusing really. Clever too."

★   ★   ★

A letter from Ian arrives after an indecently short interval:

> Barbara and I are extraordinarily happy . . . I thought I was only capable of violent affairs after the shock and disillusion of losing my wife. But now I am more completely in love and more completely loved than ever before and the whole of life has meaning and shape and value again. I hope, my dear Stephen, that you will one day be as lucky as I have been. The longer we know each other the more we discuss things about which we are in tune. All the time the ties of love increase, which is the exact opposite of what happens in an *affaire*, which starts with a bang and ends with a whimper.

> Poor Mr John Mortimer has been banished into utter darkness. He put up a pathetic effort to recapture Barbara but failed utterly, I am glad to say. I am also glad to say that she is in the process of building a new, a simple, a GOOD Henderson and that the old fire is retained to such good purpose that he has got a job as stage manager to Glyndebourne's Children's Theatre. Barbara is reviewing books for the Rank Organisation and a few days ago had John

Coast's *Railroad of Death* to do! . . . the prose is not very good but the picture he conveys is vivid.

★   ★   ★

Marriage is in the air and even Alex Hellawell cannot suppress his feelings for ever. Standing with Joy on the platform at Baker Street station he is galvanised into action, perhaps by the dramatic thunder of an approaching train:

"I say, will you . . . ? D'you think we might . . . ?"

The front of the train sweeps past, drowning his words in the rumble of the wheels. It stops with a shriek and the doors clang open.

"What, Alex?"

For a moment his natural courtesy almost intervenes to make him usher her into the carriage. But some unfamiliar daemon drives him on.

"Let's get married!"

"Yes!" cries Joy and hauls him in behind her.

★   ★   ★

Ian and Barbara are honeymooning on Capri (writes Terence). She is very nice and has the sort of sense that he tends to lack, and a conscience capable of acting when his doesn't. I enclose a cutting from the *Tatler*. You will see, under the photo of Michael Cory-Wright and the Hon Mrs Someone-or-other at the Dorchester, 'Miss Elizabeth Jennings sitting out at the Keble Ball with Mr Stuart Symons'. Elizabeth is freckled, amusing and intelligent and took a second in Eng. Lit. I imagine Stuart won't be very pleased they have spelt his name incorrectly.

★   ★   ★

I am turning my epic on Siam (writes Guthrie, announcing his marriage to a nurse) into a novel instead of an autobiography. It seems the only way to save Sheila being kicked out of bed each time I work on it late at night.

246

He has published his poems privately. They are Durnfordian in their dying fall:

> They did not complain – even uncertain as to where
> Or whose their children were, these doggedly bore
> Such sufferings as would have turned a saint.

Meanwhile, John's life in married quarters has not changed his style:

> The barges drawn inshore, shuttered at night,
> Laughter and voices, and the gentle song
> Made by a lover for his own delight. . . .

leave him 'condemned and full of care, made bitter by much longing and despair' – or, as Pharaoh Adams put it more bluntly, "consumed by a morbid war-captivity fixation'.

Is it significant that the muse inspires me to write jingles, and Guthrie and John to write high tragedy, but doesn't inspire Pharaoh, who has much more reason to let off steam, to write at all?

*   *   *

Stuart, announcing that he and Elizabeth are disengaged, has noted a promising Juliet at the Playhouse. 'Terence came down a few weeks ago and I fear the sight of my rooms in college made him feel rather sad.'

*   *   *

I was at Keble (writes Terence), and to see Stuart installed there recalled Hardy's Christminster with a vengeance. We walked miles in the rain to see some lotuses in the University Park, and I felt even worse. I have recommenced work at the bank and in consequence am almost suicidal. There is an enormous area round Moorgate station that is flat and open with only a few shattered buildings far away on the horizon. I find comfort in a silent contemplation of the scene, thousands of empty basements with a profusion of wild flowers growing in all the crevices and along the walls. It's like an overgrown Chinese graveyard. Stuart showed me his translation of 'The

Twelve Months' by a Thai poet called Thawathotsamat. This
is his 'April'. Remember?

> In the huge sky a huge sun glides:
> The land below is dry.
> No water any longer hides
> The river sandbank, white as a bone.
> Hot like the earth and sky, I wander –
> Hotter than these – my heart alone.

*   *   *

With my own heart still alone but quite cool (it is May), I leave my
friends at home hacking their way through the thickets of Civvy
Street. What the legacy of my time in Siam will be I cannot tell.
Tragedy has loomed large, and I have been dining out on it, but the
farcical element is gaining ground in the memory and may, in the
long run, prove to be the more instructive. Once war itself is seen
as farcical, rather than merely tragic, it will be less popular – and
the last days of Singapore will have been less futile than I thought.
As I am packing to board the *Gripsholm* for El Dorado, I read again
a contribution to *Punch* by 'X-P. O. W.', slip it into the diary begun
in Nacom Nyok, and put them away:

> Singapore is certainly a remarkable place, and was never more
> remarkable than the day before it surrendered. On that day I
> happened to visit the Cathay building, which is a middle-sized
> skyscraper in the centre of the city. It must surely have been
> the busiest place in the whole world. The building contained
> a hospital, a broadcasting station, a restaurant, a corps
> headquarters, the residences of several staff officers and their
> wives, and, on the ground floor, a cinema which continued to
> the end to play *Six Lessons from Madame Lazonga* to packed
> houses. The basement was regarded by about two thousand
> people as the best air raid shelter in Singapore. Among this
> workaday crowd the staff of corps headquarters looked ill at
> ease. And they were perplexed by the fact that although the
> Japanese had occupied half the island the telephone system
> was working reasonably well throughout, so that the enemy

kept on ringing up and asking in polite tones where British formations were to be found. The most bewildered man present was a major in the Veterinary Corps who had been specially flown from India that morning to certify that a shipload of three thousand goats had not got foot-and-mouth disease. I often met him during the next three and a half years when we were prisoners, and he never had another good word for a goat.

27

Sweet Kwai Run Softly

IT is now fifty years since I sang *Terang Bulan* for the last time. By 1946 our brief notoriety was over, and with the fit despatched into the labour market and the unfit tucked away in hospitals, we FEPOWs were left to fade into the background.

Since then, headlines or chance meetings have revived old memories from time to time: Philip Hay with Princess Marina at Churchill's funeral (and in Chips Channon's 1953 diary), and many years later Ailwyn De Ramsey at Cambridge (age and achievement had given his slightly Woosterish features a Churchillian mould, and he walked with a stick. "Not a bad thing to have these days!" he said, pulling out the blade of a swordstick. "How old are you? I'm seventy-seven and I'm not ready to go yet! I'll swap with you any time!"); George Bartley-Dennis, celebrating retirement by marching down Pall Mall in a golden bowler made of a metal he'd developed for the army; 'appointed to assist the Government of Colombia in developing national parks, Major Ian Grimwood, former Chief Warden of Kenya' (and former expert in English-speaking beetles); His Honour Sir Harold Cassel, headlined for suggesting in a rape case that a wife's withheld favours could influence her husband's attentions to his step-daughter. (Not reported was the story of a barrister friend of mine in another case who, anxious to keep an engagement elsewhere, deputed his Clerk, George Snow, to ask for an adjournment. The Judge had obliged because "George Snow was a very old friend"; they had been on the railway together.)

Incidents like this brought back old scenes to me, but to the general public our war would have dropped out of mind altogether had David Lean's fine but fanciful film not made us into fictional heroes overnight. But *The Bridge over the River Kwai* brought us recognition for the wrong reason. It was useless to explain that Tamarkham bridge was never blown up by land, that no pretty little girls came tripping through the jungle, that the Jap engineers required muscle, not expertise, from us, and that a colonel as bone-headed as 'Colonel Nicholson' would soon have been pounding peanuts in the cookhouse while someone more pragmatic took over. Toosey, who had made the best of a very bad job, and who saved even more lives at Tamarkham when it became a hospital camp than he did when building the bridge, was inevitably tarred with the Nicholson brush. It was a most undeserved association for a man of such enterprise and courage.

"He never forced the issue," Ian Watt wrote in *The Listener*, "so as to make the Japanese lose face. He first awed them with an impressive display of military swagger and then charmed them with his apparently unshakeable assumption that no serious difficulty could arise between honourable soldiers." Stuart Simmonds expressed the matter more pithily: "Phil Toosey was certainly not Jap-happy. But nor, if I can put it that way, was he Jap-sad." Nevertheless, once the film had become a classic we were enshrined for ever in that sunlit jungle recreated in Kandy Botanical Gardens, marching stoically to the notes of 'Colonel Bogey'. And we were caught, as it were, in the frame at an age that grew more desirable to us as we ourselves aged, and the evil associations of that photogenic little railway faded.

As the fiftieth anniversary of the victory celebrations drew near, interest was revived in that indefensible war when much of the map had still been coloured red. "What was it like on the Kwai?" "How do you feel about the Japanese?" "Have you been back, or would it upset you?" How can one answer such questions between the soup and the fish? I felt this particularly when I lunched with Masao Hirakubo, a retired London businessman who devotes himself to reconciliation. I was very interested in his experiences, both as a Service Corps officer in the Japanese army at Imphal and as a POW suffering from similar deficiency diseases to ours. Nevertheless, if we had met casually rather than by design, I think we would have talked longer and more revealingly. There is a time and place for these things; otherwise, I prefer to let sleeping dogs lie. 'No man may deliver his brother: nor make agreement unto God for him.'

However, retirement and a second marriage pointed strongly to the time and place for a rendezvous with my particular ghosts. My most formative influence had been life on the Kwai, with its mixture of beauty and squalor. It was as if the Great Artificer, demonstrating his best and worst, had bade us choose to survive for the one or succumb to the other. How were those good quiet Thais now, I wondered, and was the beauty I remembered there the truth? Then out of the blue came a letter from Phil Peachey:

> Having just learnt your address from Pharaoh Adams I felt I must drop you a line and say hello, since every year at some time or other I come across in my study a drawing that you did in Hindato camp around Christmas 1943. Do you remember that? It's a sketch map of Cambridge with some of the legend provided by me. . . . I feel honoured to have had the privilege of possessing it as a gift from you. Now I gladly give it back and hope it will become a tiny part of your family's heirlooms.

The map was in pencil and chalk on two pieces of rough paper stuck together with rice glue on a strip of a letter from my mother. I was delighted and touched to have it again but dismayed to learn how faulty my memory had been over its fate; and if faulty in such a factual detail, how reliable was my memory in general?

Others had been back: Ian Henderson when he joined Radio Malaya, Ian Watt to visit his doctor son, Terence with his eighty-five-year-old mother, and Pharaoh from Hong Kong where he was go-between in the sale of the *Queen Elizabeth* as a 'scholar-ship' to C. Y. Tung. My wife had never been to the tropics. A journey to this corner of the globe might help her to understand and tolerate the quirks in my character that I blamed on the Japanese. And so in December, a month which I had good cause to remember as being comparatively cool and dry, we went together.

I was fortunate in being briefed by the chief British expert on Thailand and Tai languages. But our venue for lunch, the Trout at

Godstow, led him to talk about his Oxford days with lecturers like Tolkien and Jack Lewis and fellow students like Kingsley Amis.

"Oh, I do so agree with you!" The voice came from an apple-cheeked woman in ankle socks, sitting with a ginger-haired man at the other end of the table. "Forgive me, but I couldn't help hearing you. Dear Kingsley and his B. Litt.! He failed, didn't he?" And off they went, capping each other's stories, until my guest – perhaps feeling he had short-changed me on Siam – got to his feet.

"I'm afraid we must be going," he said to her. "It has been a great pleasure talking to you. Strange that we don't know each other since we have shared so many experiences!"

"It is, yes . . . Are you sure we don't? My name's Elizabeth Jennings."

"Oh!" said Stuart, sitting down heavily. "Yes! We were once engaged!"

★   ★   ★

The fallibility of human memory seemed confirmed by our first sight of Bangkok. Monstrous skyscrapers with porticoed penthouses had replaced the teak houses I remembered; the *khlongs* – when not filled in for building – were black with filth, and everywhere was noise: piercing whistles from smog-masked police and tour guides, the din of demolition sites, the roar of long-tailed boats, and the howl and screech of traffic driven at breakneck speed from jam to jam. The Japanese and the Americans between them had delivered the promised Greater East Asian Co-Prosperity Sphere with a vengeance. I had spent plenty of time in tropical heat since the war, and had always found its first familiar embrace relaxing; it seemed to usher in a slower pace of life where man made less noise than nature. But in Bangkok it was the reverse.

With only light backpacks, we took a minibus to Kanburi (Kanchanaburi, to give it its official name), and as we crossed the Menam Chao Phraya I thought with a thrill of pleasure that we weren't marching all the way to Kinsaiyok, Konkuita or Nacom Nyok, and that even if we had been, there was no one to stop us buying food and drink whenever we liked. The choked highway runs much of the way through ribbon development. I failed to spot the point on the Tha Chin river where I had shared a railway wagon with Japanese casualties, and when I did see the name Nacom Pathom on a sign, as we followed trucks thundering round a by-pass, I nearly missed among new high-rise buildings the orange-glazed dome of the Phra Pathom stupa. However, the bulk of the traffic turned south before Ban Pong of evil memory, and at last the scene began to look much as I remembered it – papayas, bananas, kapok, teak huts, goats, food stalls, shrines and the odd Buddhist monk. But in the *padi* fields there were none of those endearing buffaloes, only tractors.

At Kanchanaburi a by-pass runs past the new River Kwai Hotel, skirting the town war cemetery on the left and the railway station on the right – with, beyond it, the site of my old camp. Our minibus turned at the cemetery into a still rustic lane with guesthouses overhanging the water. The river was astonishingly familiar, the same browny-blue, with scrubland on the opposite shore, and beyond that the wooded, uneven, tantalising limestone hills. Our guesthouse restaurant had wide views up and down the river. Two jolly Japanese were drinking at the bar and our host informed us that it was 'River Kwai Bridge Week', coinciding with the King's birthday celebrations; big crowds were expected.

"There is a sound and light show at the bridge tonight."

"I've had enough sound and light at the bridge. I built it!"

"Oh, then you must go! It will remind you of your time there. There are air raids and explosions and fireworks."

A bosky catwalk led to our chalet by the water's edge. With its look and smell of the river, it was a leap back in time to my old hut of bamboo. But there were a few mod cons to clear my dreams of Nip guards and free them for the company of good quiet Thais and old companions. What more, as I drifted off to sleep to the whirr of the fan, could I ask for my experiment?

Some hours later I could have done with a Nip guard or two to end the mayhem that brought us shudderingly awake. Like some monstrous May Week procession, floating discos were chugging one behind the other up towards the bridge, strobe lights flashing, and competing amplifiers blasting out Asian pop and 'All I want for Christmas is my TWO FRONT TEETH'. What goes up must come down, and up and down that tormented river went those two front teeth till four o'clock in the morning. After a shaky breakfast we hired bicycles from a gentle old man down the lane and rode up to Tamarkham. Now, the little station, with its memorial engines and railcar, is called not Tamarkham but River Kwai Bridge. It was like Blackpool. There were 'war museums', silk emporiums, discos and bars and, towering over the bridge itself, a temporary grandstand. On the scaffolding a hoarding read: 'LIGHT AND SOUND PRESENTA- TION: THE RIVER KWAI BRIDGE WEEK NOV. 28 – DEC. 6; SINGHA BEER 'THAILAND BEST SELLING BEER' : PEPSI : COCA COLA'.

It was just about there, at just about this time of year in the cool season now favoured by tourists, that Howard and Pomeroy had been led, roped together, through my working party. There had been dead silence then.

Downriver from the guesthouse a short cut leads through a monastery to the 'harbour', where the floating discos rest by day, and beyond in another *wat* is the JEATH Museum (a mnemonic for Japan, England, Australia/America, Thailand and Holland). The only surprise among the exhibits – amateurish horror paintings, the few well-known photos, and tributes to 'Weary' Dunlop, best- known of the camp surgeons (Dunlop=tyred=weary) – was a faded set of fifteen prints. These watercolours, done after the war by a Dutch prisoner, Tom Ingelse, are unusual in portraying, as well as the miseries of slave labour and the bleakness of a funeral scene, the sheer liveliness of life on the line – the improvisation, the elephants, the excitement of an air raid and the awesome weather changes; in fact, the drama and the beauty of it all as well as the horrors.

Just inland from the waterfront the old town was little changed; there were the city gate, the streets of old teak shops, and the wider street to the Governor's House with the pavilion of the flower-be- decked Golden Lingam in the middle of it. And there was the smoking chimney of the paper factory that we used to see on working parties and whose siren we heard from the airport camp.

There are two war cemeteries for the Allies, similar in layout but very different in atmosphere. Each has a dressed stone entrance, with memorial plaques to British, Dutch and Indian troops, and a large stone cross at the far end. In both cemeteries each gravestone is flanked by a flowering shrub, and here and there are trees to give shade. The Dutch plaques show the Dutch lion and a name. The British ones bear regimental badges and some have sentimental messages as well. I saw only one biblical quotation: 'In my Father's house are many mansions'. Those of my regiment were easy to spot because they carried not only the Royal Artillery gun but the Hertfordshire Yeomanry hart.

The town cemetery was a hive of activity, the St James's Park of Kanchanaburi. Tourists descended from coaches, vendors crowded the entrance, and Thai families picnicked and posed for photographs on the steps of the cross. There was an incongruous but endearing holiday air about it, as if those commemorated were not dead but still part of the scene – reincarnated; and not as old sweats like me but as men in their prime. At the gate a stall displayed a locally printed booklet written by Pharaoh Adams.

We cycled to the other cemetery a few kilometres away across the river, on the site of the old hospital camp at Chungkai. Once across the ferry we were in deep countryside, with nothing in sight but the odd small farm. Then came a leafy and silent *wat* and a little *attap* café. A beautiful avenue runs down to a landing stage on the Kwa Noy, and across the river are those tempting hills, with no sign of human life in them, still promising sanctuary. The cemetery was completely deserted, but with the graves and their flowering shrubs it seemed full of people, not dead but resting quietly, as the trees and the cross cast long shadows in the evening sun. It moved me more than any cemetery I have ever seen, even the acropolis tombs of Termessos in Turkey or overgrown graveyards in India like Sirangapatnam or Vellore; those commemorated here – so burgeoning, shining and, yes, smartly turned out were their memorials – seemed to be mustered in their old manner ready for active service together or, failing that, for irresistible claims to remembrance. And I knew so many of the names – RSM COLES, BSM NICHOLLS ('Rest after weariness, peace after pain') and there, looking as military and efficient as the best of them, was one of special poignancy:

1104097 GUNNER
F. W. HUNT
135th (HERTS. YEOMANRY)
FIELD REG. R. A.
13th AUGUST 1943 AGE 36

Bill would have been eighty-eight now. I fear he would hardly feel at home in the Tower Hamlets of today.

Not far beyond Chungkai was the level crossing on the line running back to the Tamarkham Bridge, and as I sat on my bike straddling the track I looked down it. Where there had been a mud path was a metalled road. It was empty, but I saw it thronged with people – Toosey, shirtless but still smart with the crown and two pips at his waist, doing the rounds of gangs swinging *chunkeols*, carrying baskets of soil and levelling the track. I saw the sections of embankment creeping towards each other, with ballast and sleepers and rails (oh God, those rails!) coming up from the barges, and in the distance I heard the chanting of pile-drivers going on and on – *ichi, ni no són yo, no són yo* . . . BANG! I saw the scene with Nips screaming and laying about them in *speedo* periods as darkness fell, and also in lulls when there was nothing to do but keep out of trouble and tolerate the grinding boredom. The landscape had seemed wilder then, though nothing like the jungle of the upper gorges. Now the river, too, looked tamer, and there was little on it except houseboats; no giant rafts of teak and bamboo or strings of barges. I should have liked to follow these ghosts to Konkuita, but the line stops at Tarsao, now Nam Tok, and apart from the Australian 'Hellfire Pass' tourist trail near Kanyu and the falls at Kinsaiyok and hot springs at Hindato, all reached by a new road, the upper river is not much visited. In any case it is altered by jungle clearance and by the Khao Laem dam which has submerged Konkuita. Never mind! Instead of slogging back to Tamarkham over the temporary wooden bridge for a filthy supper, a tedious roll call and a night on the *bali-bali* with a heaving mass of snoring and sweaty fellow prisoners, I could pedal gently back to the ferry and a pavement café supper of crayfish, and then, lulled by the whirring of the fan and the reassuring outline beside me, a deep and bug-free sleep.

The next day we took the train to Nam Tok, accepting the 'Special Offer For Tourists Only' of the 'Trans-River Death Railway Programme' (including the 'insurance 100,000 *baht* per seat', a poor compliment to my building skills). The journey was pleasantly rural, the country little altered except that the jungle was less intrusive, and the villages were larger with neat stations. There were more *padi* fields, papayas, bananas and Brahmin cattle (but still no buffaloes) and more *wats*. Of course the main feature was the river, and the main feature of that was the notorious Wampo Viaduct, now a favourite of photographers. More of the ubiquitous houseboats were moored below it on the river banks; there were no working craft and only one small boy was swimming in the muddy water. But the river was still beautiful, flowing between its secretive hills, looking its most gentle and innocent, and I cannot pretend that Nam Tok reminded me of my exhausted night at Tarsao, where Bill Hunt first fell out on the road to Kinsaiyok.

We broke our return journey at Tha Kilen to visit the ruins of Muang Singh in a bend of the river forty-three kilometres above Kanchanaburi. I was intrigued to learn of this thirteenth-century walled Khmer city which lay so near to our camps but had remained unknown, at any rate to me, throughout the war. After a two-kilometre walk through empty country we found a kiosk and an immaculate official to sell us tickets. We were his only customers, and the massive Khmer Prasat Muang Singh, 'Tower of the City of Lions', made a noble setting for our picnic. The views on the journey back in the sunset were even prettier than on the outward one; neatly dressed schoolchildren got in and out at the frequent halts, and basket makers sat companionably under huge trees.

We returned to Bangkok by train. As we waited in Kanchanaburi station at eight in the morning a wheezy recording of the national anthem came over a loudspeaker and everyone stood to attention. The journey was a delight, with vendors jumping on and off, offering fresh food wrapped in delicately folded leaves or plaited straw. Instead of endless traffic and new ribbon development we looked out on canals and sugar cane and tapioca and picturesque *old* ribbon development: duck farms, cow sheds, forges, village schools and, of course, *wats*. After two and a half hours we emerged at Thonburi station and a ferryboat took us across the river to the jetty near the Grand Palace.

Our time on the Kwai, since escaping from the floating discos, had made us forget the frenzy of Bangkok traffic. Now it hit us with all the more force. For the Thais the humming street life goes on for ever. And yet through all this mayhem they do still preserve an air of goodness and quietness. They are smily and 'touchy' people. If you catch their eye they smile. At Kanchanaburi station two men chattering together were constantly touching each other, one squeezing the other's knees and leaving his hand dangling companionably between them. If the women don't actually touch you, they look as if they are just going to; two girls at the town cemetery seized us round our waists for their photographs in front of the memorial plaque. And, according to one foreign resident, even the wheeler-dealers in Bangkok are 'the nicest people money can buy'.

Back once again in England, as we drove westwards from Heathrow past commuters' cars crawling towards London, their headlights sickly in the sodden dawn, the still, sunlit graves of Chungkai seemed not merely at the ends of the earth but half way to heaven. Suppose things had been the other way round, with Heathrow nodding and winking in a June sun and Chungkai dark and dripping in the monsoon, the little caf leaking and deserted and the Kwa Noy sweeping past full of menace, would I have felt the same? I think I would.

Muang Thai, 'Land of the Free', was – in spite of its new man-made horrors – still beautiful. Would we have preferred a greyer and safer imprisonment? For a vertiginous moment we had in our fashion held the gorgeous East in fee. Was it all worth it? Given our historical position we had no option. The Empire was still our responsibility as we understood it. History had not then been rewritten to justify modern developments, and national feelings were conditioned to preserving or upsetting the balance of power. It was our birthright to be preservers, and few of us – not even Norris Emmerson – could present a practical alternative to the status quo. But however disastrous the war was to the nation, those of us who survived it know that individual suffering has its rewards. As Sir Edward Dunlop said, at the opening of the Hellfire Pass Trail, a little adversity is no bad thing for the human soul.

My mind went back to the Chungkai cemetery. I had felt twenty-three again, back in my companionable military world but at the same time a privileged observer with experience of later life. The very youth of the fallen, preserved there in such splendour, was ennobling; my own dissolution would come with a queue at a crematorium and a plastic container. Then I had seen Ruth, going down the lines looking for more harts, and I had felt a rush of euphoria, glorying in the extra life I had had, compared with the lives so beautifully commemorated here but so miserably cut short.

And for what? A land fit for heroes, or one where life was a fetish and death taboo? Where, Cronus-like, the old consumed the young, an underclass the workers, the unfit the fit? I thought of Ian Henderson driving from Penang to Kuala Lumpur in 1951, crashing to his death; of Guthrie, television Controller, County Councillor and member of Synod, falling under a train in Tring in 1974; of Emmerson, shuffling through the corridors of the *Statesman of India* with his old retriever, Jane, almost to his dying day – three weeks after hers; of John Durnford, invalided out of the army and thrice divorced, his many poems still unpublished; and of Pharaoh dying in his sixties, wrecked by his privations in Japan (and perhaps, too, by smoking). I thought of Sir Philip Hay and Brigadier Sir Philip Toosey, DSO, TD, missing their three-score years and ten while colonels like Carey Owtram and the irrepressible Peanut McKellar soldiered on into their nineties. I thought of the words of Bill Drower, HM Minister in Washington: "Charity, forgiveness, imagination and a realisation of the history of Japan are all vital for us to show if we are to be looked upon as a great nation, and not as a resentful backward-looking third-rate power."

And I also thought of Terence, the answer – after all – to a maiden's prayer, giving his stylish little mother endless trips abroad and a fine home with him till she was a hundred and four. "She had better come with us," he used to say for the last thirty years or so, "she won't have much longer."

Yet, through this kaleidoscope of idealism, tragedy and farce I felt with a blinding clarity what I can only describe as a revelation of nature's interaction with man. In spite of such bitter experience of fatal interference between the two, I saw that it was not the extremes that are important but the little things – habits, instincts, the matrix of life – that go on in between. There was purpose and redemption in everything; no success without failure. The horrors of life – childhood panics, my fiasco of a war, domestic and professional failures – faded away against this timeless background. Rather than a random thread, I, like all the others, had been an indispensable part of the 'tapestry of life' – and that included Bill Hunt.

Fifty years earlier I had merely felt grief for the dead, and a fleeting envy of their 'escape'. Now these graves, and the memories of youth fused with the hindsight of later life, made everything fall into place. My own death, too, will be part of a landscape of which we are all – with or without a Great Artificer – the architects. The exaltation of those first moments may never quite recur but elements remain for reassurance at an age when it is easy to see the values of our youth crumbling everywhere. We 'ate the bitter bread of shame, we bore disgrace's heavy yoke', but those values that in the end served so many of us so well are firmly enshrined on the banks of the Kwai.

> The beauty of their graves allays our grieving.
> Their scars beneath unfading flowers fade.
> The floating discos passed as we were leaving;
> Sweet Kwai run softly by the ones who stayed.

Index

INDEX

Acknowledgments

I am grateful to the *Daily Telegraph* for permission to reproduce material from an article appearing on 5th August 1995, and to *Punch* for the 1945 contribution from the unknown 'X-P. O. W.'; also to the family of Martyn Skinner for lines quoted from *Letters to Malaya I-V* (Putnam 1941–47), and the family of John Durnford for quotations from his poems. I ask the indulgence of friends pictured within, or of their families, for the use of their verse and unguarded remarks, and I should like to thank Chris Curtis for advice on the first draft and Caroline and Patrick Taylor for their invaluable help in the later stages.